IN CONGRESS. JULY 4, 1776.

The unanimous Declaration of the thirteen united States of America,

THE DECLARATION OF INDEPENDENCE

AN ALMANAC OF LIBERTY

BOOKS BY WILLIAM O. DOUGLAS

An Almanac of Liberty

North from Malaya

Beyond the High Himalayas

Strange Lands and Friendly People

Of Men and Mountains

An
Almanac
of
Liberty

BY WILLIAM O. DOUGLAS

DOUBLEDAY & COMPANY, INC., GARDEN CITY, N.Y., 1954

Library of Congress Catalog Card Number 54–11158

To Leslie Lee and her generation,
still too young even to spell the word LIBERTY

FOREWORD

There could be as many *Almanacs of Liberty* as there are philosophies and points of view. Mine reflects, I suppose, more Thomas Jefferson and Abraham Lincoln, more Hugo L. Black, Louis D. Brandeis, and Charles E. Hughes, and more the two Roosevelts, than our other leaders; more the small town than the city; more free enterprise than big business; more the man who risks his life than he who risks his dollar; more the farmer than the middleman; more the co-operative than the cartel. My *Almanac* ranks freedom to eat with freedom to speak, the right to property with the right of privacy, the right to work with freedom from racial discrimination. My *Almanac* is concerned with the Sermon on the Mount, the United Nations, workmen's compensation, social security, as well as with habeas corpus and the Fifth Amendment. My selections, therefore, are much wider than civil liberties in the conventional sense.

My *Almanac* started many years ago, and in its inception was designed to follow the calendar meticulously. As the collection grew, difficulties developed. There was, first, the fact that some dates, such as August 1, have many claims to distinction. On the other hand, a few days are barren of significant events in this field. Again, there are sometimes several events which either cluster around a single date or which, for the sake of continuity, should be developed together. Finally, some episodes had such a slow blossoming period that they are as much identified with a month or a year as with a particular day. For these reasons, the book to a degree departs from a strict calendar of events.

This *Almanac* is for laymen. Lawyers and historians may find too much condensation to satisfy their appetites for detail. But my *Almanac* was not written for them. It was designed to show more of the forest than the trees. I wrote for the common man, hoping I could help him see the main contours, and, seeing them, better understand the high vantage point we have reached with our form of government.

One who writes an *Almanac of Liberty* must pick and choose from a vast assortment. I found that there was much to be discarded, some items as precious as any I have kept. But that is a limitation inherent in a book restricted to one page for each day of the year. The result is that I have preserved only a fraction of the extensive research which Mercedes H. Davidson headed, and to which Warren M. Christopher, James F. Crafts, Jr., William O. Douglas, Jr., and Rowland F. Kirks made important contributions. Since I have written for laymen, no footnotes or citations have been included. I have attempted to trace only the main currents or influences. They are often better indicated by a sermon or a speech than by a trial, by a veto message or by a dissenting opinion than by a law or a judicial decision, by a defeat than by a victory.

These are trying times, partly because of the holocaust that threatens the world, partly because of the internal strains and stresses that threaten a deep cleavage among us. No cleavage will occur if we remember our spiritual heritage and are true to it. There is room in this great and good American family for all the diversities the Creator has produced in man. Our *Constitution* and *Bill of Rights* were, indeed, written to accommodate each and every minority, regardless of color, nationality, or creed. That is our democratic faith. Out of that diversity can come a unity the world has never witnessed.

The need these days is to practice and preach that democratic faith. It can easily become the most contagious political force the world has ever known. But we must first redeem it. In recent years, we have let it fall to a low estate, as the people of Europe and Asia probably know better than we.

Our freedom and liberty will be easy to redeem if we remember the fundamentals. First, our way of life is greatly concerned with *method* and *means*. The history of man's struggle to be free is in large degree a struggle to be free of oppressive procedures—the right to be free from torture and the hated oaths; the right to trial by jury; the right to confront the accuser face to face; the right to know the charge and to have a fair opportunity to defend. Second, we have principles or articles of faith to which we are committed. Of these, none is more important than the right to speak and to write freely; the right to worship God as one chooses; the sanctity of the conscience; the right to be let alone; the dependency of government on "the consent of the governed."

Both the procedure which we offer for protection of the rights of man and the rights themselves are denied in the Soviet scheme of things, and are mostly withheld or suppressed in other areas, where colonial powers still rule. This gives the American ideal great advantages in the world market of ideas—if we will only be true to it, whether we hold a hearing at home or cast a vote in the United Nations.

WILLIAM O. DOUGLAS

May 18, 1954

CONTENTS

JULY

AUGUST

NOVEMBER

DECEMBER

JANUARY

FEBRUARY

MARCH

APRIL

JUNE

JULY

APPENDICES

JULY

July 4, 1776 was clear and cool in Providence and in New York City. At 6:00 A.M. the temperature was 68 degrees Fahrenheit in Philadelphia and at 1:00 P.M., 76 degrees. But though the weather was cool and calm, the political climate was turbulent.

On April 12, 1776, North Carolina instructed her delegates to the Continental Congress to obtain independence. Virginia did the same on May 15. On June 7, Richard Henry Lee of Virginia introduced a Resolution of Independence. On June 10, a committee was appointed by the Congress to draft a Declaration. That committee was composed of Thomas Jefferson, John Adams, Benjamin Franklin, Roger Sherman, and Robert R. Livingston. On June 28, the committee brought in a draft. On July 2, the Congress adopted a Resolution that "these United Colonies are, and, of right, ought to be Free and Independent States" and that "they are absolved from all allegiance to the British Crown." On July 4, the *Declaration,* drafted by Jefferson and submitted by the committee, was adopted, with modifications, by twelve of the Colonies. New York sent her approval July 15. On July 19, the *Declaration* was ordered engraved on parchment and that copy was signed on August 2 by the members then present, and later during the year by other members.

The official *Declaration of Independence* thus came on July 2. The essential purpose of the *Declaration* adopted July 4 was to proclaim to all the world the reasons for the Resolution.

Rebellion against government is a serious matter. In the eyes of established authority a revolutionary is always a subversive character. Jefferson and his associates knew these things and addressed themselves to those circumstances. The *Declaration of Independence* was aimed at people who might be won over. It was a manifesto proclaiming to the world that the cause of the American rebels was just. It sought support of world opinion by supplying a moral and legal justification for the revolution.

First, it formulated a philosophy of government: all men are created equal; "they are endowed by their Creator with certain unalienable Rights," including life, liberty, and the pursuit of happiness; governments derive "their just powers from the consent of the governed"; whenever a form of government becomes "destructive of these ends, it is the Right of the People to alter or to abolish it . . ." *Second,* the *Declaration* showed that the conditions for rebellion in fact existed in the Colonies and that the people could endure them no longer. A catalogue of oppressive measures was set forth—"repeated injuries and usurpations" by the King, with the object of establishing an "absolute Tyranny" over the Colonies.

John Adams wrote years later that there was not an idea in the *Declaration* "but what had been hackneyed in Congress for two years before." Therein lay not a weakness but tremendous political power. For it stated in resonant words the dominant sentiment in the Colonies.

Its enduring appeal lay in two of its conceptions: *first,* that revolution can be a righteous cause, that the throwing off of chains by an oppressed people is a noble project; and *second,* that all men have a common humanity, that there is a oneness in the world which binds all men together.

On July 6, the news of the *Declaration of Independence* reached New York City, where Lieutenant Isaac Bangs was stationed. He and his friends thereupon "went to a Publick House to testify" their joy "at the happy news of Independence" and spent the afternoon "merily in playing at Bowles for Wine." General Howe, Commanding General of the British Army, read the news on Staten Island July 8 from a Philadelphia newspaper dated July 6.

Official notice of the signing finally reached New York on the ninth. At 6:00 P.M. on that day, General Washington drew up his brigades "on their respective Parades" and had the *Declaration* read to them.

That winter, James Aitken, an incendiary, tried to burn London in aid of the American Revolution. He was hanged; and his mission died with him. But the *Declaration of Independence* had a more abiding effect on the minds of men. Its message traveled to all parts of the earth. It has been denounced and defended as much as any public document. Perennial discussion of it has kept it alive; its vitality has grown through the years. The political philosophy it advanced was not pure theory. The theory was hitched to practical fact: the United States thrived under independence, restated its philosophy of human rights to include blacks as well as whites, and stood before the world as a concrete example of how great and good freedom can be.

In 1861, Abraham Lincoln said that the *Declaration* gave promise that "the weights would be lifted from the shoulders of all men, and that all should have an equal chance." His prophecy came true. The *Declaration* was one political factor behind the revolutions that swept Asia in the 1940's. The nationalists of Vietnam (at that time not wholly communist) proclaimed their Declaration of Independence on September 2, 1945. It opened by quoting ours—that "all men are created equal," etc. And it listed the oppressive practices of France, the imperial power, just as we in 1776 specified our grievances against the British Empire under George III.

4

The basic premise on which the *Declaration of Independence* rests is that men are "endowed by their Creator with certain unalienable Rights." That means that the source of these rights of man is God, not government. When the state adopts measures protective of civil liberties, it does not confer rights. It merely confirms rights that belong to man as the son of God.

The *Declaration of Independence* states "That to *secure* these rights, Governments are instituted among Men . . ." The preamble of the *Constitution* says, "We the People of the United States, in Order to . . . *secure* the Blessings of Liberty to ourselves and our Posterity, do ordain and establish this Constitution . . ."

To secure sometimes means to obtain, sometimes *to safeguard.* In the *Declaration of Independence* and in the preamble of the *Constitution to secure* means *to safeguard,* as in Shakespeare's passage "Heaven secure him!" The rights and liberties *secured* were those which American citizens already had. Government merely underwrote them.

Therein lies the basic difference between democratic and totalitarian governments. In fascist, communist, and monarchical states, government is the source of rights: government grants rights; government withdraws rights. In our scheme of things, the rights of man are unalienable. They come from the Creator, not from a president, a legislature, or a court.

While there were economic and fiscal reasons behind our revolution, there were matters of principle, too.

Mellen Chamberlain relates in *John Adams, the Statesman of the American Revolution,* a conversation he had with a Yankee soldier sixty-seven years after the battles of Concord and Lexington:

"My histories tell me that you men of the Revolution took up arms against intolerable oppressions."

"What were they? Oppressions? I didn't feel them."

"What, were you not oppressed by the Stamp Act?"

"I never saw one of those stamps. . . . I am certain I never paid a penny for one of them."

"Well, what then about the tea-tax?"

"Tea-tax! I never drank a drop of the stuff; the boys threw it all overboard."

"Then I suppose you had been reading Harrington or Sidney and Locke about the eternal principles of liberty."

"Never heard of 'em. We read only the Bible, the Catechism, Watts's Psalms and Hymns, and the Almanack."

"Well, then, what was the matter? And what did you mean in going to the fight?"

"Young man, what we meant in going for those red-coats was this: we always had governed ourselves, and we always meant to. They didn't mean we should."

The idea of self-government was the most powerful force influencing the minds of men on this continent in the eighteenth century. It is that idea which more than any other inflames Asia and Africa today.

July 9, 1832 marked the end of an acrimonious debate in Congress—a debate in which religion and politics brought the discussion to the boiling point.

Cholera had reached our shores, and Henry Clay in the Senate proposed that the Congress recommend to the President a National Fast Day for prayers that would save us from "the Asiatic scourge." Andrew Jackson, a few days earlier, had declined to proclaim a National Fast Day. "I could not do otherwise," he said, "without transcending the limits prescribed by the Constitution for the President; and without feeling that I might in some degree disturb the security which religion now enjoys in this country in its complete separation from the political concerns of the General Government." Clay's resolution passed the Senate but died in the House, where the Democrats fought it vigorously. Verplanck of New York represented the opposition: "Let us leave prayer and humiliation to be prompted by the devotion of the heart, and not the bidding of the State." On that note the resolution was lost.

Prior to 1832, Congress passed several resolutions asking for days of prayer and thanksgiving, requests to which the Presidents yielded. After 1832 similar resolutions were passed, the last in 1864. Since that date Congress has not entered this religious field.

Most Presidents have proclaimed days of prayer and thanksgiving. When Jackson refused to do so, he was following Jefferson's example. Jefferson maintained that the First Amendment (October 28) forbade the federal government "from intermeddling with religious institutions, their doctrines, discipline, or exercises," and that even a recommendation of a day of fasting and prayer was forbidden. "Fasting and prayer are religious exercises," he wrote, "the enjoining them an act of discipline." And he added, "Civil powers alone have been given to the President of the United States, and no authority to direct the religious exercises of his constituents."

So it is that a subject as non-controversial as Thanksgiving Day seems to be has touched off acrimonious debate.

Spain occupied the Philippine Islands for more than the three centuries which ended in 1898. She was in possession when the American Revolution broke. It did not take long for that revolution to have its effect in the Philippines. Indeed from 1807 to 1872 the Filipinos revolted eleven times against the Spanish. From 1872 to 1896 the boiler pressure of revolt mounted. The great José Rizal was shot by the Spanish when he protested against colonial tyranny. He put the issue in simple human terms and spoke for all subjugated races when he cried out, "We are people." That plea for justice still re-echoes in Asia.

The revolution continued under Bonifacio, Macabulos, and Aguinaldo. Our Admiral Dewey and Aguinaldo joined forces, and the Islands were seized from the Spanish in 1898. McKinley proclaimed that "The Philippines are ours not to exploit but to develop, to civilize, to educate, to train in the science of self-government."

Other Presidents adopted the same policy. In 1933, we enacted a law providing for the drafting of a constitution for the Philippines and the recognition of their independence. Roosevelt was a mighty force in working out the details and resolving practical difficulties. Finally on July 4, 1946, Truman proclaimed "the independence of the Philippines as a separate and self-governing nation."

Thus ended in not much more than a generation the first and only American venture in imperialism. And our imperialism, short-lived as it was, aimed not to oppress and exploit but to liberate. In the Philippines we have been true to our ideals. As a consequence we have no closer friends, no stauncher allies. When the boots of Japanese soldiers trampled the American flag in the mud, tender brown hands of Filipinos rescued it and preserved Old Glory for the day of liberation.

Samuel Adams (1722–1803) was probably the leading democrat in American public affairs during the pre-Revolution days. His role in organizing and directing the forces of revolution is difficult to overestimate. He was the master strategist who marshaled public opinion against the royal power. For twenty years he wrote against the government, exposing its weaknesses, attacking its officials, arousing the people, preparing them for home rule. The Loyalists dubbed him an evil and vindictive man. Hutchinson, the Royal Governor, wrote, "I doubt if there is a greater incendiary in the King's dominion or a man of greater malignity of heart."

Sam Adams—loved by the common people—was the most dangerous opponent the Tories had known. He wrote under various names—Candidus, Layman, Poplicola, Puritan. He created a large cast of characters—all patriots, all troubled over the evil days which the Tories had brought upon the people.

His pen rallied America. An aristocracy was developing here that was eager to ape British ways. Sam Adams saw that. He also saw that the British, with calculated design, were making steady encroachments on the rights of home rule, which Americans had enjoyed for almost a century and a half.

Sam Adams attacked the Tory view that the few should govern the many. He attacked British law for not serving the general welfare. He championed the revolutionary principle that the people had the right to defy an abusive law imposed on them. He was responsible for the creation of the Committees of Correspondence; he was highly instrumental in organizing the Continental Congress and in drafting the *Articles of Confederation.*

Samuel Adams served as Governor of Massachusetts (1793–1797). But his great work was done before the Revolution. He not only helped prepare the American mind for revolution, he organized the people for political action, making clear where the opposition was vulnerable and what political tactics were practical. They used to say in Boston when they saw a light in his room late at night, "There is Sam Adams writing against the Tories."

On July 12, 1810, a trial of trade unionists (members of The
Journeymen Cordwainers) began in New York City for a conspiracy to raise their wages by calling a strike. They suffered the
same fate as the Philadelphia bootmakers who had been prosecuted for such a conspiracy in 1806. These New York bootmakers
were found guilty and fined one dollar each, with costs. The law
was this: "Even to do a thing which is *lawful* in itself, by *conspiracy*, is unlawful." This early view of trade unionism was short-
lived in America. The tide turned in 1842 with an historic decision
by the Supreme Judicial Court of Massachusetts.

An indictment charged that members of a bootmakers' union
agreed not to work for any person who employed a non-union
member. The purpose of the agreement was to induce all bootmakers to join the union. That purpose was not *unlawful*, said
the court, for it might aim at improving the condition of the
workers. In other words, laborers did not become conspirators by
banding together into a union for that end. The legality of an
association of laborers, the court ruled, "will therefore depend
upon the means to be used for its accomplishment." If the end
is to be reached "by falsehood or force," the project is unlawful;
if "by fair or honorable and lawful means," it is not a conspiracy.
Since no unlawful means were charged against the bootmakers,
the court held there was no indictable offense.

Since 1842, in this country the legality of union activities has
turned largely on the "end" sought and the "means" used.

July 13, 1787 is the date of the famous *Northwest Ordinance*. It established a government for the country west of the Alleghenies and north of the Ohio and provided for the formation of not less than three nor more than five States from it. The *Ordinance* set high standards for the new governments:

"No person, demeaning himself in a peaceable and orderly manner, shall ever be molested on account of his mode of worship or religious sentiments, in the said territory.

"The inhabitants of the said territory shall always be entitled to the benefits of the writ of habeas corpus, and of the trial by jury; of a proportionate representation of the people in the legislature; and of judicial proceedings according to the course of the common law. All persons shall be bailable, unless for capital offences, where the proof shall be evident or the presumption great. All fines shall be moderate; and no cruel or unusual punishments shall be inflicted. No man shall be deprived of his liberty or property, but by the judgment of his peers or the law of the land; and, should the public exigencies make it necessary, for the common preservation, to take any person's property, or to demand his particular services, full compensation shall be made for the same. And, in the just preservation of rights and property, it is understood and declared, that no law ought ever to be made, or have force in the said territory, that shall, in any manner whatever, interfere with or affect private contracts or engagements, *bona fide,* and without fraud, previously formed.

"Religion, morality, and knowledge, being necessary to good government and the happiness of mankind, schools and the means of education shall forever be encouraged. . . .

"There shall be neither slavery nor involuntary servitude in the said territory, otherwise than in the punishment of crimes whereof the party shall have been duly convicted . . ."

11

In 1798, war with France seemed imminent. About 25,000 French refugees were in the country. The French were engaged in espionage. A radical movement in this country espoused the French cause. Adams, who was President, opposed even the visit of a group of French scientists to this country on the ground that "learned societies" had "disorganized the world" and were "incompatible with social order."

As a result of this hysteria, a series of alien and sedition laws were enacted by Congress. One, which was approved July 14, 1798, made it a crime, among other things, to publish any "false, scandalous and malicious" writing against the government, the Congress, or the President "with intent to defame" them or to bring them "into contempt or disrepute" or "to stir up sedition." The crime carried a penalty of $2,000 fine and 2 years in jail. The law was to continue only until March 3, 1801.

The debate on this bill contains a famous constitutional argument. On the one side was the view that Congress had the power to curb publications "injurious to the well-being of society":

"A conspiracy against the Constitution, the government, the peace and safety of this country is formed and is in full operation. It embraces members of all classes; the Representative of the people on this floor, the wild and visionary theorist in the bloody philosophy of the day, the learned and the ignorant."

On the other side were impassioned pleas for freedom of speech and the press:

"The people suspect something is not right when free discussion is feared by government. They know that truth is not afraid of investigation."

"The Constitution . . . seems to have foreseen that majorities . . . might wish to pass laws to suppress the only means by which its corrupt views might be made known to the people, and therefore says, *no* law shall be passed to abridge the liberty of speech and of the press."

The bill passed the Senate by a vote of 18 to 6, the House, 44 to 41.

The first reign of terror in this country started shortly after July 14, 1798.

Congressman Matthew Lyon of Vermont was imprisoned 4 months and fined $1,000

—for criticizing Adams, a man who had "a continual grasp for power" and "an unbounded thirst for ridiculous pomp, foolish adulation, and selfish avarice," and

—for condemning Adams and his policy toward France.

(While in prison Lyon was re-elected by an overwhelming vote).

Thomas Cooper of Philadelphia was imprisoned 6 months and fined $400 for a publication critical of Adams for delivering up an American citizen to the British Navy for court martial.

Anthony Haswell of Vermont was imprisoned 2 months and fined $200 for denouncing the "political persecution" of Congressman Lyon.

James Thompson Callender of Virginia was imprisoned 9 months and fined $200 for calling "the reign" of Adams "one continued tempest of malignant passions" and charging him of being determined "at all events to embroil this country with France." He wrote, "Take your choice, then, between Adams, war and beggary, and Jefferson, peace and competency."

David Brown was sentenced to 18 months and fined $450 for erecting a "liberty pole" at Dedham, Massachusetts, with a sign "No stamp act, no sedition and no alien acts, no land tax. Downfall to the tyrants of America: peace and retirement to the President: long live the Vice President and the minority."

Luther Baldwin of New Jersey should not be forgotten. Adams visited Newark, and in his honor cannon were discharged. Baldwin was heard to say that he hoped the wadding behind the powder would hit Adams in the seat of his pants. For this Baldwin was fined $100.

During the reign of terror about 25 people were arrested, 15 or more were indicted, 11 tried, and 10 found guilty.

The reaction against the July fourteenth law was great, and the political lines were drawn between Adams the sponsor and Jefferson the opponent. Repeal of the law failed by a close vote in Congress in 1799.

In 1798, Kentucky and Virginia passed resolutions condemning the law. Jefferson drew Kentucky's resolution. Madison drafted Virginia's. They were a protest against usurpation of power by the national government. They maintained that it was for the States, not Congress, to legislate on matters concerning speech and press. All the state legislatures from Maryland on north took the contrary view and some of them, notably New Hampshire and Rhode Island, replied that it was for the courts, not the legislatures, to pass on the constitutionality of Acts of Congress. Kentucky replied in 1799, maintaining the right of the States to nullification. There was even talk of secession in Virginia.

The July fourteenth law was an issue in the 1800 Presidential campaign. Jefferson headed the Republican ticket. The Republicans carried the Senate and the House. The Presidential election was thrown into the House, where Jefferson was elected.

Jefferson promptly pardoned those convicted under the July fourteenth law; and for the next fifty years Congress passed laws remitting the fines. Thus in July 1840, it authorized repayment of the fine of Matthew Lyon with interest to his heirs and in July 1850 payment to the heirs of Thomas Cooper of $400 plus interest for the fine he paid.

In Shaw's play *Saint Joan* when a priest called Bishop Cauchon "a traitor," Warwick spoke up to apologize for the use of the word. "It does not mean in England what it does in France. In your language traitor means betrayer: one who is perfidious, treacherous, unfaithful, disloyal. In our country it means simply one who is not wholly devoted to our English interests."

There is similar confusion in terminology in this country. For example, the Rosenbergs, guilty of conspiring to obtain our atomic secrets for Russia, were called "traitors" and their crime was often called "treason." American citizens turned communist are also frequently charged with "treason."

Under the *Constitution* "treason" is narrowly defined: "Treason against the United States, shall consist only in levying War against them, or in adhering to their Enemies . . ." Giving secrets to an *enemy* is therefore treason. But in the constitutional sense a foreign nation is not an *enemy* until and unless war has been declared against it. One who gives secrets to a nation with whom we are not at war may be guilty of espionage. But he is not guilty of treason unless he takes up arms.

The men who drafted the *Constitution* had themselves lived under the cloud of treason. Every step they had taken down the path to independence made them potential victims. That is why Franklin said they must either hang together or hang separately. Moreover, they had ancestors who had suffered from loose use of the word "treason." After 1776, the States revised their constitutions and laws, redefining treason. A few gave it a broad sweep. Thus New York in 1781 made treasonable the utterance of an opinion that the King had authority over New York or its people.

Madison wanted treason narrowly defined, because history showed that "newfangled and artificial treasons" were the "great engines" by which partisan factions "wreaked their alternate malignity on each other." Jefferson had the like view, pointing out that the definitions of treason often failed to distinguish between "acts against government" and "acts against the oppressions of the government."

"I will prove that I was not in town in August all the month by twenty witnesses." So spoke William Ireland on trial at Old Bailey in 1678 for high treason. The treason charged was a plot of Catholics to kill the King, abolish the Protestant religion, and restore the Roman faith.

Two witnesses were required to convict. There was one who gave damaging testimony—Titus Oates, who, seven years later, was convicted of perjury for his testimony against William Ireland (September 28). The evidence of the second witness was weaker, and its veracity turned on whether Ireland had been in London during August.

When Ireland claimed he had been out of town all that month, the court said "Call your witnesses." Ireland replied that he had been prevented by his jailer from sending for witnesses. Ireland pleaded again and again for time. "Though we have no more witnesses, yet we have witnesses that there are more witnesses." The only witnesses he had were present by mere chance. The turn of the case had caught him by surprise and he needed time to reply. He called by name the men who would testify he was not in London during August. But the court would not summon them nor recess until they could be called.

The jury found Ireland guilty and he was hanged. At the gallows he was still pleading for a chance to summon a host of people who knew he was not in London during August.

The Ireland case burned itself deep in men's memories. It is a main reason why we have in the Sixth Amendment the provision that "In all criminal prosecutions, the accused shall enjoy the right . . . to have compulsory process for obtaining witnesses in his favor . . ."

Cruel and inhuman punishments have left behind them centuries of human wreckage. Convicted people have suffered all the pains and tortures that sadistic men could devise.

Since history has been recorded, people have been burned at the stake, their ears cut off, their tongues drilled or mutilated, their bodies drawn and quartered, their privy members cut off in punishment for some offense (April 2). As late as 1645, Mother Lakeland was burned as a witch in England.

Asia used the crucifixion. Sometimes a prisoner's head was twisted off or hot lead poured over his shaven pate until his eyes popped out. Sometimes he was disemboweled while alive.

Shortly before one of my visits to the Philippines, communist guerrillas had seized a priest, tied a carabao to each leg, and driven them in opposite directions, tearing the holy man in two.

The sentence placed on John Ashton, convicted of treason in 1691, was a fairly common one in England:

That ye do respectively go to the place from whence ye came; from thence to be drawn upon a sledge to the place of execution, to be there hanged up by the neck, to be cut down while ye are yet alive, to have your hearts and bowels taken out before your faces, and your members cut off and burnt. Your heads severed from your bodies, your bodies divided into four quarters, your heads and bodies respectively to be disposed of according to the king's will and pleasure; and the Lord have mercy upon your souls.

The English *Bill of Rights* of 1689 outlawed "cruel and unusual punishment." (December 16.) Perhaps that is why the Queen remitted the drawing and quartering of Ashton.

Those who drew our *Bill of Rights* knew about Mother Lakeland and Ashton. They also remembered William, Earl of Devonshire, who in 1687 was fined £30,000 for hitting an army officer with his cane. So they wrote into the Eighth Amendment the mandate against "excessive fines" and "cruel and unusual punishments."

July 1867 brought into operation in New York our first comprehensive tenement house law. Yet that law, good as it was, left New York City with 350,000 windowless rooms. Nearly 3,000 people lived on two acres of land. Blind Man's Alley, Murderers' Alley, Poverty Gap, Misery Row, Penitentiary Row—these were names of blocks on the Lower East Side. Their titles told the story of the evils of the slums—disease, juvenile delinquency, crime, discontent, suffering. There was in addition the awful toll of fire. In 1901, Theodore Roosevelt put through a more comprehensive housing reform.

Slums, however, are a malingering disease. In 1954, the Washington *Post* disclosed slum conditions in the nation's capital which in some respects were as oppressive as those which Jane Addams and Edith Abbott found in Chicago and Jacob Riis in New York. Today one out of five urban families in America lives in slums or under slum conditions. The high price of slum lands has barred their purchase for redevelopment. Slum lands, developed into modern low-cost housing, would generally not bring the return that the exploiters get from miserable shacks.

July 20, 1892 marked the first entry of the federal government into the field. It then started an investigation of the slums of our larger cities. On another July day (1949) a federal housing Act was passed which committed the national government to "the clearance of slums and blighted areas" and to the construction of a "decent home" for every American family. The Act uses both private enterprise and local housing authorities; and it furnishes federal financing. The aim is to build one and a half million building units a year until 1960.

The problem is not peculiar to America. Other countries have it too. In India, Burma, and Puerto Rico I saw modern homes supplanting miserable huts made of tin and boxes. I visited among these people and knew for the first time how it is that a house can transform a man's face.

The requirement of a speedy trial goes back to a provision in the *Magna Carta* (June 16) that two judges should go to each county "four times a year" to hold court. This provision of the Great Charter apparently was not observed. But from it developed a procedure guaranteeing that a person did not languish in prison waiting to be tried for a criminal offense. By the mid-thirteenth century, the King began to appoint, at frequent intervals, a commission "to deliver a gaol." This agency came to be a court or commission of general gaol delivery which was authorized to visit specified places and try to deliver every prisoner, whatever his crime. As a consequence all persons accused of crime, whether in jail or out on bail, were brought up for trial at least twice a year. In this way the common law worked out a procedure for guaranteeing an accused a speedy trial.

Our Sixth Amendment provides that in all criminal prosecutions "the accused shall enjoy the right to a speedy and public trial." Perhaps the most famous case involving the guarantee of a "speedy" trial arose in the Territory of Montana in 1880.

One Fox was indicted for embezzlement in 1879. His trial was continued until March 1880. At that time he demanded a trial. The prosecution refused because Congress had not appropriated money to reimburse the marshal for summoning witnesses necessary to present the government's case. The federal court adjourned after continuing the case until the next term of court, which would be held in November 1880. Fox, still being in prison, made application for a writ of habeas corpus, asking that he be discharged from prison because he was denied a "speedy" trial, which the *Bill of Rights* guarantees.

The court granted Fox the relief. It held that the prosecution had had a reasonable opportunity to prepare the case for trial and that there had been a term of court at which a trial could have been held. "The government of the United States cannot cast a man into prison and then fold its arms and refuse to prosecute."

19

A secret trial would be anathema to us. It would be unthinkable that in this country a person could be spirited away, held *incommunicado,* tried in secret, and executed. The advantages of a public trial over a secret one are obvious: a witness might testify secretly to things he would not dare say openly; lawyers and judges who could operate behind closed doors might take short cuts they would not dare take publicly; the community would not have a good measure of the manner in which justice was administered if the public were excluded.

The constitutional requirement for a "public" trial did not arise out of any special grievance in English history. But the secret trial in France and Spain was known in England as a tyrannous practice of princes. Therefore it was feared. And the common law consistently granted the right to a public trial.

The public trial can be an ominous affair. There have been times in this country when a tense, crowded courtroom turned the trial into a theatrical performance, diverting it from a calm, dispassionate search for the truth. At other times the hostility of the crowd in the courtroom has reached such proportions as to be a whip on the backs of the jury, depriving them of their impartiality.

Boisterous and disorderly people can, of course, be evicted from the courtroom. Some courts have gone further and allowed exclusion of "a crowd of idle, gaping loafers" whose presence at a rape trial was due to their "morbid curiosity" for indecent details. If an accused can show prejudice by reason of exclusion of members of the public, he gets a new trial. But if the press is represented, if the defendant's lawyers, his witnesses, and some of his friends are present, and if a select group of the public (such as members of the Bar) are admitted, the judge may in exceptional situations exclude the balance in the interest of justice.

A quiet, dignified courtroom is more likely to be a place of justice than one packed with people whose demeanor and attitude put the whole room on edge.

In all criminal prosecutions an accused is entitled to be tried "by an impartial jury of the State and district wherein the crime shall have been committed, which district shall have been previously ascertained by law . . ." This is the command of the Sixth Amendment governing trials in the federal courts. Thus a person committing a federal offense in Montana cannot be shipped out of state for trial in another jurisdiction where the Attorney General thinks the chances for conviction are better.

One of the grievances in the *Declaration of Independence* was "transporting us beyond Seas to be tried for pretended offenses." The Fathers knew the threats of the King to take John Adams, John Hancock, and others to England for trial on treason charges. They knew an American patriot would stand an excellent chance before an American jury and a poor one before a London jury.

They also knew about the trial of Roger Macguire. Lord Macguire, who lived in Ireland, was charged with high treason in 1644. It was charged that he levied war against the King, killing many Protestants. He was brought from Dublin to London for trial. He pleaded not guilty and demanded that "he might be tried and judged by his peers in Ireland." The judges ruled against him. The House of Commons, with the concurrence of the House of Lords, resolved that the court was right and urged it "to proceed speedily" according to "law and justice."

That doomed Lord Macguire, and he was shortly on his way to the gallows.

A Dublin jury might have saved his neck. A London jury was almost certain to hang him.

The right to trial by jury in criminal prosecutions is basic to us. Yet there is an important exception. If, for example, a person throws an inkwell at the judge while the court is in session, he is guilty of contempt and can be instantly arrested and fined or imprisoned without any further proof and without a jury trial (June 10).

In *Henry IV*, Shakespeare tells of the Prince who struck the Chief Justice in open court and was instantly put in prison for it. When the Prince became King, he chided the Chief Justice about it.

KING: What! rate, rebuke, and roughly send to prison
The immediate heir of England! . . .

CHIEF JUSTICE: I then did use the Person of your father;
The image of his Power lay then in me:
And, in the administration of his law,
Whiles I was busy for the Commonwealth,
Your Highness pleased to forget my place,
The majesty and power of Law and Justice,
The image of the King whom I presented,
And struck me in my very seat of judgment;
Whereon, as an offender to your father,
I gave bold way to my authority
And did commit you. If the deed were ill,
Be you contented, wearing now the garland,
To have a son set your decrees at naught,
To pluck down Justice from your awful Bench,
To trip the course of Law and blunt the Sword
That guards the peace and safety of your Person . . .

KING: . . . You did commit me:
For which, I do commit into your hand
The unstained Sword that you have us'd to bear;
With this remembrance, that you use the same
With the like bold, just and impartial spirit
As you have done 'gainst me. . . .

On July 25, 1778, a motion was made in the Continental Congress "whether it is proper that Congress should appoint any person of an ecclesiastical character to any civil office under the United States." The question raised such little interest that no vote was taken on it. Instead a Treasury report was approved which appointed inspectors of the government printing press, one of whom was a person "of an ecclesiastical character." The question whether the clergy should be excluded from public office never seems to have been raised again in the Congress. Since that time not many ministers have served in the Congress or in the executive branch. But there have been some distinguished ones.

There is a different story in the States. In the early years North Carolina, South Carolina, Mississippi, Delaware, Kentucky, Louisiana, Virginia, Georgia, and later on Texas, disqualified the clergy for all or some civil offices. New York in 1777 wrote a pervasive disqualification into her constitution that lasted until the mid-eighteenth century. Tennessee's present constitution disqualifies the clergy from the legislature so they will not be "diverted from the great duties of their functions." Maryland has a like provision.

This early ban on clergymen reflected largely, I think, the fear of a religious group dominating politics. English history had shown the evils of the merger of religious and secular power. Some clergymen in the Colonies had been very active in political affairs. Some had used the pulpit to preach against the Revolution (October 11). Some had a record of dissent in public affairs. Some, such as the Presbyterian, David Rice, of Kentucky, had led the anti-slavery crusade.

Public opinion gradually shifted to the view Madison expressed in 1788. Jefferson had prepared a draft of a constitution for Virginia excluding ministers from civil posts. Madison objected, indicating that the proposal violated "a fundamental principle of liberty by punishing a religious profession with the privation of a civil right." That was the position Jefferson later took.

During a criminal trial in New York in 1813, it appeared that stolen property had been returned to the owner by a Catholic priest. The priest was thereupon subpoenaed and asked who had given the stolen property to him. He refused to answer, saying that to do so would violate the confessional. "It would be my duty to prefer instantaneous death or any temporal misfortune, rather than disclose the name of the penitent in question," he said.

The court sustained the priest, basing its decision on the provision of the state constitution guaranteeing "the free exercise and enjoyment of religious profession and worship, without discrimination or preference." Speaking through DeWitt Clinton, the court said, "The sacraments of a religion are its most important elements. . . . To decide that the minister shall promulgate what he receives in confession is to declare that there shall be no penance; and this important branch of the Roman Catholic religion would be thus annihilated." Forcing a priest to testify concerning the confessional would produce "a horrible dilemma. . . . If he tells the truth, he violates his ecclesiastical oath. If he prevaricates, he violates his judicial oath."

This early ruling by New York has been followed in the other States either bv statute or judicial decision.

Sunday laws go back to the beginning. Efforts to relax them or to tighten them have resulted in political storms. Separation of church and state prevents enforcement of Sunday observance as a religious duty. But cessation of labor for one day a week stands on the same footing as any other regulation of hours of work.

In the 1790's, state laws against Sunday travel were invoked (unsuccessfully) to keep the mail from being carried on the Sabbath. Early in the nineteenth century, another controversy raged over Sunday mail. Beginning in 1810, the post offices were kept open for at least a part of Sunday. That brought a storm of protests. The opposition wanted to close the post offices on Sunday and to stop the transportation of mail on that day.

In 1829, Senator Richard M. Johnson of Kentucky rendered an historic report on the matter. He protested against stopping the transportation of mail on the Sabbath:

"Should Congress, in their legislative capacity, adopt the sentiment, it would establish the principle that the Legislature is a proper tribunal to determine what are the laws of God. It would involve a legislative decision in a religious controversy, and on a point in which good citizens may honestly differ in opinion, without disturbing the peace of society, or endangering its liberties. If this principle is once introduced, it will be impossible to define its bounds. Among all the religious persecutions with which almost every page of modern history is stained, no victim ever suffered but for the violation of what Government denominated the law of God. To prevent a similar train of evils in this country, the constitution has wisely withheld from our Government the power of defining the divine law. It is a right reserved to each citizen; and while he respects the equal rights of others, he cannot be held amenable to any human tribunal for his conclusions. . . . Let the National Legislature once perform an act which involves the decision of a religious controversy, and it will have passed its legitimate bounds. . . . Our constitution recognizes no other power than that of persuasion for enforcing religious observances."

On July 28, 1868, the Secretary of State certified that the Fourteenth Amendment was a part of the *Constitution*. The important reforms which this Amendment achieved were two:

1. All persons born or naturalized in the United States are citizens of the United States and of the State wherein they reside. Thus the sons and daughters of the immigrant, as well as the Negro slaves born here, become citizens.

2. The States are forbidden from
    —abridging the privileges or immunities of citizens of the United States
    —depriving any person of life, liberty, or property without due process of law
    —denying any person equal protection of the laws.

It is through the latter provisions that many of the liberties of the people are today protected.

Some of the southern States first rejected and later ratified the Amendment. Both Kentucky and Maryland rejected it in 1867 and did not later ratify it.

Denis W. Brogan in his book *The Free State* points out how it is that self-criticism, repentance, and atonement are important influences in the democratic society. Wrongs will always be done because people are people. Injuries will be unjustly inflicted. Life itself may be taken. Yet there comes a calmer day when people look back on their hysteria with sorrow. Pilgrimages are taken; verses of commemoration are written; speeches are made.

One episode that has laid heavily on the American conscience is the smashing of the Bonus Army on July 29, 1932.

During the summer of 1932, the country's worst depression lay like a blight on the land. Government did not supply adequate relief. Thousands of families were destitute. Proud and sensitive people had been reduced to making a living by selling apples on street corners or by begging.

Veterans of World War I, believing they were asserting a lawful claim, demanded immediate payment of a bonus. They marched on Washington, D.C., many bringing their families. They set up several camps, and even had a newspaper, the *Bonus Expeditionary Force News*. They were routed by federal troops under the command of General Douglas MacArthur. Tear gas was used. Cavalrymen used the flat sides of their swords to drive the veterans out.

MacArthur justified the use of force, saying the veterans were "a bad-looking mob animated by the spirit of revolution."

Fiorello La Guardia of New York said, "Soup is cheaper than tear bombs and bread better than bullets in maintaining law and order in these times of depression, unemployment, and hunger."

Will Rogers praised the veterans as the "best behaved of any fifteen thousand hungry men assembled anywhere in the world." And he added, "Just think what fifteen thousand clubwomen would have done to Washington even if they wasn't hungry."

In 1774, Jefferson wrote that the abolition of slavery was "the great object of desire" in the Colonies and that the King was wrong in encouraging the slave trade. An early draft of the *Declaration* had condemned slavery and denounced the King for promoting it. But that paragraph was stricken. The slavery issue smoldered.

The Abolitionists fanned the flames (February 19). The opening of western lands helped rouse the competing interests (February 2). John Brown (December 2) set the South on edge. And Harriet Beecher Stowe raised a veritable storm of wrath.

Uncle Tom's Cabin, published in 1851, was the first American novel with a Negro as a hero. It had such a powerful impact that within a few years there appeared about fourteen pro-slavery novels, one of which was *Uncle Robin in His Cabin in Virginia and Tom without One in Boston* by J. W. Page.

William J. Grayson came to the defense of the South with *The Hireling and the Slave*, in which he compared the miserable plight of the northern wage earner:

> *Labor with hunger wages ceaseless strife,*
> *And want and suffering only end with life,*

with the happy, secure life of the slave:

> *Safe from harassing doubts and animal fears*
> *He dreads no famine in unfruitful years.*

The man who encased southern interests in the armor of political theory was John C. Calhoun. Calhoun was indeed the last political theorist we have produced. Calhoun rejected a universal democracy. Rule by numerical majorities was dangerous. Property should have the power of referendum over hostile legislation. The States should have the power of referendum (nullification) vis-à-vis the central government.

Calhoun's democracy would give people fair trials and fair treatment. But in the fashion of the Greeks, it would be run by the select few.

On July 31, 1858, Abraham Lincoln and Stephen A. Douglas—rival candidates for the United States Senate—made final arrangements for the historic debates which bear their names. There were seven debates during the next three months. Judging by the results of the debates, Douglas won. For he defeated Lincoln for the Senate. But while Douglas won the immediate argument, the cause that Lincoln sponsored was the one that endured.

Stephen A. Douglas had the law on his side. Slaves were part of the institution of property. A slave could not become a citizen. Congress had no power to keep slavery out of a Territory. That was the law, because the Supreme Court of the United States had said so (March 6). Douglas also argued that this government was "founded on the white basis" to the exclusion of "Negroes, Indians, or other inferior races."

Lincoln maintained the Court was wrong and that its decision must be changed. He took his law from a moral authority. Lincoln did not claim social or even political equality for the Negro. "But in the right to eat the bread . . . which his own hand earns, he . . . is the equal of every living man."

Lincoln saw slavery not in process of extinction but being perpetuated. Yet he knew slavery to be such a divisive influence as to be dangerous to national unity. "A house divided against itself cannot stand." Lincoln showed his opponent to be perfectly logical, "if you do not admit that slavery is wrong." At that point there was no possibility of reconciling the differences between the two men. For Lincoln denounced slavery as "a moral, social, and political evil." No solution would work that did not first seek to contain slavery and then to bring it to an end.

These great debates were between law and morals. Stephen A. Douglas had the law on his side. But Abraham Lincoln had for his authority the conscience of the world. Lincoln lost the battle for the Senate, but he won the war for humanity.

AUGUST

On August 1, 1641, the Star Chamber was abolished. This court, which was composed of judges, clergy, lawyers, and laymen, existed about 150 years. Though it is remembered as an engine of tyranny, it was, in its early days, a useful instrument in restoring order and keeping all England quiet. The mid-fifteenth century was a turbulent one, the nobles warring with each other; and corruption among government officials was rife. The Star Chamber—which took its name from the room at Westminster where it sat—reduced that lawlessness. But as the years passed, its powers grew, the court acting as a legislature and taking unto itself almost unlimited jurisdiction. Moreover, it came to be used as an instrument to serve political ends. Authors who were critical of the Crown, political opponents of the regime, those who published or circulated literature that was unorthodox or that challenged the prejudices of the day, men who refused to submit to the Crown's illegal methods of raising revenue, all felt the vicious lash of the Star Chamber.

The Star Chamber trenched on freedom of speech and of press, of rights of conscience, of religious freedom.

Though it never applied the death sentence, its punishments were severe and barbarous. Staggering fines were imposed. Ears were cut off; cheeks branded; noses slit; tongues drilled (July 19). The pillory and whipping post were used. Convicts were paraded in public to show their offense. A man who objected on religious grounds to eating pork was put on a pork diet.

An accused could be arrested privately without any information charged against him and examined in private. Torture was used to exact confessions. So was the inquisitional oath—the oath *ex officio* (August 2).

Juries were fined and imprisoned for giving verdicts contrary to the wishes of the court.

Thus the Star Chamber became synonymous with tyranny and oppression.

The oath *ex officio* was introduced into England by Pope Gregory IX in 1236. It read, "You shall swear to answer all such interrogatories as shall be offered unto you and declare your whole knowledge therein, so God help you." Refusal to take the oath was a contempt of court. Failure to answer was to confess. Thus the oath *ex officio*, like torture, became a means of making a person accuse himself.

It was used by the clergy to inquire into the morals of people and to ferret out heresy. It was so abused that it was outlawed, only to be restored and then abolished again. When Elizabeth, in 1559, established a national church, the oath *ex officio* became the instrument for oppressing Catholics and Puritans alike.

The High Commission, whose roots went back to 1535, was created to deal with matrimonial offenses, heresy, schism, and non-conformity. Heresy and schism were not necessarily related to deviations from the established religion. Witchcraft was heresy; two women quarreling in church was schism; the failure of a minister to read prayers on Wednesday was non-conformity. But so were breaches of the rules of the Church by those who refused to conform due to indifference or to the dictates of their conscience.

The defendant took the oath *ex officio* before he knew the charges against him and often before he knew who the accusers were. The trial was based on the answers given by the defendant under oath in his preliminary examination. The oath preceded the formal accusation; the examination of the defendant preceded the trial.

The Commission had authority to impose fines and imprisonment, as well as ecclesiastical penalties such as excommunication. That fact together with the oath *ex officio* made the court a powerful body. The oath got strength from the view that without it "the stretes were likely to swarme full of heretykes."

The oath and the High Commission were both abolished by Act of Parliament in 1641. James II restored them in 1686. But they were finally outlawed by the *Bill of Rights* in 1689.

The extent of the power of the High Commission is illustrated by the case of Nicholas Fuller, who, in 1607, acted as counsel for people committed for contempt for failure to appear before the Commission. One was Richard Mansel, a minister, who had petitioned Parliament in a manner deemed offensive, and the other Thomas Ladd, a merchant, who had attended a secret meeting of an outlawed religious group. Fuller sought their release by habeas corpus in the civil courts on the ground that the oath *ex officio* was unlawful and that the Commission had no authority to impose fines or to imprison men.

In the course of his argument before the civil court, Fuller became very impassioned. He denounced the procedure whereby a man, faced with no accusers and no information, was forced to testify against himself. He complained that the High Commission could impose any punishment that three judges desired and that no review of its action was provided. For these statements, made "to the disgrace of the Commission," Fuller was tried before that tribunal. He was fined £200, and imprisoned. The civil courts held that the High Commission acted lawfully.

Moreover, the High Commission had jurisdiction over printers, publishers, and booksellers under an ordinance of 1586. Under that law all printing was confined to London, Oxford, and Cambridge. The Archbishop of Canterbury and the Bishop of London decided the number of presses needed. They also had power to grant or refuse a license to publish a book. Violations of the licensing law were prosecuted before the High Commission.

Thus the Commission extended its authority over laymen as well as clergy. The civil courts sat "to punish the outward man"; the High Commission "to reform the inward man."

There were many controversies that raged between the civil courts and the High Commission. Though the political power remained behind the Commission until 1641, the grievances against it piled high, especially from the Puritans. The Commission was the Inquisition come to England—a device to punish, not reform, those who offended the orthodox view.

John Peter Zenger, who published a New York paper, fought and won the earliest battle for freedom of the press in this country (August 24). He was prosecuted for what he published concerning the Governor of New York and the current administration. He wrote that the liberties and properties of the people "are precarious, and that slavery is like to be intailed on them and their posterity, if some past things be not amended." He complained of the removal of judges, the creation of new courts without the consent of the legislature, and the denial of the right to trial by jury. The charge was that these criticisms brought the government into disrepute.

Zenger was tried August 4, 1735. Andrew G. Hamilton of Philadelphia defended. He admitted that Zenger had published the statements. The prosecution therefore contended that Zenger should be punished, since what Zenger had written "scandalized" the government. Hamilton argued that if what Zenger had written was true, it was not a libel, that truth was always a defense. The court ruled otherwise, refusing to hear evidence on the truth of Zenger's charges. Hamilton then argued that the jury should determine whether the publications were libelous. The court first ruled that that was an issue for the judges to decide. Hamilton pressed two points:

1. All freemen have "a right publicly to remonstrate against the abuses of power in the strongest terms."

2. The jury has the right to say whether or not a statement is libelous, i.e., the jury is at liberty "to find both the law and fact."

The court changed its position in one important respect. It left to the jury the question whether Zenger's writings did not "tend to beget an ill opinion" of the government. The jury shortly returned a verdict of *not guilty*.

Zenger spent nine months in jail before he was acquitted. But as a result of his sacrifice, truth became a defense to libel and judges lost their power to determine what is libelous.

The Progressive Party in 1912 ran Theodore Roosevelt for President and Hiram Johnson for Vice-President. This movement was a revolt against "the invisible government" of the other parties. The convention met in Chicago on August 5, 1912, and adopted a platform which declared for

—direct primaries for nomination of state and national officers
—direct election of U.S. Senators
—the initiative, referendum, and recall
—equal suffrage for men and women
—limitations on, and publicity of, campaign contributions and expenditures
—registration of lobbyists
—a referendum for all laws declared unconstitutional by the courts of the States
—restriction of the use of injunctions in labor disputes and of the power of courts to hold people in contempt
—a broad program of industrial legislation, including a six-day week, prohibition of child labor, minimum wages for women, workmen's compensation laws, unemployment and old age insurance, the organization of unions
—conservation of natural resources, including retention by the States and the federal government of all coal and oil lands, water powers, and the like in order to prevent abuse by private monopolies.

Roosevelt and Johnson received 88 electoral votes and over 4 million popular votes.

In 1708, an indictment was brought in London against a printer for publishing an obscene book, *The Fifteen Plagues of a Maidenhead.* It was called a "general satyr" that "exposes fornication" and "the folly of young people." The court held that obscenity could only be punished by the ecclesiastical courts, not at common law. In 1727, the opposite view was taken in the case of the book *Venus in the Cloister* or *The Nun in Her Smock.* The book was found obscene and the printer was punished.

The law of obscenity dates from that time. Thereafter Parliament passed various laws making it a crime to expose obscene books in public places. These apparently were not effective. In 1802, the English Society for Suppression of Vice was formed. In 1857, the *Obscene Publications Act* was passed. There was considerable objection to it; and it only passed on the assurance by Lord Chief Justice Campbell that "the measure was intended to apply exclusively to works written for the single purpose of corrupting the morals of youth, and of a nature calculated to shock the common feelings of decency in any well-regulated mind."

That assurance was soon swept into the limbo. In 1868, a pamphlet, *The Confessional Unmasked,* was condemned. It was a vicious attack on the Catholic Church and contained "filthy acts, words and ideas." That case established the basic test which was also to prevail on this side of the water. The test of obscenity, it was said, was "whether the tendency of the matter charged . . . is to deprave and corrupt those whose minds are open to such immoral influences and into whose hands a publication of this sort may fall."

James Joyce's book *Ulysses* tells of the lower middle class living in Dublin in 1904. It seeks to describe not only what the characters did on a June day but also the thoughts and impulses that were passing through their consciousness at the time. Joyce shows the effects of those impressions and ideas on the behavior of the characters. The United States sued to confiscate and ban the book on the ground that it was obscene.

Judge Woolsey of the District Court held that the book was an honest and sincere effort to explore and depict psychological phenomena. Obscene in federal law means tending to stir the sex impulses or to lead to sexually impure and lustful thoughts. Woolsey held that *Ulysses* was not obscene but only "a somewhat tragic and very powerful commentary on the inner lives of men and women"; that though some scenes were "a rather strong draught" and though the effect of some passages on the reader is "somewhat emetic," nowhere does the book tend to be "an aphrodisiac."

On August 7, 1934, the Court of Appeals affirmed, saying that the effect of the book as a whole is the test and that if it could be confiscated for its erotic passages, so could *Venus and Adonis, Hamlet, Romeo and Juliet,* and parts of the *Odyssey.*

This ruling temporarily put an end to the censorship which purity leagues inaugurated in this country beginning in the 1870's.

In 1947, New York condemned *Memoirs of Hecate County* by Edmund Wilson. In 1949, Pennsylvania refused to condemn nine books, including *Sanctuary* by William Faulkner and *God's Little Acre* by Erskine Caldwell. In 1951, Massachusetts outlawed the latter. By 1953, the pendulum was swinging back to the point where intolerance reigns supreme, particularly as respects pocket books. For pocket books sell for a few cents and are read by the masses. And throughout history the censor has been particularly anxious to protect them from "dangerous," "obnoxious," or "unpopular" ideas (June 17).

One effective way in which unofficial censors operated was shown in the case involving Mencken's magazine the *American Mercury*. A society in Boston scrutinized all publications, including books and magazines. If they felt that a publication violated the law of obscenity, they contacted the large distributors and told them that prosecutions would follow if the book or magazine were sold or distributed. If their warning was ignored, they would institute prosecution.

This society notified the distributors not to handle the April 1926 issue of the *American Mercury*. The *American Mercury* sued to enjoin the society from acting as unofficial censor of its publications. Judge James M. Morton, Jr., issued an injunction. He ruled that while members of the society had a right to express their views as to the propriety or legality of a publication, they had no right to impose those views on the book and magazine trade by threatening to prosecute those who disagreed with them.

Threats from these unofficial censors had banned many books from Boston including *All Quiet on the Western Front, A Farewell to Arms, The World of William Clissold,* and *Manhattan Transfer.*

Jefferson's bookseller in Philadelphia, a Mr. Dufief, was prosecuted in 1814 for selling De Becourt's *Sur la Creation du Monde, un Systeme d'Organisation Primitive,* which contained atheistic ideas. Jefferson wrote Dufief:

"I am really mortified to be told that, in the United States of America, a fact like this can become a subject of inquiry, and of criminal inquiry too, as an offence against religion; that a question about the sale of a book can be carried before the civil magistrate. . . . are we to have a censor whose imprimatur shall say what books may be sold, and what we may buy? . . . Whose foot is to be the measure to which ours are all to be cut or stretched? . . . It is an insult to our citizens to question whether they are rational beings or not, and blasphemy against religion to suppose it cannot stand the test of truth and reason. If M. de Becourt's book be false in its facts, disprove them; if false in its reasoning, refute it. But, for God's sake, let us freely hear both sides, if we choose. I know little of its contents, having barely glanced over here and there a passage, and over the table of contents. From this, the Newtonian philosophy seemed the chief object of attack, the issue of which might be trusted to the strength of the two combatants; . . . I thought the work would be very innocent, and one which might be confided to the reason of any man, not likely to be much read if let alone, but, if persecuted, it will be generally read. Every man in the United States will think it a duty to buy a copy, in vindication of his right to buy, and to read what he pleases."

Books (and the theater as well) give entertainment—relief from the tensions, the humdrum, the sorrows of the day. But they also probe our prejudices and presuppositions, challenge our premises, and test the basic assumptions of our business, moral, and political codes.

They examine critically domestic relations and the problems of parent and child, the miscarriages of justice, the blight of racial prejudice and discrimination, the ravages of monopoly, the vested interests in slums and vice, the despair of the outcasts of society, the morbid psychology of criminals tracing back to childhood experiences. The novel (and the play) often awaken us from our slumber, startle our complacency, and put us in a way to understand little revolutions within our own neighborhood. Or they may reach across the world and give insight into people in strange and faraway places. The novel (and the play) may reaffirm our ancient faith or ridicule it. They help keep us alive intellectually and spiritually. They let us, as Milton said, "consider vice with all her baits and seeming pleasure, and yet abstain, and yet distinguish, and yet prefer that which is truly better."

Or, like classical music, they may carry us to heights we never dreamed of, give us flashes of insight that change our lives, or reassure us that the spirit of man can never be chained.

These are reasons why the very idea of a censor is instantly at war with the demands of the mind and spirit of man.

This does not mean that anything one likes may be published with impunity. There are laws of libel and obscenity. One takes the calculated risk that he may be punished for what he says or writes. But one who offends gets the benefit of a jury trial and is not subject to the mere whim or caprice of the censor. Our system develops in the end, I think, a stimulating diversity and a sense of responsibility not known when authors are dependent upon a bureau for what they may publish.

41

On this day in 1792, the first reported decision of the United
States Supreme Court was handed down. The opinion had a distinctive American characteristic—two Justices dissented. The dissenting opinion has continued as a great American tradition. It is
as true to the character of our democracy as freedom of speech
itself. Who could imagine a German judge protesting one of Hitler's orders or a Russian magistrate dissenting from a decree of
the Kremlin?

Unanimity among judges cannot always be expected. Legislative acts are often compromises between competing ideas, and
consequently pregnant with ambiguities which judges must resolve. A hiatus may have been purposely left in the statute. In
that event a problem, too explosive for the legislators to solve, is
soon transferred to the courtroom. What is "fair" or "equitable"
within the meaning of a law is a matter on which opinions frequently differ.

On constitutional questions the difficulties of getting unanimity
are compounded. The *Constitution* is written in general terms.
The language gathers meaning from a judge's experience and
philosophy. What other judges may have said it meant cannot be
binding on the newcomer. For the *Constitution* was written for all
ages.

When judges do not agree, it is likely they are dealing with
problems on which society is divided. Hughes once spoke of the
dissent as "an appeal to the brooding spirit of the law, to the in-
telligence of a future day." The dissents of the 1920's and '30's
became the law in the '40's. Even when a dissent seemed futile, it
may have pricked the conscience of our people or have let the
world know that not all of America had lost perspective.

When I took my seat on the Court in 1939, I was 40 years old, while Charles Evans Hughes, the Chief Justice, was 77. It was, perhaps, the age differential itself that drew us closely together. In any event, I very quickly discovered a warm friendship for a man whom I had previously known only by reputation. It was almost a father-son relationship that developed. One day the Chief Justice—partly reminiscing, partly advising—talked of the role of the Court in the life of the nation, the problem of getting unanimity in judicial decisions, the recurrence of the dissenting opinion. He summed up his thoughts in these words:

"I think you will find after you have been on the Court for a while that the Brethren can be brought into agreement in the vast majority of the cases. But in a fourth, or perhaps a third, of the cases, unanimity cannot be expected." As he stopped to emphasize his point, his gray beard seemed to give a Jovian authority to his words:

"No matter what President appoints the Justices, no matter how carefully he picks them, they will never be unanimous in a large percentage of the issues coming before the Court. After all the Court reflects the maturity of the community. And when there are deep cleavages of social and economic philosophy in the community that same cleavage is pretty apt to be found in the Court, too."

The First Congress received many petitions from inventors asking a monopoly for their discoveries: John Fitch had an invention applying steam to navigation; Englehart Cruse, a steam engine for pumping water; Samuel Briggs, a machine for the making of nails; Leonard Harbaugh, threshing and reaping machines; Christopher Colles, a machine to count the revolutions of a wheel; John Macpherson, a lightning rod; Abraham Westervelt, a machine for manufacturing shell buttons.

From the beginning the inventive genius of Americans pressed for recognition. Patent laws enacted by Congress (the first one being in 1790) gave powerful stimulus to it by granting inventors a monopoly of their discoveries for a limited time.

Jefferson was the first administrator of our patent system. He too was an inventor, though he never took out a patent. He invented a hemp beater, a moldboard that still governs the shape of plowshares, a pedometer, a sun dial, a leather buggy top, and the swivel chair.

Three patents were issued the first year, the first one covering the making of pot and pearl ashes. In 1953, there were 45,561 granted.

On August 13, 1813, Jefferson wrote:

"He who receives an idea from me receives instruction himself without lessening mine, as he who lights his taper at mine receives light without darkening me. That ideas should freely spread from one to another over the globe, for the moral and mutual instruction of man and improvement of his condition seems to have been peculiarly and benevolently designed by nature, when she made them, like fire, expansible over all space . . . Inventions then cannot, in nature, be a subject of property. Society may give an exclusive right to the profits arising from them, as an encouragement to men to pursue ideas which may produce utility, but this may or may not be done, according to the will and convenience of the society, without claim or complaint from anybody."

Jefferson stated the opposing interests to be balanced in the patent system: On the one side is the encouragement of inventions for the benefit of society; on the other is the protection of society against oppressive monopolies.

The first patent law granted a fourteen-year monopoly, the present one a seventeen-year one. The monopoly is "the right to exclude others from making, using, or selling the invention" in this country. The invention covers "any new and useful process, machine, manufacture, or composition of matter, or any new and useful improvement thereof."

From the beginning every conceivable type of gadget was sought to be patented. Jefferson resisted this. In time the gadgeteers won out, leading Jefferson to write in disgust, "I might build a stable, bring into it a cutting-knife to chop straw, a hand-mill to grind corn, a curry comb and brush to clean the horses, and by a patent exclude anyone for evermore using these things without paying me."

Sometimes the test of invention was lowered to let in a host of gadgets—a doorknob made of clay, rubber caps on pencils, elastic gussets in corsets, flat rather than round cords for the loop end of suspenders, putting rollers under a machine, putting rubber handgrips on bicycle handlebars, an oval rather than a cylindrical toilet-paper roll, a revolving cue rack, putting a metal washer on a wire staple, a stamp for putting initials in the side of a tobacco plug.

The Supreme Court has usually held that "inventive genius" was the constitutional test for patents. The *Constitution* says that Congress may grant patents "to promote the Progress of Science and the useful Arts." The Supreme Court early held that this made the public interest the *primary* concern of the patent system, the reward to the inventor, the means to that end, but *secondary*.

On August 15, 1894, Congress enacted an income tax—2 per cent on all income over $4,000. The constitutionality of that law was immediately challenged. While the *Constitution* gives Congress the power to tax, it circumscribes the power: "No Capitation, or other direct, Tax shall be laid, unless in Proportion to the Census or Enumeration herein before directed to be taken." In 1895, the Supreme Court ruled in a five to four decision that an income tax levied on rents from real property and on income from stocks and bonds was a "direct" tax on the property from which the income was derived and therefore must be apportioned among the States on the basis of the census. The *Constitution*, it was held, was designed to protect the rich and populous States from the smaller and poorer ones, "to prevent an attack upon accumulated property by mere force of numbers."

There was much history and logic on the side of the dissenters. Moreover, the discrimination implicit in the majority decision cut deep: an income tax on wage earners and salaried people would be constitutional but not one on investors. Harlan pointed out that the propertied classes had now received "a position of favoritism and advantage." Brown deplored the use of "the spectre of socialism" to contract the *Constitution* and to surrender "the taxing power to the moneyed class."

There was a long agitation for a constitutional Amendment. By the time the joint resolution passed the Congress in 1909, about the only objection voiced was that an income tax would tend "to make a nation of liars," that it would create "a tax upon the income of honest men and an exemption, to a greater or less extent, of the income of the rascals."

The Sixteenth Amendment was ratified in 1913, Connecticut, Rhode Island, and Utah rejecting it and not subsequently ratifying.

Franklin D. Roosevelt came to the Presidency in the midst of the worst depression the nation had known. Farm prices, relatively speaking, reached their lowest point since the Civil War. Deflation, forced sales, food surpluses, lack of buying power depleted the country. Perhaps Roosevelt's leading measure was his agricultural program. Farmers received benefit payments if they reduced production of products in oversupply. The funds to make the benefit payments were raised by a tax on the processing of farm commodities.

A cotton mill resisted the tax. The case was decided by the Supreme Court early in 1936 (January 6). A majority of the Court held the tax unconstitutional. Congress can levy taxes for the "general welfare" (September 30). But reduction of acreage and control of production, the Court said, are not included; they are matters purely of local concern.

Most everyone, except the Justices, seemed to know that farm prices and farm surpluses were very relevant to the "general welfare" of the nation. Certainly a tax to aid the farming community was no more revolutionary than the protective tariff. The decision came with a shock. It, more than any other episode, convinced Roosevelt that the judiciary needed reorganizing (February 29).

Not many months passed before Roosevelt was telling the nation: "The Court has been acting not as a judicial body, but as a policy-making body . . . the majority of the Court has been assuming the power to pass on the wisdom of . . . Acts of Congress—and to approve or disapprove the policy written into these laws. . . . We have . . . reached the point as a nation where we must take action to save the Constitution from the Court and the Court from itself."

In the field of constitutional law, judges do not feel bound by rulings of their predecessors. It is the *Constitution* they swore to support and defend, not the gloss which an earlier Court has put on it. And so it is that decisions on the construction of the *Constitution* have been constantly re-examined.

der Cases, which first came before the Court in 1869. Greenbacks

Perhaps the most dramatic in our history were the *Legal Ten-* had been issued to help the North finance the war, and the question was whether Congress had power to make them legal tender for payment of private debts. The Court was composed of eight Justices, who voted five to three against the constitutionality of the law.

One Justice resigned, and Congress increased the number of Justices to nine. That gave Grant, who thought the *Legal Tender* decision wrong, two appointments to the Court. He nominated Strong and Bradley, whom the Senate confirmed, in face of newspaper clamor that Grant was "packing" the Court. A rehearing was granted in the *Legal Tender Cases* over the dissent of four Justices. On re-argument the new majority overruled the earlier case and held the greenbacks to be legal tender.

Age does not necessarily give sanctity to a decision. In 1937, the Supreme Court overruled a ninety-five-year-old decision and in 1938 a sixty-eight-year-old one. These involved constructions of the *Constitution*. Decisions on private law are usually more stable. But there are many exceptions. In 1867, the Supreme Court overruled a private law decision fifty-seven years old. From 1937 to 1949, the Supreme Court overruled 30 decisions, 21 involving constitutional questions. The great majority of the 30 had been decided within the previous twenty years.

In general each generation has taken unto itself the construction of the *Constitution* that best fits its needs (August 11).

August 18, 1823 marked a high tide of intolerance in Maryland. Benjamin Galloway announced his candidacy for the legislature on the "Christian ticket." He came out against the "Jew Bill," and asked for only Christian support, not that of "Jews, Deists, Mohammedans, or Unitarians." His opponent was Thomas Kennedy, a Scotch Presbyterian. Galloway won the election, but the cause Kennedy sponsored was soon to carry the day.

Maryland's constitution, adopted in 1776, required a public officeholder to make "a declaration of a belief in the Christian religion." This barred Jews from holding office. Thomas Kennedy led the campaign to end the discrimination. He started his drive for reform in 1818. His measure was voted down or defeated again and again. He himself was defeated in 1823, only to win the next election. He was in the Maryland legislature in 1826, when the law qualifying Jews for public office was finally passed.

Kennedy was not eloquent. His sentences were blunt and ragged. But they had the passion of justice in them: "There are few Jews in the United States; in Maryland there are very few. But if there was only one—to that one, we ought to do justice."

A monument commemorating his fight for tolerance stands in the cemetery at Hagerstown.

In August 1937, the first Soil Conservation District was organized in Anson County, North Carolina. By 1954, there were 2,586 such districts, covering nearly one and a half billion acres of land and nearly 4,800,000 farms throughout the nation.

This program was part of Roosevelt's undertaking to save the country's topsoil (January 5). "The nation that destroys its soil destroys itself," he wrote in 1937. This is the idea that induced every State to pass Soil Conservation District Laws. The federal Soil Conservation Service renders technical aid to these local groups.

A survey is made to ascertain the best use for a tract of land. A conservation plan is drawn up, which may include terracing, strip cropping, stubble-mulching, contour cultivation, seeding of pastures, drainage, construction of ponds, planting of shelter belts. Some lands may be retired from cultivation and put back to trees or grass. Crops may be changed or rotated. Each meadow, each slope is studied to ascertain the best productive use to which it can be put. Plans are projected for the entire watershed as well as for each farm.

The farmers themselves form and manage the districts. This is in the tradition of self-government, as related by Parks in *Soil Conservation Districts In Action*. Over half the state laws permit the districts to adopt land-use regulations and to enforce them. Little coercion has been used to date. The achievements—and they have been great—have resulted largely from co-operation. Yet can a farmer be prevented from farming his land as he chooses? Can he be stopped from breaking sod in the "dust bowl"? The first legal test was in Colorado, where the land-use regulations were sustained in 1948.

I remember a visit to a conservation farm in Texas. It had some patches of woodland, and rolling acres of lush meadows. There was no trace of wash on the slopes, even after a hard rain. The farmer next door was beginning to be ashamed that his land was streaked with gullies, that gravel had taken the place of much of his choice topsoil.

In colonial days, American judges, appointed at the pleasure of the King, were customarily Tories. Great pressure was put on them to bow to the royal will. To their great credit, they often refused. The record of independence which they wrote is part of our tradition. The attempt of the King to control them made firm the resolve to keep our courts free from the executive. A series of episodes relating to search warrants illustrates the point.

Customs officers wanted search warrants good for all times and all occasions, so that they could search any place day or night for contraband goods. These were the general writs of assistance that James Otis protested against (February 24). Some judges issued the writs, notably in Massachusetts. Most of the judges in the other colonies refused. Prominent in the opposition was Chief Justice William Allen of Pennsylvania, who said, "If you will make oath that you have had an information that they [taxable goods] are in any particular place, I will grant you a writ to search that particular place, but no general writ to search every house."

On August 20, 1768, William de Grey, Attorney General of England, rendered an opinion in which he chided Allen and emphasized the legality of the general writ. Allen was adamant. The Connecticut judges were also opposed to De Grey. The New York judges delayed action for five years, finally refusing the writ. The same happened in Maryland. The judges in Florida and Georgia also stood firm. A violent storm developed in Virginia between the Crown and the judges. The judges were unanimous, being unmoved by arguments, legal opinions from overseas, and threats of impeachment. A measure of the opposition to the general writ is its condemnation in Virginia's *Declaration of Rights*, which preceded the *Declaration of Independence* (June 12).

On August 21, 1721, James Franklin, brother of Benjamin Franklin, started publication in Boston of America's fourth newspaper, the New England *Courant*. (The first was the Boston *News Letter*, April 24, 1704; the second, the Boston *Gazette,* December 21, 1719; the third, the *American Weekly Mercury* of Philadelphia, December 22, 1719). Benjamin worked as an apprentice on the *Courant,* and he also contributed items to it that were anonymous even to his brother.

Some political comment made in the *Courant* irked the Colonial Assembly. James was arrested, censured, and imprisoned for a month. During that month Benjamin—then seventeen years old—ran the paper. He reported in his *Autobiography* that he "made bold to give our rulers some rub," with the result that he was considered "a young genius that had a turn for libelling and satyr."

When James was released from jail, the Assembly ordered that "James Franklin should no longer print the paper called the New England *Courant.*" The brothers had a consultation and decided the paper should be printed thereafter under the name of Benjamin Franklin. This was a dodge; but the paper was published that way for several months, until differences between the brothers took Benjamin to New York.

The New England *Courant* was our first paper to denounce the colonial regime, and one of the first to feel the full brunt of censorship. Prior to it was *Publick Occurrences,* a single issue of which had appeared in Boston in 1690. It was quickly suppressed because not licensed, the theologian Increase Mather joining with those who denounced it.

Behind the New England *Courant* was the Hell-fire Club, whose members threw their darts at both church and state. The paper drew not only the wrath of the government but also the ire of the theologian Cotton Mather, who said it reflected a "wickedness never parall'd anywhere upon the Face of the Earth."

On August 22, 1911, Taft vetoed the joint resolution admitting New Mexico and Arizona into the Union. His objection was the provision in the Arizona constitution providing for the recall of judges:

" . . . the unbridled expression of the majority of a community converted hastily into law or action would sometimes make a government tyrannical and cruel. Constitutions are checks upon the hasty action of the majority. They are the self-imposed restraints of a whole people upon a majority of them to secure sober action and a respect for the rights of the minority, and of the individual in his relation to other individuals, and in his relation to the whole people in their character as a state or government . . .

"By the recall in the Arizona constitution it is proposed to give to the majority power to remove arbitrarily, and without delay, any judge who may have the courage to render an unpopular decision. . . . We can not be blind to the fact that often an intelligent and respectable electorate may be so roused upon an issue that it will visit with condemnation the decision of a just judge, though exactly in accord with the law governing the case, merely because it affects unfavorably their contest."

Arizona changed its constitution to meet Taft's objection, and after admission restored the provision for recall of judges. Today eight States have similar provisions.

The first judge in the United States to be recalled was Charles Weller, of the San Francisco police court. The incident which gave rise to it was Weller's reduction of bail (November 10) in the case of a man charged with an assault upon a young girl. The accused fled, forfeited his bail, and escaped trial. Investigation showed laxity in supervising other cases involving assaults against girls. The women of San Francisco became aroused and led the recall campaign in 1913.

Nicola Sacco and Bartolomeo Vanzetti were Italians. Sacco worked in a shoe factory; Vanzetti was a fish peddler. Each was industrious; and neither had a criminal record prior to his arrest in 1920 for the murder of two men in a pay roll robbery at Braintree, Massachusetts. The accused were pacifists and anarchists, but not communists. During World War I, they had "dodged" the draft. In 1920, they were active in "radical" circles in Massachusetts and on the suspect list of the Department of Justice.

In 1920, the federal government undertook the wholesale arrest and deportation of aliens who were suspected of being in sympathy with communist Russia. Hysteria seized many communities having a large proportion of foreign labor. Boston was as badly infused with the fear as any city. It was in this atmosphere that Sacco and Vanzetti were tried.

They were convicted on the flimsiest of evidence. They were denied a new trial after an offer of proof which went far toward exonerating them by seriously implicating other men. Many disinterested observers felt that the trial was infected with passion, prejudice, and unfairness. It seemed that the hysteria of the day had seized even the courts. A reading of the record years later leaves the impression that Sacco and Vanzetti, charged with murder, were convicted because they were pacifists, draft dodgers, and radicals. Perhaps they were guilty; perhaps not. That is not the question. What will always lie heavily on the conscience of America is that they went to their death on August 23, 1927, as a result of a trial which in retrospect seems not to have been a fair one.

Long before the American Revolution, seeds of our civil liberties were sprouting in the Colonies. The records of trials before the colonial courts show an acute awareness by defendants of the requirements of due process.

On August 24, 1692, William Bradford, Pennsylvania printer (February 12), was charged with printing "a malicious and seditious" paper without disclosing that he was the printer. The Quakers had quarreled among themselves, dividing into two factions. The condemned publication contained an attack by the minority on the dominant group, including the magistrates.

Bradford demanded an immediate trial. He said that "speedy justice" was "the right of every free born English subject." (July 21.) Bradford did not get a "speedy" trial. He was held in jail until the following December.

When he came to trial, he demanded to know the charges against him (November 21), saying "ye never let me have a copy of my presentment, nor will ye now let me know what law ye prosecute me upon."

Bradford challenged two of the jurors because they had aligned themselves with the majority group. He wanted an "impartial" jury. His objections were overruled.

The court first ruled that the jury were to determine only whether Bradford had printed the paper. Bradford objected, saying the jury were also to find "whether this be a seditious paper or not." He claimed that the "jury are judges in law as well as the matter of fact." (August 4.) Some jurymen spoke up, saying, "they did believe in their consciences, they were obliged to try and find whether that paper was seditious." The court finally left that issue to the jury.

The jury, after ten days, could not agree and they were discharged. Bradford then asked that he be discharged. The court ruled he would have "to answer next court, as before." At the next court Bradford protested that he could not be put in jeopardy twice (November 16).

He was not tried again and shortly left for New York.

When Sacco and Vanzetti were convicted, the Supreme Judicial Court of Massachusetts had only a limited power of review. It could review only questions of law, e.g., whether the jury was properly instructed. It could not review the weight of the evidence. It could not consider whether, on the whole record, an injustice was being done. It could not order a new trial, though it felt that justice required it. As a consequence of the Sacco-Vanzetti case, the power of the Supreme Judicial Court was broadened in all capital cases. By an Act passed in 1939 it was granted review of the whole case—of the law and the evidence; and it was given power to order a new trial, if satisfied that justice required it. No longer was the trial judge absolute master; no longer could his prejudice or partisanship determine the fate of men.

The execution of Sacco and Vanzetti had repercussions abroad. In 1909, Oscar Slater had been convicted in Scotland of murder. There was no provision at that time for review of criminal appeals. In 1927, a law was passed granting review. Slater appealed. In 1928, his conviction was reversed and he was released, the government paying him £6,000 as compensation for his eighteen years of false imprisonment (May 9).

"The right of citizens of the United States to vote shall not be denied or abridged by the United States or by any State on account of sex." On August 26, 1920, the Secretary of State proclaimed that this, the Nineteenth Amendment, had become part of the *Constitution,* 36 of the 48 States having ratified it.

Susan Brownell Anthony, the woman who gave her life to this cause, died in 1906 before the final accomplishment. But she, more than any other single person, was responsible for it. There was a powerful complex of forces at work in this woman. She never put aside this cause for any other. She never formed a tie, personally or professionally, which would interfere with it. Every speech, every trip, every letter was for its promotion. Many other American women also led the crusade. During World War I, some chained themselves to the gates of the White House to dramatize their demand for the franchise.

The United Nations, whose Charter proclaims "the equal rights of men and women," supplied an international forum for suffragettes. The leaders have been Mrs. L. N. Menon, of India, and Miss Minerva Bernardino, of the Dominican Republic. In 1953, they persuaded the General Assembly to adopt an international convention granting women equal political rights. Before 1953 ended, 27 nations signed it. From 1945, when the United Nations was formed, to 1953, suffrage rights were extended to women by 24 countries. By the end of 1953, there were only 17 countries in which women had no political rights.

The communists also promote the cause. They try to generate unrest in the feudal Middle East by advertising the prominence of women in the communist regimes.

In 1952, there were almost 2 million more women eligible to vote than men in the United States. In 1953, women could vote in all elections on an equal basis with men in 60 countries, including the Moslem nations of Indonesia, Pakistan, and Syria.

The *Constitution* provides that federal judges "shall hold their Offices during good Behaviour, and shall, at stated Times, receive for their Services, a Compensation, which shall not be diminished during their Continuance in Office." It also provides that civil officers, including judges, "shall be removed from Office on Impeachment for, and Conviction of, Treason, Bribery, or other high Crimes and Misdemeanors." Impeachment is by the House; conviction is on the concurrence of two thirds of the members of the Senate present.

At the Constitutional Convention, John Dickinson of Delaware, on August 27, 1787, moved to insert after the words "good Behaviour" the words "provided that they may be removed by the Executive on the application by the Senate and the House of Representatives." Gouverneur Morris of Pennsylvania and Edmund Randolph of Virginia opposed the motion. Of the eight States on the roll call and voting, only Connecticut voted in the affirmative.

Thus an independent judiciary was provided for, and one of the grievances against George III rectified. For the *Declaration of Independence* stated, "He has made Judges dependent on his Will alone, for the tenure of their offices, and the amount and payment of their salaries."

The Senate has sat as a Court of Impeachment nine times in cases involving judicial officers.

Of these, one—George W. English of Illinois—resigned before trial and his impeachment was dismissed in 1926.

Four were removed from office: John Pickering of New Hampshire in 1804; West H. Humphreys of Tennessee in 1862; Robert W. Archbald of Pennsylvania in 1913; and Holsted L. Ritter of Florida in 1936.

Four were acquitted: Samuel Chase of Maryland in 1805; James H. Peck of Missouri in 1831; Charles Swayne of Florida in 1905; Harold Louderback of California in 1933.

The record proves that the Senate has used its power sparingly and has been reluctant to weaken the independence of the judiciary. At the same time a tradition of fearless and honest decisions regardless of consequences has developed, so that the judiciary has indeed become an integral part of the system of checks and balances in our government.

In 1953, a House committee was investigating certain federal grand jury investigations in California. The grand jury had been impaneled by Louis E. Goodman, U. S. District Judge. He was subpoenaed by the committee and asked questions concerning his conversation with the foreman of the grand jury. The functioning of a federal grand jury, Judge Goodman asserted, was part of a "judicial proceeding," and the conduct of a federal judge in a "judicial proceeding" was beyond the competence of Congress to inquire into, except in impeachment proceedings.

Judge Goodman and his six colleagues on the District Court bench stated their views as follows:

". . . The judges signing below, being all the judges of the court, are deeply conscious, as must be your committee, of the constitutional separation of functions among the executive, legislative, and judicial branches of the Federal Government. This separation of functions is founded on the historic concept that no one of these branches may dominate or unlawfully interfere with the others.

"In recognition of the fundamental soundness of this principle we are unwilling that a judge of this court appear before your committee and testify with respect to any judicial proceeding. The Constitution of the United States does not contemplate that such matters be reviewed by the legislative branch, but only by the appropriate appellate tribunals. The integrity of the Federal courts, upon which liberty and life depend, requires that such courts be maintained inviolate against the changing moods of public opinion. We are certain that you as legislators have always appreciated and recognized this, and we know of no instance in the history of the United States where a committee such as yours has summoned a member of the Federal judiciary. . . ."

On August 30, 1917, the High Court of Impeachment of Texas convened to try Governor James E. Ferguson. On September 25, 1917, he was removed from the Governorship and disqualified to hold any office of honor, trust, or profit under the State of Texas. The offenses related for the most part to improper financial transactions. One offense concerned the Governor's interference with the management of the affairs of the University of Texas by the Board of Regents. "The Governor . . . not only filed charges against certain members of the faculty, as he had the right to do, but after the members were exonerated by the Board of Regents he has sought to have the members of the faculty expelled from that institution because he desired it . . . and to assert . . . his own aristocratic will" instead of the legal judgment of the Board.

The impeachment of Ferguson might, indeed, never have taken place but for his attack on the University of Texas. He sought to impose his will on the University by vetoing its entire appropriation, except the salary of one officer. In this manner he sought to dictate educational policies. The faculty, the students, and the alumni rose in mighty protest. Though the impeachment of the Governor rested mainly on corrupt actions, it was in effect one of the greatest victories for academic freedom the nation has known.

During the late 1940's and early 1950's, many investigating committees leveled their guns on faculty members of colleges and universities. Some institutions knuckled under to the committees, discharging those who once had been communists or who refused to testify on the grounds of self-incrimination. During this period, Harvard Corporation maintained a position of stout independence. For example, in 1953 it had before it two faculty members who once were communists but no longer were, yet who had invoked the Fifth Amendment as respects their former activities. One of these in 1944 had lied to an agent investigating a person for government work. A third professor had never been a communist but had invoked the Fifth Amendment because of her fear that the investigations would destroy our civil liberties. Each of the three had good teaching records; none was under communist domination or permitted his connection with the communist party to affect his teaching. None used his position to influence the political thinking of the students.

After a full review of the facts, the Corporation removed none of the three. It placed on a three-year probation the one who had lied to the investigating agent. It took no action against the other two.

Alan Barth of the Washington *Post* wrote that "It is an abdication of academic independence for any university to serve indiscriminately as the executor of punishments arbitrarily imposed by a congressional committee," that institutions of higher learning cannot make "their vital contribution to a free society, if they are subject to political control." That is the concept of academic freedom which Harvard exemplified, to her eternal credit, even when hysteria was at its worst.

SEPTEMBER

In 1920, Governor Alfred E. Smith of New York vetoed a bill requiring each public school teacher to obtain a certificate from the Commissioner of Education that he is of good moral character, will support the state and federal constitutions, and is loyal "to the institutions and laws" of New York and the nation. The bill also gave power to the Commissioner to revoke the certificate if he found the teacher was not "loyal." The Governor said in a notable veto:

"The test established is not what the teacher teaches, but what the teacher believes. . . . It permits one man to place upon any teacher the stigma of disloyalty and this even without hearing or trial. No man is so omniscient or wise as to have entrusted to him such arbitrary and complete power not only to condemn any individual teacher, but to decree what belief or opinion is opposed to the institutions of the country.

"No teacher could continue to teach if he or she entertained any objection, however conscientious, to any existing institution. If this law had been in force prior to the abolition of slavery, opposition to that institution which was protected by the Constitution and its laws would have been just cause for the disqualification of a teacher. . . .

"Opposition to any presently established institution, no matter how intelligent, conscientious, or disinterested this opposition might be, would be sufficient to disqualify the teacher. Every teacher would be at the mercy of his colleagues, his pupils, and their parents, and any word or act of the teacher might be held by the commissioner to indicate an attitude hostile to some of the institutions of 'the United States' or of the State.

". . . The bill confers upon the Commissioner of Education a power of interference with freedom of opinion which strikes at the foundations of democratic education."

1

Dr. Robert M. Hutchins, formerly President of the University of Chicago, testified as follows before a House committee in 1952:

"Now, a university is a place that is established and will function for the benefit of society, provided it is a center of independent thought. It is a center of independent thought and criticism that is created in the interest of the progress of society, and the one reason that we know that every totalitarian government must fail is that no totalitarian government is prepared to face the consequences of creating free universities.

"It is important for this purpose to attract into the institution men of the greatest capacity, and to encourage them to exercise their independent judgment.

"Education is a kind of continuing dialogue, and a dialogue assumes, in the nature of the case, different points of view.

"The civilizations which I work and which I am sure every American is working toward, could be called a civilization of the dialogue, where instead of shooting one another when you differ, you reason things out together.

"In this dialogue, then, you cannot assume that you are going to have everybody thinking the same way or feeling the same way. It would be unprogressive if that happened. The hope of eventual development would be gone. More than that, of course, it would be very boring.

"A university, then, is a kind of continuing Socratic conversation on the highest level for the very best people you can think of, you can bring together, about the most important questions, and the thing that you must do to the uttermost possible limits is to guarantee those men the freedom to think and to express themselves.

"Now, the limits on this freedom cannot be merely prejudice, because although our prejudices might be perfectly satisfactory, the prejudices of our successors, or of those who are in a position to bring pressure to bear on the institution, might be subversive in the real sense, subverting the American doctrine of free thought and free speech."

No person shall be incompetent as a witness or juror "on account of his religious belief, provided, he believes in the existence of God, and that under His dispensation such person will be held morally accountable for his acts and be rewarded or punished therefor in this world or the world to come." So provides the constitution of Maryland. Arkansas has a similar provision. And a few States have a like rule by statute or judicial decision. This was, indeed, the rule of the common law, which reflected the view an English judge expressed to a witness during a famous trial in 1685 that God "may justly strike thee into eternal flames and make thee drop into the bottomless lake of fire and brimstone, if thou offer to deviate the least from the truth and nothing but the truth."

The opposite view is supported by most of the States. They reject the idea that the veracity of a witness turns on his belief or disbelief in God. Fear of Divine punishment is one inducement for a person to tell the truth. There are, however, others. For an atheist or agnostic may have a moral sense, a high standard of right and of wrong, an innate instinct for decency and fair play.

Some States, though allowing an atheist or agnostic to testify, permit his disbelief to be shown in order to impeach his credibility. Kansas and most of the States do not allow that "stigma" to be cast on him. As a New York judge once said, an inquiry into the religious beliefs of a witness allows a lawyer to prejudice a jury because of the unpopular religious faith or creed of the person who is testifying. Religious animosities are easily aroused and give rise to passions which through the years have done great injustice.

The accommodation of our law to the unorthodox theological view is seen in the almost universal rule that a witness who does not choose to take an oath may make affirmation instead.

Most States have laws protecting employees from being controlled or coerced by their employers in the exercise of their suffrage. For example, some make it an offense for an employer to discharge or threaten to discharge an employee because he votes a certain way. Beginning last century, some States enacted laws requiring employers to give their employees time out for voting during regular working hours, without any deduction from their wages. The time allowed varies from one to four hours. The aim was not so much discouragement of coercive practices of employers as a desire to stimulate voting by employees. If they would lose part of a day's wages by voting, many might not go to the polls.

Is it a taking of the employer's property without due process of law to require him to pay wages while his employees are voting? In 1952, the Supreme Court held, in a case from Missouri, that it was not. Getting out the vote is a legitimate public end. The "political well-being" of the community is as much a part of the public welfare as its "physical well-being." Minimum wages can be fixed to protect the health and morals of the worker. An election law which imposes a minimum wage requirement for the protection of the right of suffrage is within the police power. The police power, though not unlimited, includes "all the great public needs."

Charles II adopted severe measures against nonconformists, closing their churches and arresting those who met for religious worship. Among these were the Quakers, who showed extraordinary resistance to the oppressive measures. When the police raided their meetings, none would move or seek to escape. They would go as a congregation to prison and stay there until dismissed. They would not seek release nor would they pay the fines that were imposed on them. And when they were released, they would repair once more to their meetinghouse. If the meetinghouse had been closed by the police, they would assemble in the street before the door and there worship God.

William Penn was charged with such a meeting in Grace Church Street, London. The indictment stated that he preached there, causing "a great concourse and tumult of people" to the "great disturbance" of the peace and to the "great terror and disturbance" of the people. The only violence or disorderliness was supplied by the police who broke up the meeting.

Penn's trial took place at Old Bailey and lasted five days. The jury, in spite of threats and coercion by the court, refused to convict Penn. On September 5, 1670, they returned a verdict of not guilty.

Penn then demanded his liberty. But though the jury had acquitted Penn, the judge was bent on having his own way. He held Penn for fines.

"Fines for what?" Penn asked.

"For contempt of court," was the answer. And Penn was hauled away to Newgate.

The judge who committed William Penn for contempt was a victim of the hysteria of his day. During the trial, when he saw that the jury was out of hand and was obstinate against a verdict of guilty, he remarked:

"Till now I never understood the reason of the policy and prudence of the Spaniards in suffering the Inquisition among them. And certainly it will never be well with us till something like the Spanish Inquisition be in England."

William Penn's judge took a short cut to make this unpopular minority feel the displeasure of the government and to seek revenge on them for not conforming. Short cuts are always tempting when one feels his cause is just. Short cuts have always been justified on the ground that the end being worthy, the means of reaching it are not important. Short cuts, however, are dangerous. If they can be taken against one person or group, they can be taken against another. Our greatest struggle has been to provide procedural safeguards that will protect us against ourselves and make as certain as possible that reason and calm judgment will not be swept away by passion and hysteria. Experience shows that it is the William Penns of the world, not the criminals, who suffer most when the procedural safeguards for fair trials are relaxed.

A judge's self-interest in a case may vitiate a trial. Chief Justice Taft, writing for the Supreme Court, so held in 1927. The judge in that criminal case was on a salary; but when he convicted a defendant, he got an additional fee. That system was held to deny a defendant due process of law.

But the conduct of a judge at the trial may be equally damaging to an accused. Holt, Lord Chief Justice, presided at the trial that sent Haagen Swendsen to his death in 1702. The crime was spiriting off Pleasant Rawlins for the purpose of marriage. There was evidence of force in spiriting her away; and they were, indeed, married. There was testimony by the parson who married them that Pleasant was willing and did not object. Haagen testified that Pleasant had encouraged him, kissing him and squeezing his hand when they walked in the garden.

Holt conducted most of the examination of the witnesses. He seemed to relish baiting Haagen. He put questions like this: "If she did know anything of, or was consenting to the arrest, why did you *force* her to the tavern, and marry her with a parson you had provided for that purpose?" The use of *force* was the gist of the offense. If any *force* was used, Haagen was guilty, even if Pleasant consented to be married. Holt, by his questions, firmly implanted in the jury's mind that Haagen did use *force*. That cost Haagen his life.

At William Ireland's famous trial when he pleaded for time to call his witnesses (July 18) Scroggs, Lord Chief Justice, implanted in the minds of the jury that the witnesses, if present, would testify falsely. "We know you can call heretics, and ill names, fast enough."

Those convictions would today be set aside for the conduct of the judges. As a federal court recently said, the judge is responsible "for a courtroom atmosphere in which guilt or innocence may be soberly and fairly tested"; he must not exploit "the authority of the bench" toward a conviction which privately he thinks is deserved or required.

Ordinarily when a lawyer is charged with a crime, the court of whose bar he is a member will not disbar him until he is tried and convicted. But there are exceptions; and one occurred in 1882, when a federal court disbarred J. B. Wall, an attorney, after a summary hearing before the judge sitting without a jury and on the judge's own charge that this lawyer had helped lynch a prisoner a few days earlier.

The exceptional circumstances which the Supreme Court held justified the summary proceedings were these:

Proof of the lawyer's active participation in the lynching was clear and his denial was evasive.

The prisoner was hanged at the door of the courthouse while the court was in session.

The lawyer's participation in the lynching showed "a gross want of fealty to the law and repudiation of legal government"—an attitude making a person unfit to be an officer of the court.

Abraham Lincoln, who was licensed to practice law on September 9, 1836, had an encounter with the authorities when he was eighteen years old. He was hailed into court for operating a ferryboat across the Ohio River without a license. Displaying the common sense that marked his life, Lincoln proved that he was not operating across the river, but only from the shore to passing steamers in midstream.

By 1834, he was representing his neighbors without pay before the local justice of the peace in Springfield.

By 1841, he had advanced professionally so far that he argued 14 cases before the Illinois Supreme Court and won all but 4.

Lincoln "rode circuit" several months a year. As a "circuit rider" he went horseback or by train to distant counties to try cases. These were Lincoln's happiest times. Court was a gala occasion in the county seats, and Lincoln was the star performer, both in court and after hours. With his office in his coat pockets and his arguments in his head, Lincoln charmed the juries, not only as counsel for criminals and widows but also for railroads and landlords. He won cases far more often on wit and common sense than on precedent. His ability to laugh his way to some victories did not mean he failed to take his obligations seriously. He was at heart a conciliator, always counseling people to discourage litigation.

The lessons Lincoln learned, representing both poor and the rich before judges and juries, served him well in the crucial years that followed. Carl Sandburg has said that a study of Lincoln's pre-Presidential years "would imply that if he was what he was during those first 52 years of his life, it was nearly inevitable that he would be what he proved to be during the last four."

Banishment is a penalty known to some countries. It was practiced in America during the colonial period. In Russia, exile to Siberia has long been a form of sentence, following conviction for a political or other crime. Other countries of Asia have used banishment as a means of getting rid of "troublesome" or "undesirable" people. In the summer of 1951, I visited Hunza, a small principality in the northern part of West Pakistan. Hunza, about half a mile wide and eighty miles long, is jagged, bleak country that lies snug against the border of Sinkiang. Hunza is an absolute monarchy with a Mir as ruler, who has a place of banishment named Shingshal that lies about 13,000 feet high. It has short summers and long, bitter winters. I did not visit it, but I heard cruel tales of the men and women who were sent there.

Some Americans have known the bitterness of banishment. Bert L. Scott, a native of Yakima, Washington, was convicted by a justice of the peace for negligent driving. He was fined $50 and given a ninety-day jail sentence. The judge suspended the jail sentence and all but $25 of the fine, provided Scott left the State and stayed away for five years. That was banishment imposed as the price of avoiding jail. On September 10, 1950, when the judge was up for re-election, the Yakima *Republic* (not noted for its defense of civil liberties except when Robert Lucas was its editor) denounced him for what he had done in that case and in others like it. The paper then fought two long, legal battles in the courts to vindicate itself. The St. Louis *Post Dispatch*, meanwhile, reviewed the Scott case and stated:

"The place to protect civil rights is not in Washington or some other seat of government but in each city, town and village in the land. Local police stations and local courts are the focal points. It is the duty of the bar and of the press to watch these everywhere with the vigilance of Editor Lucas of the Yakima *Republic*."

On September 11, 1919, Calvin Coolidge, Governor of Massachusetts, broke a strike of policemen in Boston by calling out the state guard.

The police were notoriously underpaid, drawing smaller wages than streetcar conductors; and they were unable to get more wages or benefits, though other workers were obtaining increases. The police, in contravention of an order of the Boston Police Commissioner, formed a union and affiliated with the American Federation of Labor. The Commissioner thereupon placed nineteen of the leaders on trial. The police defended on the ground of their low pay and long hours, and refused to surrender their A. F. of L. affiliation. The Commissioner suspended the nineteen policemen, and the police went on strike.

Eleven hundred and seventeen patrolmen out of 1,544 quit duty on September 9. That night and the next day there was considerable rioting and robbery—"the devil was on the loose in Boston," said the news reports. By the evening of the tenth, mobs filled the streets. Coolidge acted vigorously on the eleventh.

During this controversy, Coolidge engaged in an argument with Samuel Gompers of the A. F. of L. Coolidge wrote to Gompers, "There is no right to strike against the public safety by anybody, any time, anywhere."

That message—and the action of Coolidge in breaking the Boston strike—made him a national hero overnight and headed him toward the White House.

Coolidge represented the *status quo*. His antithesis was Robert M. La Follette, whose liberalism was Jeffersonian, romantic, and idealistic. La Follette threw his great energies behind the creation of an administrative machinery of government to deal with the powerful forces of his day. There was first the rise of big business, its increasing domination of our natural resources, and its exploitation of labor. Second was the growing inequality in the distribution of wealth in the nation. Third was the decline in honesty and efficiency in government.

La Follette made Wisconsin an experimental laboratory for progressive ideas. He broke the power of "the bosses," instituted effective controls over railroads and other utilities, introduced industrial reforms, revised the tax system, raised the standard of public administration, and made the University a powerful force in the State. La Follette then brought Wisconsin's progressive political creed to the national scene. He headed a third party in the 1924 Presidential election. His electoral vote was small, but he garnered one sixth of the popular vote.

La Follette was the voice of labor crying out against oppression, the voice of small business protesting against monopolies, the voice of farmers pleading against oppressive freight rates, the voice of the conservationist denouncing the plundering of the public domain, the voice of the unemployed asking for more than crumbs from the table.

No man in American public life ever expended more energy than he in his crusades. His confidence in people was never shaken. He had Jefferson's passion for more democracy as a cure for all the evils, from boss-ridden cities to greedy trusts. La Follette hoped he would be remembered for his devotion to "the ideals of American democracy." A measure of it was his message in 1909 to Tom L. Johnson (December 1) after the latter's defeat for a fourth term as Mayor of Cleveland, "Fight on, brave heart, fight on."

La Follette's philosophy was a liberalism indigenous to America, true to our character, untainted by foreign influence.

The class warfare which Marxism preaches has never taken hold here. Perhaps the closest we came to it was in the bitter industrial conflicts near the end of the last century. Yet even then the ideology of class conflict was largely foreign and unacceptable. Our moral fiber rejects it. Our social, economic, and political democracy is a great leveler that will stop its growth here.

In 1776, there was a deep schism in the country. Merchants and plantation owners, who at first had opposed the British colonial policy, soon became alarmed at the tumultuous forces they had helped loosen. Some turned Loyalist, and joined forces with the King. Others stood silent and neutral, biding their time. Many left the country; over 40,000 (including Jonathan Odell, the famous Tory satirist) went to Canada; thousands went to the Bahamas; thousands more returned to England.

The political philosophy that had taken hold here split the classes. The farmers, the small merchants, the mechanics, the laboring class—they were the ones who fed the flames of revolution, they were the ones who outraged their betters. The landed gentry, the aristocrats, the gentlemen, looked with suspicion on those commoners. The aristocracy even had jokes about them:

> *Down at night a bricklayer or carpenter lies*
> *Next sun a Lycurgus, a Solon doth rise.*

The commoners replied that the aristocrats could go to "Hell, Hull, or Halifax," so far as they were concerned.

This schism in the classes resulted in the liquidation of the colonial aristocracy and the emergence of a dominant middle class. It was then that we supplanted colonialism with Americanism and put at work great leveling forces that have often been blocked, but never long suppressed.

Lloyd H. Fisher, author of *The Harvest Labor Market in California,* concluded, after years of study of the problems of migratory labor, that the brightest prospect of this lowly class of workers was in the abolition of the jobs they sought and the creation instead of industrial work. He wrote about the wetbacks, the okies, the human tumbleweeds, the Joads, the destitute families who in the summer follow the sun north in search of work, or who are refugees from disasters such as the dust bowl. John Steinbeck wrote of some of them in *Of Mice and Men, In Dubious Battle,* and *The Grapes of Wrath.* Those books stung America's conscience. The I.W.W.'s drew heavily on these migrants for their membership in the 1920's. They have been the subject of more investigations than probably any other group, the most recent being the report of *The President's Commission on Migratory Labor,* 1951.

The problems they create in the communities they touch are considerable. Housing, labor camps, sanitation, hospitalization, medical care, education are part of them. The low wages they usually receive, the use of aliens on a seasonal basis, the practices of contractors, unemployment, juvenile delinquency, and crime are part of the problem. Effective unionization of the seasonal worker to date has been virtually impossible. The migrant laborer has had no champion in politics. His cause is just, but his sponsors in high places are few.

Fortune wrote in 1939 that California's agricultural system could not exist without this migratory group, this "unwanted glut of humanity."

The political weakness of this vast, ever changing migrant group (which amounted to 1 million people in 1953) is emphasized by an episode that happened when Roosevelt and the New Deal were strong. A group of officials insisted that cotton benefit payments be divided with *share croppers.* The reaction was violent. It was indeed the cause of the now famous purge of the Agricultural Adjustment Administration.

September 15, 1787 was the last working day of the Constitutional Convention. There had been many differences, many debates, many divisions. But the one that struck deepest, and came closer than any other to defeating the Convention, was the struggle between the small and the large States, the slave States and the free States over representation in Congress.

The *Constitution,* as adopted, gave each State two Senators and one Representative for every 30,000 people, as determined by a decennial census. In determining the number of people in each State all "free persons" were counted, plus "three fifths of all other persons," except Indians not taxed. Congress was granted power to apportion "direct taxes" among the States on the same basis. And all bills "for raising revenue" had to originate in the House. This is what is known in our history as The Great Compromise.

1. The Senate was conceived as a curb on the House. Washington suggested the analogy of drinking coffee: "We pour legislation into the Senatorial saucer to cool it."

2. The slave States got their slaves counted in the census, with the result that five free persons in Virginia had as much power in choosing Representatives as seven persons in New York. (But they could be subject to "direct taxes" on the same basis.)

3. Equal representation of each State in the Senate reassured the small States and gave the North the balance in that chamber.

4. The power of the House to originate revenue bills put "the purse strings" in the hands of the people.

Yet the compromise only passed by a vote of five to four, Massachusetts being divided. If it had failed, the *Constitution* would have failed. For as Luther Martin said, "We were on the verge of dissolution, scarce held together by the strength of a hair."

"The people of the States will never be such fools as to give up so important an interest." So spoke John Rutledge of South Carolina at the Constitutional Convention. What he referred to was slavery, and the occasion for his pronouncement was a motion by Luther Martin to give Congress power to tax or to prohibit the importation of slaves.

The question of slavery had already entered the debates. For the South had got its voting strength increased in the House by including three fifths of the slaves in the census (September 15). But that was a political issue. Luther Martin's motion introduced a moral one. The delegates did not line up on a sectional basis. George Mason of Virginia denounced "this infernal traffic" in slaves. Oliver Ellsworth of Connecticut thought the "morality or wisdom of slavery" was a question for the States. The weight of the Convention was on the side of avoiding the moral issue. For the wiser ones knew that if Luther Martin's motion were pressed, some of the South would be permanently alienated.

And so it was that a compromise was worked out. It was proposed that Congress could not prohibit the slave trade prior to 1808 but that it could place a tax, not exceeding ten dollars each, on slaves imported. North and South united to adopt this provision, the four middle States (New Jersey, Pennsylvania, Delaware, and Virginia) voting no. George Mason later told what happened. A few southern States made a bargain with New England: If New England avoided the slavery issue, the South would vote down the proposal (February 9) to require a two-thirds vote of each House of Congress to make a regulation of commerce.

The use of the word "slaves" was sedulously avoided. It does not appear in the *Constitution,* for, as Luther Martin commented, its use might be "odious to the ears of Americans."

On September 17, 1787, the Constitutional Convention voted to adopt the *Constitution*. Before the vote was taken Benjamin Franklin, one of the wisest of men, addressed the delegates:

"I agree to this Constitution with all it faults, if they are such; because I think a general Government necessary for us, and there is no form of Government but what may be a blessing to the people if well administered, and believe farther that this is likely to be well administered for a course of years, and can only end in Despotism, as other forms have done before it, when the people shall become so corrupted as to need despotic Government, being incapable of any other. I doubt too whether any other Convention we can obtain may be able to make a better Constitution. For when you assemble a number of men to have the advantage of their joint wisdom, you inevitably assemble with those men, all their prejudices, their passions, their errors of opinion, their local interests, and their selfish views. From such an Assembly can a perfect production be expected? It therefore astonishes me, Sir, to find this system approaching so near to perfection as it does. . . . Thus I consent, Sir, to this Constitution because I expect no better, and because I am not sure, that it is not the best. The opinions I have had of its errors, I sacrifice to the public good."

On September 18, 1850, the *Fugitive Slave Act* was passed. It allowed a slave owner to get a certificate from a court in his home State that he owned a certain slave who had escaped and, armed with that certificate, to go to the asylum State and apply to a federal judge for the return of his property. In the trial the facts recited in the certificate were conclusive once the slave was identified; and the slave could not testify.

There was a sizeable Negro community in Boston, among whom were many escaped slaves. William Lloyd Garrison was making Boston notorious as an abolition center (February 19). Hence many desired to vindicate the law by returning a fugitive to slavery from New England soil. In 1851, one Shadrach was arrested, but in the midst of his trial was rescued by friends. Though the rescuers were tried, the jury would not convict. Later the same year one Sims was tried and returned to Georgia. Then in 1854 came the famous case of Anthony Burns.

Burns was defended by the great Richard Henry Dana. The judge was Edward S. Loring. A mob, headed by a clergyman, tried to effect a rescue of Burns but failed. Thereupon the marines and militia were called out and the trial took place before fixed bayonets. Loring ordered Burns returned, and the Negro was marched to a boat under heavy guard while most of Boston and the North muttered ominously. The case became a *cause célèbre*. It was not only the return of a free man to slavery that aroused people. Northern officials had become "slave-hunters" and northern courts had become instruments of a "fearful slave-power." Moreover, the case against Burns was weak. His identification was somewhat dubious. And two strong points were foreclosed by the certificate brought up from Virginia: there was evidence that the wrong man claimed him and that he had not "escaped."

The sense of injustice in Burns' case was so great that no Negro was ever again returned from Massachusetts.

"Permanent, inveterate antipathies against particular nations and passionate attachment for others should be excluded . . . Just and amicable feelings towards all should be cultivated. The nation, which indulges towards another a political hatred, or an habitual fondness, is in some degree a slave . . . Against the insiduous wiles of foreign influence . . . the jealousy of a free people ought to be constantly awake."

So spoke Washington in his Farewell Address on September 19, 1796. Washington had seen the revolutionary movement in France stir people here. He had seen the Jacobins try to get America aligned with France against England, and he had denounced them for it. Washington in his Farewell Address spoke, therefore, for an attitude not so much of isolationism as for neutralism in world affairs. He did not want America to become the agent or executioner for another nation's policy. He wanted America to be the friend of all peoples, not the champion of one country against another.

There is an enduring wisdom in Washington's advice which America has often forgotten. Our failure to respect his advice is the cause of the great decline in American influence and prestige in Asia and the Middle East since World War II:

We stood *against* the independence of Indonesia from 1945 to 1949, favoring the Dutch against a subjugated people.

We connived with Britain to salvage an infamous British oil concession in Iran, aligning ourselves *against* Iran's democratic forces.

We became underwriters of French colonial policy in Indo-China and Morocco (October 19), helping to *crush* and *subdue* nationalist movements that were anti-communist.

"He whom the blazing fire burns not, whom the water forces not to come up, who meets with no speedy misfortune, must be held innocent on his oath." So spoke Manu, the ancient Hindu lawgiver.

An appeal to the supernatural has been a method used by many peoples for proving guilt, in England as well as in India.

In an elaborate ecclesiastical ritual, the accused would remove a rock from boiling water with his bare hand. The hand or arm would be bound up for three days. If at the end of that time the skin was healed, the accused was declared innocent. If he had a blister, he was guilty.

Ordeal by fire followed a similar pattern. The accused picked up a red-hot iron and carried it for three steps. His hand was then bound up and inspected the third day.

Ordeal by water had a different twist. The accused was bound hand and foot and cast in a pool. If he sank, he proved his innocence. If he floated, without swimming, he must have the devil in him.

These ordeals flourished in England for centuries, supported by the belief that God intervened on behalf of the guiltless. By 1215, the Catholic Church was done with them. In 1262, they were abolished by the King.

But wager of battle was not abolished in England until 1818. It gave the accused the option of resolving the controversy in battle with the accuser. The weapons used were a sword or an ax. If the accused slew his opponent, or made him call out the word "craven," or was able to fight until the stars came out, he was acquitted. If he was overcome or unable to continue, he was adjudged guilty. If the accused were a woman, child, priest, or invalid, a man was hired to do battle.

It took centuries for men to be rid of the idea that God was always on the side of him who was the stronger or had the greater skill.

Witchcraft prosecutions flourished in England for 160 years. During that time a conservative estimate of the number who were hanged or burned is 600. The Witch Finder General—the most notorious investigator of them all—was Matthew Hopkins, a Puritan, who ruled supreme in 1645 and 1646.

An Act of Parliament imposed a death penalty on any person who "shall use, practice, or exercise any witchecrafte, enchantment, charme, or sorcerie, whereby any person shall happen to bee killed or destroyed." Hopkins and his cohort, John Stearne, formed a flying squadron that went from county to county on their investigations and hearings. Usually two men and two women would be used as "searchers." Suspects were stripped and examined for marks of the devil. Then they were put cross-legged on a stool, or walked up and down, or otherwise kept awake without food for several days. Meanwhile the imps that witches commanded were watched for, and these might appear in the form of a spider or a fly that could not be killed.

Hungry days and sleepless nights were methods of torture that produced the confessions.

A man said in a quarrel that he wished his neighbor's tongue would rot. The neighbor died of cancer and the man was convicted. An eighty-year-old pastor was trotted around a room for several nights, until he confessed he had sunk a ship, drowning fourteen sailors. A woman was convicted who "felt something come into the bed about her legges but could not finde anything."

Hopkins waxed strong, collecting fees from each community. He and Stearne probably were responsible for the hanging of 200 or more people in two years.

The hysteria of witchcraft came in wave after wave, usually following religious controversies. Two great figures thundered against it. Shortly before 1600, Reginald Scot published *Discoverie of Witchcraft*, which had little deterrent effect. Francis Hutchinson in 1718 published his *Historical Essay on Witchcraft*, which, by a devastating analysis of the trials, laid the ghost that had haunted England for so long.

On September 22, 1692, the last persons were hanged in this country for witchcraft. During the four months ending then, the number arrested exceeded 250, while those hanged numbered 19. In addition, 1 was pressed to death for refusing to plead; 2 died in prison from ill-treatment.

The story has been told by Starkey, *The Devil in Massachusetts* and by Miller, *The Crucible*. The hunt started with fantasies of little girls which were given credence by excitable teen-agers. The "witches" tried were rich and poor, black and white. The court was composed of laymen. (One Nathaniel Saltonstall, to his eternal credit, resigned from it in disgust.) The theory of the trials was that the devil assumed the shape of a human and worked violence and injury on people.

The trial was before a jury. The judges were guilty of three cardinal errors. They accepted as evidence of guilt (1) an unusual excrescence on the body of the accused ("devil's mark" it was called); (2) any mischief (such as the death of a cow) which followed a quarrel between the accused and a neighbor; and (3) the appearance of the accused in the dream or fantasy of the accuser ("spectral evidence") to do harm and evil. Thus evidence of the emotional state of the accuser became proof of the behavior and guilt of the accused.

The search for witches, encouraged by the clergy, set neighbor against neighbor. Every quarrel became quickly related to the failure of bread to rise, to the falling of a brick, or to the sickness of a child. Suspicion reigned supreme.

People were tried in an atmosphere dominated by mob psychology. The trials read much like those before the People's Court in Red China in 1952, as related by Hutheesing in *The Great Peace*. No conviction in the Salem witch trials of 1692 would stand the test of due process of law. They are eternal warnings that there is danger to liberty (1) whenever the accusation is itself sufficient to condemn a man; and (2) when short cuts are taken, forsaking the procedural safeguards erected to guarantee that all trials will be fair (March 18).

Today, if a person charged with a crime is asked to plead guilty or not guilty and stands mute, he is taken to plead not guilty. That was not always so. Until 1772, a person who, in a treason or misdemeanor case, did not plead was presumed to plead guilty. He was thereupon convicted and punished. If it happened in a felony case (murder, robbery, etc.), his refusal to plead brought dire consequences. In the early years, he was put in solitary confinement and given bread one day and water the next, until he pleaded guilty or not guilty, or died from starvation. The bread was the "coarsest" that could be got, and the water was taken from "the next sink or puddle to the place of execution." Later on, "pressing" was used—the notorious *peine-forte et dure*. The prisoner would be stretched and weights laid on him, being gradually increased until he died or agreed to plead guilty or not guilty. To hasten death a stake was often placed under him. Men were "pressed" on this continent for their refusal to plead. As the years passed, this torture was somewhat lessened—a prisoner who stood mute had his two thumbs tied together, so that the pain might compel him to plead; or he was placed in chains.

This barbarism ended in 1772, when Parliament provided, in a law applicable to America, that a prisoner who stood mute should be taken to plead guilty. Not until 1827 did England provide that standing mute in a criminal case was the equivalent of a plea of not guilty.

The history of the *peineforte et dure* is one chapter in our long and tortuous escape from torture and compulsion in criminal trials.

In 1789, while the Congress was considering the *Bill of Rights*, the States General in France adopted the *Declaration of the Rights of Man and the Citizen*. It has much in common with our *Bill of Rights* and doubtless received inspiration from the constitutions of our States. (At this period in history, American ideas were influencing Europe; European ideas were not potent forces here.)

The French *Declaration* states in part:

—"Men are born and remain free and equal in respect of rights."
—Man has "natural and imprescriptible rights"—"liberty, property, security, and resistance to oppression."
—Everyone is "counted innocent until he has been convicted."
—"No man is to be interfered with because of his opinions."
—"Every citizen may speak, write and publish freely, provided he be responsible for the abuse of this liberty."
—The right to property is "inviolable and sacred" and no one shall be deprived of it except in case of "evident public necessity" and "previous just indemnity."

As Chafee, *How Human Rights Got Into The Constitution*, says, the French *Declaration* is more of a political treatise than our *Bill of Rights*. Ours is a lawyer's document, designed for practical application and administration. The French *Declaration* is more a philosophical dissertation. Ours is hitched to enforcement machinery and a procedure whereby rights may be protected. The French *Declaration* is a ringing pronouncement of faith. Even more important, ours is a reservation of rights which Englishmen had already largely *secured*. The French *Declaration* is a reaching for rights which man on the Continent had not yet acquired.

On September 25, 1789, Congress proposed the *Bill of Rights*. In 1953, Irving Dilliard of the St. Louis *Post-Dispatch* had this to say:

"What I think about the state of our liberties is the blackest thought I have had in my lifetime. I am convinced that the Bill of Rights would not be submitted and ratified as part of the Constitution were it presented in Congress today."

As to the First Amendment rights, he said:

"There is widespread indifference among newspapers generally to freedom of the press itself. . . . Many newspapers never have an editorial which touches the issue of the separation of church and state. Freedom of speech for the individual is often trespassed on without causing so much as a word of protest."

As to unreasonable searches and seizures:

". . . these basic protections are trampled time and again, and a large part of the press takes no notice."

As to protection against self-incrimination:

"This basic protection of an accused person is grounded deep in history. . . . Yet it could not be made a part of the Constitution today. Indeed, there is a campaign on . . . to undercut the guaranty against self-incrimination if not to eliminate it altogether. And in saying this I do not approve of the Fifth Amendment's abuse by those who hide behind it."

As to the right to counsel and to bail:

"Many an accused person has gone to prison in recent years lacking assistance of counsel to tell him of his rights, many a time excessive bail is required—with little or no objection in the press."

As to the attitude of the press, Dilliard said:

"No amendment to the Constitution can be adopted without a fighting campaign, and I do not find the press today fighting for the principles and causes that the Bill of Rights embodies . . . I find no reason to believe therefore that the press would lead a national campaign to adopt the Bill of Rights were its protections and guaranties introduced in Congress today."

The *Hatch Act*, passed in 1939, forbade officers and employees in the executive department (with exceptions) from taking "any active part in political management or in political campaigns." A rule of the Civil Service Commission, while permitting employees to vote, contained the same prohibition. Violation of this mandate carried the penalty of dismissal from the service, with a loss of all seniority and other civil service benefits, and a permanent ban against re-employment in the same position.

On September 26, 1944, the sanction was enforced against a roller in the mint, who was a ward executive committeeman in Philadelphia and, in that position, visited residents of his ward, solicited their support for his party, acted as a watcher at the polls, circulated campaign literature, and helped organize political rallies and assemblies.

The Supreme Court, by a divided vote, sustained application of the law to this skilled mechanic. Reasonableness of the Congressional regulation was found in three main considerations that may have motivated Congress:

—Political activity of the employee might promote or retard his advancement or preferment by his superiors.

—Government employees were "handy elements for leaders in political policy to use in building a political machine."

—There would be a cumulative adverse effect on employee morale if all of them could be induced to participate in political activity.

There is a famous dictum of Holmes, dating back to 1892, that a person has "no constitutional right to be a policeman." That dictum has pernicious implications. Since no one has the right to work for the government, he can be discharged for a good reason or for a bad one. Moreover, he can be discharged after a trial which violates the standards of decency and fair play (November 18, March 21, 22).

If the dictum is true as respects government employment, it holds true for employment by a college, a railroad, or an oil company. If the dictum is valid, a man or woman can be branded a "security risk" by any group, put on a black list, and barred from all employment.

The doctrine that a person has "no right" to work is un-American. It is contrary to the freedom of opportunity which Lincoln talked about in 1860: "When one starts poor, as most do in the race of life, free society is such that he knows he can better his condition; he knows that there is no fixed condition of labor for his whole life." That is the philosophy stated by Ralph Waldo Emerson in his *Essay on Politics:* "A man has a right to be employed, to be trusted, to be loved, to be revered." That should be our standard.

The *Bill of Rights* does not say who may be a policeman or a doctor or an engineer. It does not say what government must give. It does, however, say what may not be done, what may not be taken away. A man's liberty may not be taken away without due process of law. And to most men the right to work is as precious as life itself.

A person may not be qualified for many jobs. But if he is to be *officially disqualified* for one, it should only be after a fair trial. And that disqualification should not carry over to others. If it does, then a person who has committed no crime can be branded and cast into the outer darkness. That happens in a police state. It should never happen in free America.

September 28, 1678 was an ominous day for Londoners. That night Titus Oates was out with his constables making arrests. Before he was done, thirty-seven men were executed (July 18) and hundreds were ruined in reputation and livelihood.

Titus Oates was a notorious informer. He masqueraded as a doctor of divinity. Then he turned to Catholicism and attended Jesuit schools in Spain and in France. He was, in due course, expelled from them and returned to England, claiming knowledge of the secret design of the Catholics toward England. He drew up the plot of the Papists to murder the King, burn London, and massacre the people. Oates forged letters, laid his plans carefully, and managed to be summoned before the Privy Council to tell the whole story.

Oates was a good stage manager. He told his story in tidbits, first accusing three Jesuits. He was authorized to arrest them in a nocturnal raid. When word spread to the populace, fear gripped London. People were ready to believe that the Catholics were guilty. Oates, a hero overnight, was placed on a salary and given an office at Whitehall.

Parliament investigated the Popish Plot, but no move was made to investigate the informer. He stood above the turmoil, the savior of the nation. Oates emphasized his intimacy with the accused; and when one of his accusations failed, he always had ready a diversionary charge.

The Catholic hunt was on; homes were ruthlessly searched; the prisons were filled. For almost a year London was on edge, as Oates did his devilish work.

The national neurosis gradually wore itself out. When James II, a Catholic, came to the throne in 1685, Oates was tried for perjury, found guilty, fined, whipped, and sentenced to life imprisonment. And the court decreed annual commemorations of his false swearings. Four days each year for the rest of his life he was to stand in designated pillories.

Not until recent years did an informer enjoy such acclaim as Oates knew.

Judges have often read their own notions of *laissez faire* economics into the Due Process Clause of the Fourteenth Amendment. One such episode figured prominently in Roosevelt's plan for reorganizing the judiciary (February 29).

The Supreme Court wrote into the *Constitution* what some called "the freedom of the sweatshop." It struck down, in 1923, a District of Columbia law fixing minimum wages for women and children. Employees and employers, the Court said, have "an equal right to obtain from each other the best terms they can as the result of private bargaining." That "freedom of contract" was protected by the *Constitution*.

In 1936, the Court applied that doctrine to nullify a New York law regulating the wages of women and minors. Both decisions were by a divided Court. The injustice of the rulings was emphasized by Stone's dissent: a wage is not always the result of "free bargaining," but often "forced upon employees by their economic necessities and upon employers by the most ruthless of their competitors."

When Washington's law fixing minimum wages for women and children came before the Court in 1937, one Justice changed his mind, enabling Chief Justice Hughes, on the heels of Roosevelt's court reform program, to write for a majority and overrule the two earlier decisions.

Liberty under the *Constitution*, wrote Hughes, is "liberty in a social organization which requires the protection of law against the evils which menace the health, safety, morals and welfare of the people."

Any regulation is apt to affect values adversely. For example, a zoning ordinance, price control, limitation of oil production, or the like might substantially reduce the value of the regulated property or business. But that does not mean that the regulations exceed the police power of the States. A classic statement of Holmes put the matter this way: under the police power "property rights may be cut down, and to that extent taken without pay." If a State acts within the limits of rationality, it is not taking property without due process of law.

What of the federal government? Does it have police power?

When Congress legislates concerning the District of Columbia, it legislates over a federal domain. It may, therefore, pass a rent control law for the District. How about rent control or price control for the nation? We have had those laws and they have been sustained —but only under the war power. Rent control was upheld even after the President proclaimed an end of hostilities of World War II, since the effect of that war on deficit housing had not yet been eliminated. Suppose it had been eliminated. Could Congress pass a valid rent control law or price control in times of peace?

The *Constitution* says, "The Congress shall have power to lay and collect Taxes . . . to pay the Debts and provide for the common Defense and general Welfare of the United States."

To date the latter phrase has been construed to qualify the power "to lay and collect" taxes, not to give Congress power to legislate for the "general Welfare." (August 16.)

93

OCTOBER

We Americans have never been apostles of vengeance. Though our tempers have at times run high, we have in the end bowed to moderation. For example, most of our treason trials ended in forgiveness. Shays' Rebellion (January 25) and the Whisky Rebellion (January 27) were genuine revolts against our government. The Whisky Rebellion resulted in prosecutions and convictions for treason (May 30). But no one was hanged; the President pardoned the culprits. When the Civil War ended, the South was cruelly oppressed. But none of the top rebels—Lee, Hampton, Longstreet, Stephens, Jeff Davis—was ever tried for treason.

By the 1940's, we were members of an international community, where compassion also has an important role to play. But we took a different view at the end of World War II, because of the heinous crimes of Hitler and his gang. The judgments entered at Nuremberg on October 1, 1946, illustrate this break in tradition.

By our standards no one can be tried for violating an *ex post facto* law. An *ex post facto* law is one which punishes a person today for an act which, when he did it, was not a crime (January 14).

The Nuremberg trials, in my view, applied to the defendants such a law. Hitler and his colleagues were guilty of murder over and again and deserved the death penalty under the common law of those crimes, as Radin, *The Day of Reckoning*, makes clear. But they were not tried for murder. The Kellogg-Briand Pact of 1928 renounced war "as an instrument of national policy," and Germany was a signatory. And so the defendants were tried for the crime of waging an aggressive war. But no matter how many books are written or briefs filed, no matter how finely the lawyers analyze it, the crime for which the Nazis were tried had never been formalized as a crime with the definiteness required by our legal standards (February 28), nor outlawed with a death penalty by the international community. By our standards that crime arose under an *ex post facto* law.

Goering et al. deserved severe punishment. But their guilt did not justify us in substituting *power* for *principle*.

In 1856, Washington was a Territory. Isaac I. Stevens was Governor and Edward Lander was Chief Justice of the Territorial Supreme Court. There were some marauding Indians operating in Pierce County. Some white men who had married Indian women were thought to be involved, but there was no evidence against them. Stevens, however, had them arrested and held in jail without any charges being preferred against them.

Their lawyers applied to Lander for writs of habeas corpus. Stevens countered by declaring martial law. Lander, in defiance of the Governor, held court to hear the cases. The Governor had the Army arrest the Judge and remove him to Thurston County. The lawyers for the prisoners applied to Lander in Thurston County for habeas corpus. Stevens declared martial law in that county also. Lander held court in defiance of Stevens' proclamation. Once more Stevens arrested Lander. When Lander was released, he held court, cited Stevens for contempt, and fined him $50. One account has it that Stevens pardoned himself!

Caleb Cushing, Attorney General of the United States, rendered an opinion that Stevens' declaration of martial law was unlawful, that conditions in the Washington Territory were not so serious as to make suspension of the civil authority and substitution of military rule warranted (December 17).

Lander, in defying Stevens, did honor to the independency of the judiciary. In his action on the habeas corpus cases he recognized that in America there is no such thing as protective custody, that a man cannot be held in jail, unless he is charged with a crime and informed of the accusation.

In the early 1930's, Texas undertook a program for the conservation of oil by limiting production. There was such opposition to the program that in 1931 the Governor declared "martial law" in one region, putting it under military command. The well owners then obtained an injunction from a federal court restraining enforcement of the regulation limiting production. The Governor flouted that order, and directed his military commander to enforce the regulation. Thereupon, the well owners sued the Governor and the military commander, claiming that the enforcement of the conservation program by troops was unconstitutional. The federal court so held and in 1932 the case reached the Supreme Court.

The Court, speaking through Chief Justice Hughes, ruled that the declaration of "martial law" was unconstitutional. There were no conditions of insurrection creating a state of war; the courts were open; and the controversy over the conservation program was being adjudicated in an orderly manner by the judiciary. If the action of the Governor were sustained, the settlement of a controversy involving the constitutional rights of property owners would be taken from the courts and given to the executive. Then "the fiat of a state governor, and not the Constitution of the United States, would be the supreme law of the land," said Hughes (December 17, 18).

The importance of the decision is in the ruling that whether "the allowable limits of military discretion" have been exceeded is a judicial question. Thus the courts look behind a Governor's proclamation of a state of insurrection to see if there is need for it. In the Texas case Hughes said that, if the proclamation were justified, it should have been used "to maintain the federal court" rather than "to attempt to override it."

The *Constitution* extends "judicial power" to "cases" and to "controversies." In the Constitutional Convention, Charles Pinckney proposed that "Each branch of the Legislature, as well as the Supreme Executive, shall have authority to require the opinions of the Supreme Judicial Court upon important questions of law and upon solemn occasions."

Some of the States have like provisions in their constitutions. In that way, the legislature or the Governor may get an advisory opinion from the courts on the constitutionality of legislation before it is enacted.

But Pinckney's proposal was not adopted. Washington, however, in 1793 asked the opinion of the Justices of the Supreme Court on questions arising under certain treaties. They respectfully declined to answer, saying that since they were judges "of a Court in the last resort" and since the three branches of government were "in certain respects checks upon each other," there were "strong arguments against the propriety of our extra-judicially deciding the questions alluded to."

That early precedent has been consistently followed. The Supreme Court will not render advisory opinions; it decides only actual controversies. A friendly suit, designed to get an adjudication on the constitutionality of a law, will be rejected. Issues concerning property, personal and other rights must be in issue; and the cause must be a fighting one, not feigned.

Thus the judicial power is held in close restraint and denied a roving commission to look into affairs of state.

Not all controversies arising under the *Constitution* can come to the courts. Many are left for decision to the *political* branches.

When Georgia, in 1867, sought to enjoin the Secretary of War from enforcing the odious Reconstruction Acts, the Court held the issue was *political,* not *justiciable.*

In 1841 and 1842, Rhode Island, as a result of Dorr's Rebellion, had two governments, each claiming sovereignty. The Court declined to resolve the controversy, saying it was one for the *political* branches.

The initiative and referendum, adopted by Oregon (June 2), was said to be inconsistent with the "republican form of government," which under the *Constitution* the United States guarantees to each State. That question, the Court held, was for Congress to determine, as it could when Oregon's delegates sought to be seated.

The process of amending the *Constitution* likewise is in the hands of Congress and the Executive.

In recent years, a sharply divided Court has declared that the validity of acts apportioning a State into Congressional districts presents *political,* not *justiciable* issues.

This self-limitation on judicial power rests on the belief that there is political wisdom in courts abstaining from certain controversies, because their vastness, complication, or sensitive nature make them unsuited for judicial decision. The point is illustrated by the suit which the Duke of York brought for the throne of England centuries ago. The judges ruled that they "durst not enter into any communication thereof, for it perteyned to the Lordes of the Kyngs blode."

Thomas Paine was a Britisher who came to America at Franklin's invitation late in 1774. Parrington, *Main Currents in American Thought,* calls Paine one of the first real internationalists. Paine did, indeed, say, "My country is the world." And he did spread the ideas of the American Revolution to England, France, and other discontented places. But when Paine first landed here, the Revolution had not yet happened. It was, however, in the wind; and Paine's keen scent picked it up.

Paine dropped his idea of establishing a school in Philadelphia and instead went to work on a political tract. In a little over a year, this newcomer had mastered the facts of life in the American Colonies, shaped up the issues, and marshaled the arguments for independence. *Common Sense,* published early in 1776, pointed out that it was to America's self-interest to be free of England. *Common Sense* attacked the divine right of kings and ridiculed the principle of a hereditary monarchy. *Common Sense* denounced the British constitutional system that lawyers on both sides of the ocean had usually praised. The "aristocratical tyranny" of the King and the House of Lords, Paine argued, were sufficient to place control in the hands of the landed interests and against the people.

The power of *Common Sense* was in its timing. Grievances had piled high. Yet the people here had lived under the King for a century and a half. That long alliance had produced loyalties and habits that made it difficult, even for the lower classes, to break with England. *Common Sense* produced a profound psychological effect. It dissolved the remaining fogs of sentiment and made revolution seem eminently practical.

Tom Paine soon was to be proscribed by the Tories of Europe and America. John Adams, indeed, called him "the filthy Tom Paine." But he was a stout champion of the rights of man and on the eve of our revolution rendered this nation a great service.

On October 7, 1872, an indictment was returned against the notorious city boss—William Marcy Tweed (1823–1878). The indictment contained 220 counts, and Tweed was found guilty on 204 of them. Each count charged a separate offense. Having served the greatest sentence imposed under any count and paid the fine, Tweed applied for release from prison in 1875. He gained his freedom because New York law did not permit a trial under one indictment for separate, distinct crimes.

He was at once rearrested on a civil action to recover 6 million of his "stealings." Bail was set at 3 million, which he could not furnish. So he went to jail pending trial. He escaped and went abroad, only to be returned to New York, where he spent his few remaining months in jail.

Tweed had built himself a "ring" in New York which controlled the government, and exacted from the public purse and from business a heavy toll. He had puppets in the Governor's mansion, the legislature, the courthouses, as well as in municipal offices. He had a rule that all bills submitted to the City and County of New York were to be at least 50 per cent fraudulent, the graft being divided among designated officials. He helped plunder the Erie Railroad, and he exacted heavy bribes from many companies. He and his "ring" misappropriated from New York City at least 30 million, perhaps 200 million, dollars.

Disclosure of the misdeeds of Boss Tweed was due to the New York *Times* and *Harper's Weekly*. George Jones wrote for the *Times*, and Thomas Nast drew cartoons for *Harper's*. They were on Tweed's trail for some time. Finally a member of the "ring" brought incriminating documents to George Jones. Tweed, learning of it, offered Jones 5 million dollars and Nast a half million to stay silent.

The *Times* and *Harper's* could not be bought. They broke the story, laying bare the sordid details.

The *Times* and *Harper's* showed American journalism at its best—courage, integrity, and pitiless publicity of the facts.

In 1943, Congress attached to an appropriation Act a rider that no part of the funds appropriated should be used to pay the salaries of Robert M. Lovett, Goodwin B. Watson, or William E. Dodd, Jr., after November 15, 1943. This was done over the protest of the agencies where the men were employed. The three men were kept on the pay roll after that date; but not being paid, they sued for their salaries.

They had been condemned by the Committee on Un-American Activities headed by Martin Dies. Congressman Dies had called them "irresponsible, unrepresentative, crackpot, radical bureaucrats" affiliated with "communist front organizations" and unfit to hold a government post. His charges precipitated a sharp debate on the floor of the House, with the result that the matter was referred to the Appropriations Committee for an investigation, so that each "man would have his day in court" and have a chance to prove himself "innocent." The Committee held hearings in a secret, executive session. The accused employees were allowed to testify, but all lawyers were excluded from the hearings.

When the litigation reached the Supreme Court in 1946, the law was held unconstitutional, as a bill of attainder. A bill of attainder is an act of the legislature that punishes individuals or members of a group without a *judicial trial.* Its vice is that it condemns a person by legislative fiat, that a person is punished without the benefit of a trial having all the safeguards which the *Bill of Rights* provides (January 14). Exclusion from government employment on the ground of "subversive activity" deprived these men of the opportunity to follow their careers. It was therefore a form of punishment which Congress is precluded by the *Constitution* from imposing on any person.

Judges like Brandeis, Cardozo, Hughes, Murphy, Stone, and Rutledge brought to the bench a libertarian philosophy and used it to shape the law to the needs of an oncoming generation. In that sense they were "activists," criticized by many. But history will honor them for their creative work. They knew that all life is change and that law must be constantly renewed if the pressures of society are not to build up to violence and revolt.

When one looks down 500 years of legal history, he comes to know that those judges were the exception. Most judges never knew their lesson. The majority were apostles of the *status quo*. Their inventive genius was used to defeat social legislation, to undermine the *Habeas Corpus Act* or the *Federal Employers' Liability Act,* to use the *Constitution* to protect the vested interests of the day. At times the bench has even been swept by hysteria, becoming little more than an executor for those who preached intolerance.

A sad example was the manner in which the judges smote Eugene V. Debs, who led the railway workers in the famous Pullman strike of 1894. The company reduced wages but not salaries, and increased dividends. Management refused to make any concessions to the workers. When they went out on strike, the federal government allied itself with the company. Federal troops were called out; and the Department of Justice got an injunction against Debs which directed him in sweeping terms to have nothing to do with the strike (October 18, March 23). He defied the decree and was jailed for contempt. The Supreme Court sustained his commitment on grounds that would have made Hamilton and Marshall twinge. Federal courts, it was held, had an *implied* authority to supervise interstate commerce and transportation of the mails, even in absence of any Act of Congress granting the courts jurisdiction.

No greater claim to judicial supremacy has ever been made, and significantly it was made on behalf of vested interests that were callous to human rights.

When William E. Borah was a young lawyer in Boise, Idaho, he heard that a mob was trying to break into a jail in a nearby town and lynch a Negro. He got an engineer to give him a ride in the cab of the engine to the town. Mounting a box in front of the jail, he addressed the mob on the basic principles of due process of law and fair play. Shortly the mob melted away into the night, and the prisoner was saved.

The struggle for liberty has been in large measure a struggle to be free of the mob. As Le Bon wrote in *The Crowd,* the mob gives passions free play; it has no inhibitions; it wants blood, not justice. A mob can infect a trial, making it a mockery. In 1923, the Supreme Court held that where a state trial is dominated by a mob and a mere mask for its will, where counsel, jury and judge "are swept to the fatal end by an irresistible wave of public passion," the federal courts will secure the prisoners their constitutional rights through habeas corpus if the state courts fail to do so.

In 1902, Georgia made an historic decision giving a man convicted of rape a new trial because the crowd in the courtroom put on a demonstration against him during the trial and another one outside the courthouse while the jury deliberated. A classic opinion was rendered by South Carolina in 1912. At a murder trial there were mutterings of lynching so ominous that defense counsel, just appointed, did not dare ask for a continuance in order to prepare the case. A hostile crowd packed the courtroom, milling around so that counsel could not see the witness on the stand, or even the jury. The court said that the dock, the witness chair, the jury box, counsels' table were "inviolable precincts." If the crowd could surround those places, the jury would be apt to be overawed, defendant terrified, counsel confused, and witnesses induced to testify falsely.

Judges cannot control public sentiment, but due process demands that they control their courtrooms and make them places of quiet dignity.

Prior to our *Declaration of Independence,* there were Tories in the pulpits denouncing the revolutionary theories of Jefferson and Madison. The leading Tory minister was Jonathan Boucher, an Anglican.

He preached that man's sacred duty was obedience to government, that rebellion against lawfully constituted authority was an unforgivable sin. "Obedience to government is every man's duty, because it is every man's interest; but it is particularly incumbent on Christians, because . . . it is enjoined by the positive commands of God."

Boucher defended the divine right of kings. Even if the government was not a good one, it nevertheless is "our duty not to disturb the peace of the community by becoming refractory and rebellious subjects, and resisting the ordinances of God."

"Everything our blessed Lord either said or did pointedly tended to discourage the disturbing a settled government," Boucher preached.

Boucher searched "all the Scriptures" and could find no reference to "civil liberty." True liberty, he maintained, consisted "in subserviency to law." "To suffer nobly indicates more greatness of mind than can be shown by acting valiantly."

These were the political tenets which Boucher delivered from his pulpit in Virginia. Popular opinion mounted against him. He began to keep a pair of loaded pistols on the pulpit. One Sunday his church filled up with armed men. His friends persuaded him not to preach that day; and shortly after, Boucher left for England, never to return.

Boucher symbolized to Madison the evils of the established church. Boucher's efforts to robe the King in ecclesiastical garments was one potent reason why the Fathers thought that it was evil to make the church the instrument of the state.

The right to revolt has sources deep in our history.

Thomas Jefferson wrote to Madison: "I hold it, that a little rebellion, now and then, is a good thing, and as necessary in the political world as storms in the physical. . . . It is a medicine necessary for the sound health of government."

Alexander Hamilton said in the *Federalist:*

"If the representatives of the people betray their constituents, there is then no resource left but in the exertion of that original right of self-defence which is paramount to all positive forms of government . . ."

Abraham Lincoln said in his *First Inaugural:*

"This country, with its institutions, belongs to the people who inhabit it. Whenever they shall grow weary of the existing government, they can exercise their constitutional right of amending it, or their revolutionary right to dismember or overthrow it."

The famous *Habeas Corpus Act* of 1679 (May 27) did not, by terms, extend to persons being held or detained for reasons other than a criminal charge. Prior to 1679, the grievances that had arisen resulted from the arrest and detention of people for actual or alleged crimes. But it soon appeared there were other instances where a person being detained should be released. One was the case where a child was being kept from his parents, or where one parent prevented the other from having access to the child. Under the early bankruptcy laws, the commissioners had large powers to commit bankrupts to prison and keep them there interminably. Or a wife might be put in jail for refusing to give testimony which would prove her husband to be bankrupt.

In England no statute allowed relief in such cases until 1816. But long before then the courts had been giving relief by way of habeas corpus on the theory that if the writ is applicable "to one species of unlawful imprisonment," it is "in reason equally applicable to another." The grant of relief in the family cases and in bankruptcy cases probably antedates 1700. It was well established by that time.

One Thomas Brailsford had gone into bankruptcy in 1722, and in May 1723, had been committed to the Fleet, the infamous debtors' prison (June 19). He had languished in the Fleet for over two years, being intermittently questioned concerning his affairs. On October 13, 1725, Chancellor King ordered the bankruptcy commissioners to discharge Brailsford from the Fleet.

And so it was that, in 1769, Dr. Johnson told Boswell, "The habeas corpus is the single advantage our government has over that of other countries."

The First Continental Congress met in Philadelphia in September 1774, and on October 14, passed a *Resolution* protesting encroachments by the Crown on the liberties of the people. Numerous grievances were recited. Two have significance in our daily affairs even now.

"That the respective colonies are entitled to the common law of England, and, more especially, to the great and inestimable privilege of being tried by their peers of the vicinity according to the course of that law. . . .

"That they have a right peaceably to assemble, consider of their grievances, and petition the King; and that all prosecutions, prohibitory proclamations, and commitments for the same are illegal."

The right to be tried "by an impartial jury of the State and district wherein the crime shall have been committed" is now guaranteed by the Sixth Amendment (July 23), and the right peaceably to assemble and petition the government (January 4) by the First Amendment.

Behind the October *Resolution* were some explosive events.

In 1767, Parliament imposed duties on glass, paper, painters' materials, and tea imported into America. These taxes raised a storm. The Massachusetts legislature, in 1768, petitioned the King in protest. Massachusetts was in turn rebuked and asked to rescind its action. Massachusetts refused. On learning that new troops were coming to enforce the tax laws, a convention of ninety-six Massachusetts towns met in Boston in the fall of 1768 and protested to the King the use of coercion. Parliament and the King severely censured that action, and directed the Governor of Massachusetts to transmit to London full information "touching all treasons" in Massachusetts in order that the offenders might be tried "within the realm."

Resistance to the taxes grew, until, in 1770, Parliament removed all duties except those on tea. Opposition to the tax continued. Finally came the Boston Tea Party in 1773. Then in 1774 came repressive measures.

The Port of Boston was closed.

The people of Massachusetts were deprived of a large measure of self-government. Thus town meetings were outlawed except those called with the written consent of the Governor.

In a case of "murder or other capital offense" (which would include the "treasonable acts" of the colonists in resisting the invasions of their liberties), the Governor was granted power to have the trial in another colony or in Great Britain, if he concluded that "an indifferent trial" could not be had in Massachusetts.

Selection of jurors was taken from the people and their courts and given to sheriffs appointed by the Governor. Vacancies in the courts were to be filled by the Governor, and the judges named were to serve at the pleasure of the King. The Council (the upper house of the legislature) was thereafter to be appointed by the King.

These were the explosive events behind the October fourteenth *Resolution* of the First Continental Congress.

The King made new appointments to the Council. But of those appointed some were frightened into not serving, others were forced to resign. The result was that there was no quorum left.

The community reaction to the efforts of the King to control the juries was also violent. Jurors summoned refused to act. One group said that if they served, they would betray "the just and sacred rights of our native lands," which were "purchased solely with the toil, the blood and treasure" of their ancestors. The people congregated at the courthouses, making it impossible for trials to be held. And when the sheriffs of the Governor ordered them to give way, they refused, saying they recognized no courts except their own.

In Boston, the legislature impeached judges who undertook to act under the new laws. In Worcester, 5,000 people formed a double file and made the judges, lawyers, and sheriffs walk bareheaded down it, swearing they would not hold court under these laws. In Great Barrington, the citizens filled the courthouse, leaving no room for judges or jurors.

"The fences of law are broken down," said the royalists. And so they were. Popular feeling ran so high that no judge, no jury, no sheriff dared enforce a law against the general bent of the people.

The philosophy behind the 1775 measure removing cases to a distant place for trial was expressed in a contemporary letter by Jared Ingersoll:

"There is no safety in trusting the breach of revenue laws to a Jury of the Country where the Offense is committed . . . they find even in England they never can obtain verdicts where Smuggling is practised and therefore always bring the Causes up for trial to London."

In Parliament, the American jury system was criticized: "To these men offenders know how to apply; and when any riot happens between the military power and the people of the town, the jury, being taken principally out of that town, the power of life and death of the offender is lodged in those who are offended."

A jury reflects the attitudes and mores of the community from which it is drawn. It lives only for the day and does justice according to its lights. The group of twelve, who are drawn to hear a case, makes the decision and melts away. It is not present the next day to be criticized. It is the one governmental agency that has no ambition. It is as human as the people who make it up. It is sometimes the victim of passion. But it also takes the sharp edges off a law and uses conscience to ameliorate a hardship. Since it is of and from the community, it gives the law an acceptance which verdicts of judges could not do.

Shakespeare, in *Measure for Measure*, was more critical:

> *The jury, passing on the prisoner's life,*
> *May, in the sworn Twelve, have a thief or two*
> *Guiltier than him they try. What's open made to justice,*
> *That justice seizes: what know the laws*
> *That thieves do pass on thieves?*

That is the argument in favor of "blue ribbon" juries. The Supreme Court upheld them by a five to four vote. Frank Murphy, dissenting, maintained that a constitutional jury was one drawn from a cross-section of the community.

It was long the practice of courts to issue injunctions in labor controversies and use their coercive power to break strikes. These injunctions were often issued without notice, without the moving party being required to put up any bond, and without specifying in detail what the union members were forbidden to do. Moreover, these labor injunctions were used to deprive unions of valuable rights, such as collective bargaining. One who violated the injunction, even though a stranger to it, could be punished for contempt (October 9).

In simple terms, this meant that a single judge could issue a labor injunction, interpret it, find it had been disobeyed, and fine or jail the violators as he chose. No jury trial was allowed. In practice, union members were often convicted, under the guise of trials for contempt, of substantive crimes for which, if indicted, they would have had a constitutional right to a jury trial.

In 1914, Congress, by the *Clayton Act*, dealt with these abuses in which federal courts had long indulged. It exacted more onerous requirements for issuance of injunctions. That victory was a pyrrhic one. At once the federal courts undertook an emasculation of the law. Only one small advantage to labor managed to survive. Congress required, in a narrow group of cases, that if a trade unionist were hauled into court by his heels for contempt, he could get a jury trial. Some courts, however, held that the judiciary had an "inherent power" to punish for contempt which could not be modified by the legislative branch. Hence they denied labor leaders jury trials. In 1924, the Supreme Court took the opposite view. It sustained that part of the *Clayton Act*, and held that Congress could provide a jury trial in these criminal contempt proceedings.

That small victory for labor was about all that survived the mighty effort that Wilson and his cohorts put into the labor provisions of the *Clayton Act*.

France, plagued by a rising tide of nationalism and independence in Morocco, ousted the Sultan in the summer of 1953 and installed a colonial government. The Moroccan matter came before the General Assembly of the United Nations. Many thought France's action violated the declaration in the *Charter* that one of the purposes of the United Nations was "To develop friendly relations among nations based on respect for the principle of equal rights and self-determination of peoples." This principle, proclaimed by our *Declaration of Independence*, was one of Woodrow Wilson's famous fourteen points, which he penned in 1918.

Bolivia presented a resolution which read:

"The General Assembly . . . *Recognizing* the right of the people of Morocco to complete self-determination in conformity with the Charter,

"*Renews* its appeal for the reduction of tension in Morocco and urges that the right of the people of Morocco to free democratic political institutions be ensured."

On October 19, 1953, the resolution was voted on in committee, paragraph by paragraph. In each instance, Henry Cabot Lodge, Jr., representing the United States, voted "No." Nevertheless, the resolution was voted out of the committee. When it came before the General Assembly, the United States once more opposed it. It failed to pass the Assembly, less than the two thirds necessary for approval voting in the affirmative.

In 1953, we sometimes lost sight of the great vision which John Adams had of America—"the opening of a grand scheme and design in Providence for the illumination and emancipation of the slavish part of mankind all over the earth."

114

Joel Barlow, a most conservative and respectable Connecticut Yankee, spent 1788 to 1805 in France, and thereupon became a great apostle of the American creed. His *Advice to the Privileged Orders,* long buried in American letters, ranks with Paine's *Rights of Man.* The Pitt ministry suppressed it in England.

In Europe, Barlow saw the feudal system at work, the *established* church in operation, the dominance of the military, laws that laid heavy hands on people. In France, he saw judicial offices auctioned by the King. He saw the "door of justice" barred "against the poor." He saw taxes levied to support the luxury of a small clique.

Barlow not only inveighed against these evils; he brought to Europe an American message:

"In the United States of America, the science of liberty is universally understood, felt, and practiced, as much by the simple as the wise, the weak as the strong. Their deep rooted and inveterate habit of thinking is that all men are equal in their rights. . . . This point once settled, every thing is settled. Many operations, which in Europe have been considered as . . . dangerous experiments, are but the infallible consequences of this great principle. The first of these operations is the business of election. . . . There is no jealousy on the occasion, nothing lucrative in office; any man in society may attain to any place in the government."

"Banish the mysticism of inequality," he said, "and you banish almost all the evils attendant on human nature."

He pointed out that "the word *people* in America has a different meaning from what it has in Europe. It there means the whole community, and comprehends every human creature."

In the 1940's and '50's, Asia and Africa were as heavily oppressed by feudalism as Europe was in Barlow's day. But we did not emulate Barlow. We relied mostly on guns and money, propping up feudal overlords. We forgot Barlow's message—that ideas of freedom are the most potent force in the world.

On October 21, 1953, the General Council of the Presbyterian Church adopted an important religious and political manifesto on communism.

It warned against communism, which at bottom, it said, was "a secular religious faith of great vitality" that has no loyalty to truth and that is committed to a "philosophy of lying." It praised some of the services which Congressional committees have rendered.

The Council protested, however, against certain practices of those committees. "Some Congressional inquiries have revealed a distinct tendency to become inquisitions. . . . Treason and dissent are being confused. The shrine of conscience and private judgment, which God alone has a right to enter, is being invaded." (March 15).

The Council objected to a purely negative program against communism. "Ideas are on the march, forces are abroad whose time has come. They cannot be repressed and they will bring unjust orders to an end. . . . All forms of feudalism . . . are foredoomed. So too are all types of imperialism. . . . Many of the revolutionary forces of our time are in great part the judgment of God upon human selfishness and complacency, and upon man's forgetfulness of man."

Communism is "foredoomed to failure" because it leaves God out of account. On the other hand, when governments do not interest themselves "in the common people, violent revolt eventually takes place." The threat of communism can be met "only by a sincere attempt to organize society in accordance with the everlasting principles of God's moral government of the world."

The Council also urged conference table discussions with Russia—"talk, unhurried talk, talk which does not rule out in advance the possibility of success, talk which takes place in private," with all conclusions being made public. "Direct personal conference has been God's way with man from the beginning."

When the Colonies broke with England in 1776, they faced the problem of transforming their colonial governments into a commonwealth. How should this be done? The idea of using a Constitutional Convention came from *Resolutions* adopted October 22, 1776, by the Concord Town Meeting. The reason for the use of the Convention was stated in one of the *Resolutions:*

"That the Supreme Legislative, either in their Proper Capacity or in Joint Committee, are by no means a body proper to form & Establish a Constitution or form of Government; for Reasons following:

1—Because we Conceive that a Constitution in its Proper Idea intends a System of Principles Established to Secure the Subject in the Possession & enjoyment of their Rights & Privileges, against any Encroachments of the Governing Part.

2—Because the Same Body that forms a Constitution have of Consequence a power to alter it.

3—Because a Constitution alterable by the Supreme Legislative is no Security at all to the Subject against any Encroachment of the Government part on any, or on all of their Rights and privileges."

The "yellow dog" contract has had an infamous history. It was a device used by employers to keep unions out of their plants. The contract required an employee to promise that, while employed, he would not become or remain a member of any labor organization. An attempt by Congress to outlaw the "yellow dog" contract was nullified by the Supreme Court in 1908. An attempt by the States to outlaw it was defeated by the Court in 1915.

The *Constitution* provides that no person shall be deprived of "property" or of "liberty" without due process of law. Those rights, it was said, prevented government from compelling either an employer "to accept or retain the personal services of another" or an employee "to perform personal services for another." Thus it was held that employer and employee had an "equality of right," which government could not constitutionally disturb.

This construction of due process threw the weight of government behind business and against labor. As Holmes said in a famous dissent, unionization might well be necessary to establish that "equality of position," without which there could be no liberty of contract. The laboring man on his own could hardly muster the strength to bargain effectively.

The "yellow dog" contract was swept into the limbo in 1937 when the Court, speaking through Chief Justice Hughes, upheld the provisions of the *Wagner Act*, forbidding employers from discouraging membership in a union by such contracts of employment, and granting employees the right of self-organization and collective bargaining (March 29). But that victory was narrowly won, four Justices dissenting on the ground that the *Wagner Act* deprived employers of the "right to contract" with whomever they pleased.

118

The *Charter* of the United Nations was unanimously approved in San Francisco by the heads of 50 delegations in June 1945. It came into force October 24, 1945, when the 5 permanent members of the Security Council and 24 other signatory States deposited their ratifications with the United States.

The aim of the *Charter* was:

—to save succeeding generations from the scourge of war
—to reaffirm faith in fundamental human rights, in the dignity and worth of the human person, in the equal right of men and women and of nations large and small
—to establish conditions under which justice and respect for the obligations arising from treaties and other sources of international law can be maintained
—to promote social progress and better standards of life

The subscribing nations proposed:

—to practice tolerance and live together in peace as good neighbors
—to maintain international peace and security
—to insure that armed force shall not be used, save in the common interest
—to employ international machinery for the promotion of the economic and social advancement of all people.

The United Nations has suffered failures and defaults. But it has also achieved great successes. It is as imperfect as all human institutions and more imperfect than many. But it serves an essential function. It provides machinery to the world community for co-operative undertakings. Moreover, it provides a forum for argument and debate, a pulpit where pleas to the conscience of the world may be made. Through the channels provided by the United Nations, even a voice from the wastelands of the earth can be heard. Through the good offices of the United Nations, the members of the world community are coming to know that all problems have a common denominator. It is that understanding which in time will furnish the cement necessary to bind all peoples closely together.

There followed in 1948 a *Universal Declaration of Human Rights* adopted by the General Assembly of the United Nations. It proclaimed among other things that:

—all human beings are born "free and equal in dignity and rights"

—everyone has the right to "life, liberty, and security of person"

—no one shall be subjected to "torture or to cruel, inhuman, or degrading treatment or punishment"

—no one shall be subjected "to arbitrary arrest, detention, or exile"

—everyone is entitled to "a fair and public hearing by an independent and impartial tribunal" in criminal proceedings and has the right "to be presumed innocent until proved guilty"

—no one shall be convicted of crimes under *ex post facto* laws

—everyone has the right to freedom of movement and residence within each nation

—everyone has the right to "freedom of thought, conscience, and religion," to "freedom of opinion and expression," to freedom of "peaceful assembly and association," and to "equal access to public service in his country"

—"the will of the people shall be the basis of the authority of government"

—everyone has "the right to work," "the right to rest and leisure," and "the right to education."

These and other rights gain much of their inspiration from our own *Declaration of Independence* and *Bill of Rights*. This *Declaration* may in legal effect have no binding consequences in any land; it may be only a reaching for the stars. But it lifts the hearts of men the world around. For it states in solemn and dignified terms the aspirations of men and women of good will of every race.

The Continental Congress appealed to Quebec to send delegates to a meeting of the Congress called for May 10, 1775. The appeal was a *Letter to the People of Quebec,* approved by Congress October 26, 1774. This *Letter,* more than any other document, shows the civil rights which the fathers prized the most and which they felt were being denied them by the royal authority.

"The first grand right," the *Letter* says, is representative government, making people "ruled by laws, which they themselves approve, not by edicts of men over whom they have no controul."

The "next great right" is trial by jury—the guarantee that life, liberty, and property will not be taken without a fair, public trial before a jury from the neighborhood.

Then comes the right to habeas corpus—the procedure whereby a court can quickly inquire into the legality of a man's imprisonment.

The fourth right is the free ownership of land, farm laborers being paid for their work, not rendering service by reason of subservience to some overlord.

The last right mentioned in the *Letter* is freedom of the press. The fathers conceived of this right in broad terms. It was designed not only for dissemination of political ideas and the criticism of government, but also for "the advancement of truth, science, morality, and arts in general."

These were "the invaluable rights"—the rights "without which a people cannot be free and happy," the rights in jeopardy when the "legislative, executive and judging powers are all moved by the nods of a Minister." These were the rights in the forefront of events leading to the *Declaration of Independence.*

Michael Servetus, prosecuted by John Calvin, was burned at the stake in Geneva on October 27, 1553. On October 27, 1903, some of the lineal descendants and disciples of Calvin erected an expiatory monument on the site.

At the stake Servetus cried out, "Oh Jesus, Son of the Eternal God, have pity on me." If he had been willing to confess Jesus as "the Eternal Son of God," he might have been saved. But by the prevailing theological view Servetus put the adjective in the "wrong" place.

Servetus thought that baptism of infants, who as yet had no personal faith, was not consistent with true Christianity. He rejected the doctrine of the Trinity. Jesus, he thought, was man deified. "The nature of humanity," he taught, "is of such character that God can communicate divinity, and this not by degradation of divinity but by exaltation of humanity." Servetus believed that Calvin's doctrines of original sin, the depravity of man, and predestination were monstrous. He published his views in *The Restoration of Christianity*, which was burned with him.

These views were heretical under the Code of Justinian and punishable by death, as Roland H. Bainton has faithfully recorded in *Hunted Heretic*.

There is no doubt that Calvin sincerely believed that the very stability of Christendom depended on the outcome of the trial. There is no doubt that Calvin's fanatical faith left room for no dissenters, no doubters. He demanded faith in one orthodox creed. Servetus had ideas which were dangerous to that orthodoxy, and he lived at a time when a man spoke his deepest convictions only at great peril.

The problem of Servetus was in a sense the problem of this age. Those who speak out against the neurosis that has seized us in the mid-twentieth century risk much. But if they stay silent, they are unworthy of their inheritance. Then they lose the fight for freedom by default. If a few sick minds can transfer their psychosis to the whole community, anyone can readily become a victim of the calumny and lies which the modern hunt for heretics has produced.

The first Ten Amendments to our *Constitution*—commonly referred to as the *Bill of Rights*—were held to be restrictions on the power of the federal government, not the States. Madison had endeavored to include provisions that no State should infringe "the equal rights of conscience, nor the freedom of speech or of the press, nor of the right of trial by jury in criminal cases." But that proposal was rejected.

Though the Fourteenth Amendment, adopted after the Civil War, says that no State shall deprive any person of "life, liberty, or property, without due process of law," it was assumed, up to 1925, that "liberty," as so used, did not include freedom of speech. In that year the Supreme Court, in passing on the constitutionality of a New York law which made it a crime to advocate the overthrow of the government by force or violence, assumed that freedom of speech and of the press, protected by the First Amendment, were also included within "liberty," as that word is used in the Fourteenth Amendment. In 1927, the first state law abridging free speech was struck down on that ground. Since then, that rule has been repeatedly applied to cases where the States have restrained free speech and freedom of the press. Soon it was applied to situations involving freedom of religion and to rights of assembly.

That is the reason why First Amendment rights are often said to have a preferred position in our constitutional scheme. They are preferred because the *Constitution*, as construed, protects them against abridgment by either the States or the federal government.

Few other provisions of the *Bill of Rights* have ever been applied in full force to the States (February 17, May 1).

The First Amendment provides that Congress shall make "no law . . . abridging the freedom of speech, or of the press." The prohibition on its face is absolute (June 13). But the courts have construed it as though it read that Congress may make "some laws" abridging the freedom of speech and of press. During World War I, a man circulated a pamphlet denouncing conscription. Another published twelve newspapers attacking the war. One made a speech against our participation in the war. Another circulated two socialist tracts critical of the war. One published a German-language paper critical of capitalism and the war. A minister attacked the purposes of the war and our participation in it. Their convictions were all sustained by the Supreme Court under the federal espionage act.

In 1925, the Court sustained a conviction under a New York law making it a crime to advocate the necessity or propriety of overthrowing the government by force. The defendant had circulated a manifesto extolling Marxism and calling on the proletariat to revolt. In 1927, the Court upheld a like conviction of a communist under a California statute. She had helped organize a group which advocated overthrow of the government by force.

In 1940, Congress made it a crime to teach or advocate the overthrow of the government by force. The communist leaders in America were convicted of a conspiracy to use the communist party for that purpose. There was no evidence that the accused had done anything but teach the condemned doctrine. They had taken no steps to translate their creed into action.

The theory underlying the cases is that if an act can be punished, its advocacy can be, *provided* the utterance is a call to action immediately or as speedily as circumstances permit, and not merely a reflection of a philosophical attitude.

The law has therefore moved a long way from John Stuart Mill's dictum:

"If all mankind minus one, were of one opinion, and only one person were of the contrary opinion, mankind would be no more justified in silencing that one person, than he, if he had the power, would be justified in silencing mankind."

Madison, in the *Federalist*, spoke of the singular achievements of the Framers of the *Constitution*. "They accomplished a revolution which has no parallel in the annals of human society. They reared the fabrics of government which have no model on the face of the globe." Madison did not refer to the right to habeas corpus, the prohibition of bills of attainder, and the other restraints on government which British subjects had won after long struggles. Those guarantees were not novel. The novel thing was that men were to govern themselves as they had never done before.

"We the People of the United States" established the *Constitution*. "We the People" are the source of all governing power. The executive, the legislative, and the judicial branches are our agents, commissioned to express our will. "We the People" no longer have to beg for rights. We are the source of political power, and we may not be deprived of any of that power by any branch of the government.

This is the philosophy behind the command of the First Amendment that Congress shall make "no" law abridging freedom of speech and of the press. "We the People" are the governing body, who are not dependent on the legislature for what we may say or print. Our philosophy is premised on the belief that national security will be better assured through political freedom, than through repression. Once we start restraining that political freedom, we evince a lack of faith in the boldest political principle the world has known.

This is the theme of Alexander Meiklejohn, former President of Amherst, who, in 1953, wrote a devastating criticism for the *University of Chicago Law Review* of the Supreme Court decisions which have allowed freedom of speech to be abridged.

On October 31, 1791, Philip Freneau (1752–1832) launched the *National Gazette* in the nation's Capital. Freneau, poet of the Revolution, had planned to open a paper in New York. Jefferson and Madison persuaded him to come to Philadelphia. The capital had only a conservative, Federalist paper run by John Fenno. Jefferson and Madison wanted Freneau's great pen aligned with them against Hamilton and the aristocracy.

As inducement, Jefferson offered Freneau a "clerkship for foreign languages" in the Department of State, which paid $250 a year and required only "a moderate knowledge of French."

The other paper preached as gospel, "Take away thrones and crowns from among men and there will soon be an end of all dominion and justice." Its social items aped the Court of St. James.

Freneau resorted to satire. He published an account of the trial of "James Barefoot, laborer, for carelessly treading on the great toe of My Lord Ohio." Barefoot was convicted, His Lordship's toe was in "a fair way of recovery," and the chance for a pardon was slight because of "the enormity of the offense."

Freneau singled out Hamilton for special attack. He gave Hamilton a formula for converting a republic into a monarchy: "confer titles of rank," "harp incessantly on the dangers of the mob," "secure a rich manufacturing class by making laws in their interests." He campaigned against the Bank (December 23), against the practice of the Senate having private sessions.

When France became a republic in 1792, Freneau espoused the French cause, even against the neutrality policy of Washington. Washington protested to Jefferson about "that rascal Freneau." Jefferson stood firm, replying that Freneau's paper "has saved our constitution which was galloping fast into monarchy."

Freneau, our first true opposition editor, drilled Jeffersonian principles into the people. He showed what power the press can have over public affairs. John Adams, indeed, laid his defeat to Freneau and "other troublesome newspaper men."

NOVEMBER

On November 1, 1765, the *Stamp Act* became effective. It imposed a duty on most of the documents used in judicial proceedings and in commercial transactions. Newspapers, pamphlets, and books were included. So were deeds, bills of lading, invoices, and the like. The Act gave the admiralty courts jurisdiction to try those who violated the Act. There was no jury in the admiralty court. The case was heard and decided by a judge. The judges who would try the American colonists would be judges serving at the pleasure of the King.

The purpose of the *Stamp Act* was to raise money to help defray the cost of stationing British troops here. When the proposal was first made, a storm of protest arose in the Colonies. Opposition mounted. Resistance to the law became so great that it was never enforced; and it was repealed in 1766.

From this opposition three principles of a fighting faith emerged:

There should be no taxation without representation.

Taxes on the privilege of publishing are as obnoxious as censorship itself.

Trial by jury is "the inherent and invaluable right" of the citizen.

"To lay with one hand the power of government on the property of the citizen, and with the other to bestow it upon favored individuals to aid private enterprises and build up private fortunes, is none the less a robbery because it is done under the forms of law and is called taxation." So ruled the Supreme Court in 1875 when it refused to enforce against Topeka, Kansas, bonds given a company to induce it to establish a factory there.

In 1919, North Dakota undertook an experiment in socialism. It established a bank and a warehouse, elevator, and flour mill system, and launched a home building program—all under the ownership and management of the State. The Supreme Court ruled that it was not a taking of property without due process of law to levy taxes to finance that program.

Between the Kansas case and the North Dakota case was one from California decided in November 1896. Irrigation districts were organized, and they were financed by taxation. Was taxation for irrigation taxation for "a public purpose"? The Supreme Court held that it was, otherwise millions of acres of cultivable land would be left in an "arid and worthless condition."

Yet might not construction of a factory in a community likewise serve the public interest by bringing employment to a destitute area?

At Alton, Illinois, is the grave of Elijah P. Lovejoy, whom Irving Dilliard of the St. Louis *Post-Dispatch* has called "the first martyr to freedom of the press in the United States," an editor "who knew no compromise on right and wrong as his conscience understood them."

Alton was divided on the issue of slavery. Lovejoy, an abolitionist editor, was outspoken. An aroused community destroyed several of his presses. Finally a public meeting was called at which a resolution was adopted demanding that Lovejoy end his career as editor in Alton. Lovejoy addressed the gathering on November 3, 1837.

"Have I, sir, been guilty of any infraction of the laws? Whose good name have I injured? When and where have I published anything injurious to the reputation of Alton?

"What, sir, I ask, has been my offense? Put your finger upon it—define it—and I stand ready to answer it. If I have committed any crime, you can easily convict me. . . . But if I have been guilty of no violation of the law, why am I hunted up and down continually like a partridge upon the mountains? . . .

"If the civil authorities refuse to protect me, I must look to God; and if I die, I have determined to make my grave in Alton. I have sworn eternal opposition to slavery and by the blessings of God I will never turn back. With God I cheerfully rest my cause. I can die at my post but I cannot desert it."

Four nights later a mob attacked the warehouse where Lovejoy's new printing press was stored. Lovejoy was killed in the encounter.

Recently American journalists erected bronze markers at the place where Lovejoy fell. By that act they illustrated a trait in the American character. At times we indulge in violent excesses. But the American conscience usually speaks up, and on a later day pilgrimages are made to atone for the injustice (July 29).

Prior to 1719, there had been censorship of the press in Massachusetts. But on November 4, 1719, a series of events started which effectively put an end to it. Shute, the Royal Governor, on that day addressed the General Court (composed of the Council and the House), charging the Colony with neglect in conserving the forests as souces of naval supplies. This criticism stung to the quick. The House drew up a *Remonstrance* charging the Royal Surveyor of the woods with gross misconduct.

Shute came to the defense of the Surveyor and ordered the House not to print the *Remonstrance*. The House insisted. Shute replied that if the criticism of the Surveyor were left in the *Remonstrance,* he would use his power as licensor of the press to prevent the *Remonstrance* from being printed. The House stood firm. Shute sent orders to the printers not to print the document. One Nicolas Boone, on urging from the House, disobeyed the order and the *Remonstrance* was printed.

Shute stormed and fretted. The Council was indecisive; Shute took no action against Boone; the force of public opinion carried the day. Defiance of Shute established a precedent which soon meant official recognition of the end of censorship of the press in Massachusetts.

On November 5, 1917, the Supreme Court struck down a city ordinance making it unlawful for a colored person to occupy a house located in a block where the majority of the residents were white. A similar provision barred whites from colored blocks. The suit arose in an attempt to enforce a contract against a Negro buyer, who defended on the ground that his purchase would be illegal, since the property was in a white block.

The Court invalidated the ordinance on the ground that the Fourteenth Amendment qualifies a person to acquire property without discrimination against him because of his race or color. The Fourteenth Amendment does not make a white person deal with a Negro or a Negro deal with a white. The Fourteenth Amendment constrains only "state" action. But a city ordinance is "state" action.

How about a restrictive covenant in a deed? Can parties agree that a residential lot will not be sold to a Negro?

Some thirty years later the Supreme Court held that buyers and sellers could make such restrictive covenants as they liked and by their voluntary action agree to keep Negroes from a residential area. But once the parties sought enforcement of those covenants in the courts, the situation changed. If the courts of a State ordered the restrictive covenant to be enforced or granted damages for its breach, then the State entered a forbidden domain. For action of the courts of a State, like action of the State legislature, is "state" action within the meaning of the Fourteenth Amendment. Imposing damages for failure to observe the restrictive covenant, like a decree requiring its enforcement, puts the State behind a practice which discriminates against a Negro because of his race or color.

Restrictive covenants in real estate deeds are old and ancient devices for controlling the use of property. They have been used for many purposes, including the protection of a residential area from invasion by minority groups. Covenants forbidding the sale of houses and lots to Negroes have been common. Wholesale use in recent years of racial restrictions in newly developed urban areas closed them to Negroes. Their use within cities resulted in "black belts" being encircled by territory into which the colored people could not move. The consequences were serious, because the Negroes since the turn of this century moved more and more into the cities. In New York City, Negroes were 1.9 per cent of the population in 1910 and 6.1 per cent in 1940. There were other like increases in other large northern and midwestern cities.

Restrictive covenants bottled up the Negro population in overcrowded places that were unwholesome in terms of health and morals, and that were breeding grounds for crime, racial friction, and riots. Housing shortages increased the resistance of the whites against Negro expansion, and at the same time increased the pressure within the "black belts" to break the bonds.

Restrictive covenants were used primarily to exclude Negroes. But they were by no means so restricted. Many excluded all non-Caucasians; many were aimed at the Semitic races. Yet prior to the recent Supreme Court decisions the courts of at least nineteen States and the District of Columbia enforced these racial restraints.

The Sixth Amendment provides that "in all criminal prosecutions" the accused has the right to "the assistance of counsel for his defense." This provision governs trials in the federal courts. But unlike some other guarantees of the *Bill of Rights* (October 28), it has not been made applicable to the States through the Fourteenth Amendment. The Due Process Clause of the Fourteenth Amendment (July 28) has been construed, however, to require the appointment of counsel for a defendant in certain cases.

The famous Scottsboro trial of seven young Negroes brought the problem to the Supreme Court in 1932. Until the morning of the trial, no lawyer had been named to represent the defendants, who were both ignorant and illiterate and charged with an atrocious crime, carrying the death penalty. The lawyers named had no chance to investigate or prepare a defense. The Supreme Court reversed convictions obtained in that way, as violative of "due process." "The right to be heard would be, in many cases, of little avail if it did not comprehend the right to be heard by counsel."

But in 1942, the Court, by a divided vote, greatly limited that doctrine. A farm hand, who demanded a lawyer because he was too poor to hire one, was put to trial for robbery and forced to defend himself. He was sentenced to eight years. The Court concluded that even without a lawyer the accused had had a fair trial. The result is that it is mandatory for state courts to appoint counsel only in capital cases.

The 1942 case has been severely criticized on numerous grounds, one being the objection stated in the dissent that it "subjects innocent men to increased dangers of conviction merely because of their poverty." A rich defendant, a defendant with friends and allies, always has counsel. The impoverished defendant, the waif, the unpopular one, may be forced to stand trial without knowing whether the charge against him is valid or what a valid defense might be (April 2).

134

"You are banished from out of our jurisdiction as being a woman not fit for our society, and are to be imprisoned until the court shall send you away." This was the verdict of the forty theologians who condemned Anne Hutchinson on November 8, 1637, at Newtown, Massachusetts.

Anne Hutchinson, heavy with child, was tried for heresy. She claimed that the Calvinist ministers of Massachusetts taught "the covenant of works" or salvation by ministry and authority and that they were therefore not able ministers of the *New Testament*. She maintained that true salvation was by "the covenant of grace," i.e., by the free inner light that comes from communion with God and the revelations which He brings.

Anne Hutchinson appeared without defense counsel. While the trial was filled with subtleties of theology, she pleaded for freedom of conscience. She claimed that the Lord had let her see "which was the clear ministry and which the wrong." Her position was this: "Now if you condemn me for speaking what in my conscience I know to be truth, I must commit myself unto the Lord. . . . You have power over my body but the Lord Jesus hath power over my body and soul . . . Having seen Him which is invisible, I fear not what man can do unto me."

Anne Hutchinson's child was delivered dead, and the birth was called a "monstrous" one. Later she was driven to the wilderness and murdered by Indians. These events may have quieted the consciences of those who had condemned her. But the doctrinal duel she fought and lost in the cause of religious toleration helped stir the revolutionary forces that demanded a preferred position for liberty of conscience in our scheme of things.

On November 9, 1670, Chief Justice Vaughan issued a writ of habeas corpus that brought eternal credit to himself and great strength to the jury system. William Penn, the Quaker, had been tried for preaching in the Grace Church Street of London, so as to cause a great "concourse and tumult" of people and a "great disturbance" of the peace (September 5).

The jury found him guilty only of speaking, not of breaching the peace. The jury, though reprimanded by the court and sent back for further deliberations, returned the same verdict. The court thereupon ordered the jury kept all night without food, drink, fire, or chamber pots. The next day the jury returned the same verdict. Once more, the court locked the jury up for the rest of that day and the following night. The next day the jury returned a verdict of *not guilty*.

The court immediately fined the jurymen forty marks each and had them locked up in Newgate until their fines were paid. They were, however, shortly released on writs of habeas corpus, Chief Justice Vaughan holding that on questions of fact the jury had the final say. Thus the independence of the jury was established. A citizen became entitled to be tried by his fellow citizens, not by a judge. The jury system became a bulwark of free men, rather than a coercive instrument of the powers-that-be.

In November 1951, the Supreme Court rendered an historic decision concerning the right of an accused to bail. The Eighth Amendment provides that "Excessive bail shall not be required." American communists, under arrest and charged with advocating the Marxist theory of overthrow of the government, applied for bail in a federal court. Bail was fixed in the amount of $50,000 for each of the accused. They moved for its reduction, claiming that $50,000 was "excessive" under the *Constitution*. Chief Justice Vinson rendered the decision.

Federal law has always provided that an accused in a *noncapital* case *shall* be admitted to bail before trial. From the viewpoint of the accused, bail serves two main functions—it permits the unhampered preparation of a defense, and it serves to save the accused from being punished prior to his conviction. From the viewpoint of the government, bail gives assurance that the accused will stand trial and submit to sentence if found guilty. Admission to bail always involves the risk that the accused will take flight. But that is a risk inherent in our system of justice, contrasted to the system of law in totalitarian countries such as Russia.

In fixing bail the judge cannot make the sky the limit. He must take each case on its own peculiar facts—the wealth of the accused, his character and prior record, the likelihood of an attempt to escape, the nature of the offense.

Chief Justice Vinson acted in the finest tradition when he held that fixing of bail at the uniform amount of $50,000 for each communist was arbitrary. The amount was far in excess of the bail required in comparable cases. The record disclosed no facts indicating that $50,000 was needed to assure the appearance of the defendants for trial. If this order of bail had been allowed to stand, then people could be held in jail upon mere accusation, until it was found convenient to give them a trial. That is the Russian, not the American, system (January 7).

Our public school system goes back to November 11, 1647, when Massachusetts provided that every town having 100 or more families or households should have a grammar school supported by the taxpayers. The preamble of the law referred to that "ould deluder, Satan," who tries to keep men from knowledge of the Scriptures; and it stated as its purpose the training of children so that they may know the Word firsthand and not be deceived by those who put "false glosses" on it.

Horace Mann, the great educator, once said that this law "laid the foundation" of the present system of free schools. The idea of an educational system that was at once both universal and free and available to all the people, rich and poor alike, was revolutionary. No other nation ever had such an institution; three centuries later it is a stranger to the bulk of the people of the world.

The free public school system which the Puritans conceived has been in large measure the secret of America's success. In these classrooms children of all races, nationalities, and tongues learned a common language and became imbued with one central idea—the American conception that all men are created equal, that opportunities are open to all, that every minority, whether respected or despised, has the same guaranteed rights as the majority. The public school system was indeed the true "melting pot." Parents who landed here often brought with them the antagonisms, rivalries, and suspicions of other continents. But their children became one and united in pursuit of the democratic ideal.

Massachusetts again led the way when it enacted, in 1852, the first general compulsory attendance law in America. It required every child between 8 and 14 to attend some public school for at least 12 weeks a year. Since 1918, when Mississippi adopted such a law, all the States have required compulsory attendance at some school.

Today there are forty-one States which require attendance until the child is 16, three until he is 17, four until he is 18. Five require 8 years of attendance, thirty-four require 9, five require 10, three require 11, and two (Ohio and Utah) require 12.

Oregon, in 1922, adopted a statute requiring all children between the ages of eight and sixteen to attend a public school until they finished the eighth grade. The Oregon law had been adopted under campaign slogans such as these:

"We must now halt those coming to our country from forming groups, establishing schools, and thereby bringing up their children in an environment often antagonistic to the principles of our government.

"Mix the children of the foreign born with the native born, and the rich with the poor. Mix those with prejudices in the public school melting pot for a few years while their minds are plastic, and finally bring out the finished product—a true American."

The constitutionality of the law was challenged by the Society of Sisters, who conducted an orphan home, where they taught the subjects usually pursued in public schools, and in addition gave systematic religious and moral instruction according to the tenets of the Roman Catholic faith.

The case reached the Supreme Court in 1925 and a unanimous decision held the law unconstitutional. The Court said that the Oregon statute unreasonably interfered "with the liberty of parents" in the upbringing and education of their children:

"The fundamental theory of liberty upon which all governments in this Union repose excludes any general power of the State to standardize its children by forcing them to accept instruction from public teachers only. The child is not the mere creature of the State; those who nurture him and direct his destiny have the right, coupled with the high duty, to recognize and prepare him for additional obligations."

The decision conformed with the pattern of the school laws in this country. While all the States by this time required parents to send their children to some school, they gave, with the exception of Oregon, the choice of the public, private, denominational, or parochial school.

On November 13, 1853, Margaret Douglass was convicted of violating a Virginia law making it a crime for a white person to "assemble with Negroes for the purpose of instructing them to read or write." The evidence showed that she ran a school for twenty to thirty Negro children in her home in Norfolk. For this crime she was sentenced to a month in jail.

The purpose of the law was stated by the judge at the time of imposing sentence:

"Our mails were clogged with abolition pamphlets and inflammatory documents, to be distributed among our Southern Negroes to induce them to cut our throats. . . . Under such circumstances there was but one measure of protection for the South, and that was adopted."

Margaret Douglass, a Southerner, said in her plea to the jury:

"I deem it the duty of every Southerner, morally and religiously, to instruct his slaves, that they may know their duties to their masters, and to their common God. . . . I am a strong advocate for the religious and moral instruction of the whole human family. I have always instructed my own slaves and will continue to do so as long as I remain in a slave state."

On November 14, 1904, the Collins Committee of Inquiry in England made a report on the appalling miscarriage of justice in the case of Adolf Beck.

Beck, an innocent man, was convicted not only once but twice. The charges were defrauding women of jewelry or money. Beck was convicted in 1896 and sentenced to seven years. He was identified by the victims; and a handwriting expert swore the checks that had been passed were written in Beck's hand. Beck defended on the ground that the criminal was an ex-convict named John Smith, who, in 1877, had been convicted for like offenses and had used the same techniques. The police, indeed, thought that Beck was Smith.

If the prison records had been faithfully kept, they would have shown that Smith was circumcised, which alone would have saved Beck. Moreover, at the 1896 trial the judge ruled that the defense could not show that the documents in Smith's 1877 trial were in the same handwriting as those in Beck's trial.

Beck had evidence that the same man wrote both. That man could not have been Beck, for in 1877 Beck was in South America. When the judge excluded the evidence, Beck was, in effect, denied the one good defense he had.

Beck was released from prison in 1901 and rearrested in 1904 for a similar offense and once more convicted. He did not, however, serve a second time, as meanwhile Smith was arrested on similar charges for crimes committed while Beck had been in prison. Investigation led to the release and pardon of Beck and eventually to a grant to him of £5000 indemnity by Parliament.

When Beck was convicted, his case could be reviewed on appeal only if the trial judge submitted a question of law to the appellate court. As a result of Beck's case, the Court of Criminal Appeal was established in 1907, to which there may be appeals as of right on the kind of rulings that resulted in Beck's wrongful conviction.

On a bleak morning in 1902, J. B. Brown was led to the gallows in Florida and the rope placed around his neck. All was in readiness for the execution. Only the death warrant had to be read and the trap door tripped. But when the death warrant was read, it was apparent that someone had made a serious error. The person ordered to be executed was not Brown, but the foreman of the jury which had found Brown guilty of the murder of Harry E. Wesson.

Brown was led back to his cell, and his attorneys took instant advantage of the delay. They persuaded the Governor to commute the sentence to life imprisonment.

The Supreme Court of Florida, in affirming the conviction, said there was "very little testimony" to connect Brown with Wesson's murder, except a "confession" which Brown, after his arrest, had made to another prisoner. Brown took the stand at the trial, denied that he had made the "confession," and swore he was innocent. The courts held that the issues presented were for the jury to resolve.

Eleven years passed when one J. J. Johnson, who had been indicted with Brown but never tried, made a deathbed confession, admitting that he had killed Wesson and wholly exonerating Brown. Florida officials investigated and were convinced that Brown was innocent (May 9).

In 1913, Governor Park Trammell gave Brown a full pardon. In 1929, Brown, who was then "aged, infirm, and destitute," was given a pension by the Florida legislature in compensation for the twelve years he spent in prison for a crime he did not commit.

". . . nor shall any person be subject for the same offence to be twice put in jeopardy of life or limb." Such is the command of the Fifth Amendment. And all the States have a like provision either in their constitutions or in their common law.

During the reign of the Stuarts, a jury was often discharged during the course of a trial if the prosecution saw the proof was deficient, so that better evidence could be secured for a second trial. The practice was an abhorrent one, which was finally condemned by British judges in 1746. And early American decisions took the same stand.

Today, a second trial will be allowed for failure of evidence only in extreme circumstances, as, for example, where it was the defendant's fault that the crucial testimony was not available at the first trial. Only North Carolina allows a second trial when the prosecutor simply failed to have his evidence ready at the first trial.

Generally, the trial judge has discretion to discharge a jury and order a retrial if the interests of justice require it, as, for example, when a juror is found to be prejudiced against the prosecution or the accused.

Under our federal system one act, e.g., possession of liquor, may violate both *state* and *federal* law. It is not double jeopardy to convict under *federal* law, though the same act was previously punished under *state* law.

At times the people have cried for blood and weak judges have obliged. Anne Redfearne was tried and acquitted of witchcraft in Lancashire, England. The verdict was so unpopular that she was tried again on precisely the same charge, viz., that eighteen years earlier she had summoned the Evil One and helped murder Christopher Nutter through the use of an image of clay. A lady saw her mold the clay; Nutter on his death had accused Anne Redfearne of his bewitchment. She was convicted on the second trial and hanged. This was in 1612, after the principle of double jeopardy had been established.

Sir Walter Raleigh had been a favorite of Elizabeth. But when James came to the throne, Raleigh's political fortunes waned and political rivals plotted his destruction. He was soon arrested and charged with treason. There were treasonable projects afoot, since James would not tolerate the Catholic religion in the realm. Plots were laid to kidnap him and force concessions from him. One plot was to put Lady Arabella Stuart on the throne in his place. Raleigh was charged with promoting the latter plan with Lord Cobham.

There was hardly a shred of evidence against Raleigh that was competent by modern standards. The prosecution relied mainly on depositions and letters written by Cobham. Cobham was alive and could have been produced. Raleigh asked that Cobham confront him. "Call my accuser before my face," he demanded. Raleigh knew that Cobham had retracted the confessions. Raleigh knew that they could not stand up under cross-examination.

The judges feared the same thing. So they refused to make the prosecution produce Cobham, giving as their excuse "many horse-stealers may escape, if they may not be condemned without witnesses."

Raleigh was convicted on November 17, 1603, and later beheaded. He went to his death without meeting his accuser face to face. Perhaps Cobham's confessions had been forced by torture. Perhaps Cobham had lied. Whatever the truth, Cobham never had to suffer the torment of cross-examination. The jury never had a chance to determine whether Cobham was telling the truth.

The Raleigh trial was a notorious one, long remembered. It was one of the reasons why, prior to the federal *Constitution*, some of the States wrote into their constitutions provisions giving an accused in a criminal trial the right to be confronted with the witnesses against him. It led likewise to the inclusion of the same protection in the Sixth Amendment.

Dorothy Bailey, an employee of the federal government with a civil service classification, was discharged in 1948 after a finding of the loyalty board that it had "reasonable grounds" to believe that she was "disloyal" to the United States. The controversy moved from the loyalty board to the Supreme Court, where her dismissal was affirmed by a divided vote.

Miss Bailey testified that she had not been a communist, and she submitted many affidavits as to her character and as to the public positions she had taken contrary to the communist party line. No person appeared against her. The evidence on which she was discharged was secret information in the files of the loyalty board. It was given by people who were not under oath and whose identity was unknown, both to Miss Bailey and to the loyalty board.

The anonymous accusers of Dorothy Bailey may or may not have been respectable or trustworthy. They may have been wholly malicious. They may have carried old grudges. They may long have nourished smoldering jealousies. They may have been demented.

Dorothy Bailey, whether innocent or guilty, was condemned for public employment by faceless and unknown accusers, whose testimony was not under oath and who were not presented for cross-examination.

The use of depositions and statements of unidentified persons became increasingly common following World War II. They were used not only in loyalty proceedings, but in hearings to determine the legality of the classification which a local draft board gave a man under the *Selective Service Act*. The practice was sustained by the courts over vigorous dissents.

The use of statements by informers who need not confront the person under investigation or accusation has such an infamous history that it should be rooted out from our procedure. A hearing at which faceless people are allowed to present their whispered rumors and yet escape the test and torture of cross-examination is not a hearing in the Anglo-American sense. We cannot be proud of the practice—whether the life of a man is at stake, or his reputation, or any matter touching upon his status or his rights.

If F.B.I. reports were disclosed in administrative or judicial proceedings, it may be that valuable underground sources would dry up. But that is not the choice. If the aim is to protect the underground of informers, the F.B.I. report need not be used. If it is used, then fairness requires that the names of the accusers be disclosed. Without the identity of the informer, the person investigated or accused stands helpless. The prejudices, the credibility, the passions, the perjury of the informer are never known. If they were exposed, the whole charge might wither under the cross-examination.

The devastating effect of a cross-examination is illustrated by a trial in England before Lord Denman in which the forgery of a will was the issue. Samuel Warren (1807–1877) had a witness on the stand. Putting his thumb over the seal, he held up the will and proceeded with the examination:

Q: And did you sign the will as subscribing witness?
A: I did.
Q: Was it sealed with red or black wax?
A: With red wax.
Q: Did you see the testator seal it with red wax?
A: I did.
Q: Where was he when he signed and sealed this will?
A: In his bed.
Q: Pray, how long a piece of red wax did he use?
A: About three inches long.
Q: How did he light that piece of wax?
A: With a candle.
Q: Who lit that candle?
A: I lit it.
Q: With what?
A: With a match.
Q: Where did you get that match?
A: On the mantle-shelf in the room.
Q: Now sir, upon your solemn oath, you saw the testator sign that will—he signed it in his bed—you signed it as a subscribing witness—you saw him seal it with red wax—a piece of wax about three inches long—he lit the wax with a piece of candle—you lit the candle.
A: I did.
Q: Once more, sir—upon your solemn oath, you did?
A: I did.

Warren, taking his thumb off the seal and turning to the judge, said, "My lord, it is sealed with a wafer!"

"In all criminal prosecutions, the accused shall enjoy the right
. . . to be informed of the nature and cause of the accusation."
This is the command of the Sixth Amendment for all criminal
trials in the federal courts.

To be held in custody without any charge is revolting to our
sense of justice. Convicting a man of vagrancy because he is a
communist or convicting him of tax evasion because he is a rack-
eteer is bad enough. But bringing him to trial without disclosure
of the precise accusation would be even worse. For it would in
effect often be a denial of an opportunity to defend.

In England, the matter came to a head in the *Petition of Right*,
which complained to the King that "divers of Your Subjects have
of late been imprisoned without any Cause shewed; and when
for their Deliverence they were brought before your Justices by
Your Majesty's Writs of *Habeas Corpus* . . . and their Keepers
commanded to certify the Causes of their Detainer, no Cause was
certified, but that they were detained by Your Majesty's special
Command, signified by the Lords of Your Privy Council, and yet
were returned back to several Prisons, without being charged
with any Thing to which they might make Answer according to
the Law."

The issue was forced by reason of the practice of the King in
requiring forced loans from citizens and putting them in jail if
they refused (May 26).

Thomas Darnel was one victim. In November 1627, he sought
release from prison by habeas corpus. The court required the
jailer to disclose by what authority Darnel was held. The jailer
showed that Darnel was detained by special order of the King.
Darnel argued that if that was a justification for his detention,
citizens may be "restrained of their liberties perpetually."

The court was apparently troubled, for it heard long arguments
and deliberated some days. Finally the judges delivered a long
opinion, saying that they were required to "walk in the steps of
our forefathers" and deny the relief (August 17). The word of
the King was sufficient to hold a man, they said, for "we trust
him in great matters."

148

On November 22, 1927, there started in Minnesota a legal proceeding that was to make history for freedom of the press. A state law permitted the abatement as a public nuisance of a newspaper or magazine found to be "malicious, scandalous, and defamatory." The State brought such a proceeding against a publication called *The Saturday Press* and obtained a decree which ended its publication and made further publication punishable as contempt.

The Supreme Court set the decree aside, condemning it as censorship, as a prior restraint on publication. A publisher may be held accountable by libel for what he prints. But once he is restrained from printing, government enters a forbidden domain. A degree of abuse is inherent in all human institutions, including the press. But we believe with Madison that "to the press alone, chequered as it is with abuses, the world is indebted for all the triumphs which have been gained by reason and humanity over error and oppression."

The same power that could suppress a "defamatory" paper today could suppress an "unorthodox" or unpopular one tomorrow. It was censorship that in an early day was used to stifle the efforts of patriots to inform the people of the duties of kings and the rights of subjects.

Not until 1952 did the Supreme Court rule that motion pictures were protected by the guarantees of freedom of speech and press contained in the *Constitution*. The Court did not outlaw all censorship of movies. It merely held that a censor could not ban them because he thought they were "sacrilegious" or "prejudicial" to the interests of the people.

149

In the 1930's and '40's, there came before the Supreme Court a series of cases involving attempts by municipalities to exact a license from Jehovah's Witnesses for the distribution of their religious literature. They are a religious sect who spread through pamphlets their religious beliefs and interpretations of the *Bible*. A city ordinance, which required a license to distribute literature, was applied against one of them, with a resultant fine for offering religious tracts without a license.

In 1938, the conviction was reversed by the Supreme Court on the ground that under our system the right to publish cannot be licensed. Included in the press is "every sort of publication which affords a vehicle of information and opinion." Circulation as well as publication is protected.

And in subsequent cases the Court held that a tax could no more be levied for the privilege of distributing literature than it could for the privilege of delivering a sermon, or making a speech, or exercising any constitutional right. For the power to tax a privilege is the power to control or suppress its enjoyment. One cannot be compelled to purchase through a license tax or otherwise a privilege freely granted by the *Constitution*.

In one case the victorious counsel was one Rutherford, a tall, rangy man with a heavy mane of hair, a light tan cutaway suit, wing collar, flowing tie, and a massive gold watch chain. His voice was loud and booming. McReynolds, who was given to sharp encounters with lawyers, interrupted Rutherford: "Instead of applying for a permit, which seems to me a reasonable requirement, this lady defied the law. Tell me, why did she do it?"

Rutherford's answer disclosed the fanatic zeal of this sect. Pointing with his finger to the sky, he fairly bellowed: "This lady did not get a permit, because Jehovah God told her not to."

Early in the sixteenth century, printers, binders, publishers, and dealers in books were organized into the Company of Stationers, which, among other things, granted or withheld licenses to print, searched out and destroyed literature printed in violation of law, and helped the regime stamp out treasonable, seditious, and heretical books. Before long, the government felt that it needed more power over political and religious dissenters. Hence in 1586, it imposed comprehensive regulations over the press, including the restriction of all printing to London, Oxford, and Cambridge, the control of the number of presses that might be used in the nation, and the licensing of books. Those who granted the licenses were the Archbishop of Canterbury and the Bishop of London (August 3).

By 1637, the seething political and religious controversies produced more stringent measures. A more detailed and strict licensing system was instituted. Even when revolution abolished the Star Chamber in 1641 and restored power to Parliament, the licensing of the press continued. The argument was that "it is not meere printing but well ordered printing that merits so much favour and respect, since in things precious and excellent, the abuse . . . is commonly as dangerous, as the use is advantageous." The reason was fear of the Catholics and protection of the Protestant religion.

In one form or another licensing of the press continued until 1694, when the *Licensing Act* expired, never to reappear.

The reasons for abolishing the system that gave government control of the press were numerous. Some related to the oppressive practices of the Company of Stationers that long had had a monopoly. Others concerned the rights of authors and students, and the boycott of foreign books. Moreover, the advocates of a free press, though losing the cause in the mid-seventeenth century, nevertheless had planted ideas that could not be destroyed.

John Selden had spoken against restraints on publications. If a censor could keep a book out of the country, "then Lord have mercy upon all schollers," he said.

John Milton wrote more eloquently in his famous *Areopagitica,* a book condemned in 1644 by Oliver Cromwell and a Protestant Parliament:

". . . books are not absolutely dead things, but do contain a potency of life in them to be as active as that soul was whose progeny they are . . . I know they are as lively, and as vigorously productive, as those fabulous dragons' teeth; and being sown up and down, may chance to spring up armed men. And yet on the other hand unless wariness be used, as good almost kill a man as kill a good book; who kills a man kills a reasonable creature, God's image; but he who destroys a good book, kills reason itself; kills the image of God, as it were in the eye. Many a man lives a burden to the earth; but a good book is the precious life-blood of a master spirit, inbalmed and treasured up on purpose to a life beyond life."

The Postmaster General is directed by Congress to admit periodicals to second-class mail (which carries a low postage rate), if they are published "for the dissemination of information of a public character, or devoted to literature, the sciences, arts, or some special industry, and have a legitimate list of subscribers." The Postmaster General denied *Esquire* magazine use of the second-class mail privilege, not because its writings and pictures were obscene, but because they were "morally improper and not for the public welfare and the public good."

In 1946, the Supreme Court sustained *Esquire's* position, refusing to read the postal law as giving the Postmaster General the power of censorship:

"What is good literature, what has educational value, what is refined public information, what is good art, varies with individuals as it does from one generation to another. There doubtless would be a contrariety of views concerning Cervantes' *Don Quixote*, Shakespeare's *Venus and Adonis*, or Zola's *Nana*. But a requirement that literature or art conform to some norm prescribed by an official smacks of an ideology foreign to our system. . . . to withdraw the second-class rate from this publication today because its contents seemed to one official not good for the public would sanction withdrawal of the second-class rate tomorrow from another periodical whose social or economic views seemed harmful to another official."

Book banning is probably as old as books. In A.D. 35, Caligula suppressed the *Odyssey* because it contained ideas of freedom deemed dangerous to Rome.

Art of Love by Ovid was burned in Rome in 1497 and in England in 1599, and was barred by U. S. Customs in 1928 and by San Francisco in 1929.

Tyndale's translation of the *New Testament* was suppressed in England in 1525 and Martin Luther's translation of the *Bible* was burned in Germany in 1624. Martin Luther suppressed the translation of the *New Testament* by Eisner, a Catholic priest, in 1532.

The Divine Comedy by Dante was burned in Italy in 1497.

Savonarola was hung on a cross and burned with all his books in Italy in 1498. Servetus suffered the same fate in 1553 (October 27).

Il Decamerone by Boccaccio was burned in Italy in 1497 and placed under ban in Boston in 1935.

In 1642, Galileo's teachings that the earth revolved around the sun were destroyed as heretical.

Candide by Voltaire, first printed in 1758, was barred by U. S. Customs in 1929 as obscene.

Uncle Tom's Cabin by Harriet Beecher Stowe was banned in Russia in 1852 (Alexander II abolished slavery in Russia in 1861).

The Adventures of Tom Sawyer and *Huckleberry Finn* by Mark Twain were banned from a few public libraries in this country in 1876 and in 1885 respectively.

The works of George Bernard Shaw and Upton Sinclair were banned by Yugoslavia in 1929. Of the many books banned by Soviet Russia, one of the earliest was *My Life and Work* by Henry Ford.

This is only a partial list. It does not include those books put on the *Index Librorum Prohibitorum* of the Catholic Church. Nor does in include perhaps the biggest burning in history—the bonfire at the University of Berlin in May 1933, when 25,000 volumes by Jewish authors were burned by the Nazis.

In 1953, the State Department banned a long list of books from the libraries of the Information Service abroad. Among these were:

Witness by Whittaker Chambers
The Selected Works of Tom Paine by Howard Fast
Thunder Out of China by Theodore White
Washington Witch Hunt by Bert Andrews
The Loyalty of Free Men by Alan Barth
Mission to Moscow by Joseph E. Davies

The reasons for banning these books are not known. Certainly *The Loyalty of Free Men* and *Washington Witch Hunt* would help Asians and Europeans understand America better. Those books show that America does not stand for intolerance, that for every one in America who preaches hate or who assassinates character, there are several who preach and practice fair play. Asia and Europe need that lesson. For in 1953 and in 1954, those who saw America from abroad would get few glimpses of our warm heart and bright conscience.

In 1953, American public opinion against book banning was so outspoken that the State Department revised its policies. It removed some books from the proscribed list and set up somewhat more lenient standards for selection of books for our overseas libraries. Some of the standards established, however, had no relevancy to literary qualities. For example, books of persons "who publicly refuse to answer questions of Congressional committees regarding their connections with the communist movement, shall not be used, even if their content is unobjectionable."

In 1953, the American Library Association voted a significant declaration on *The Freedom to Read,* which in summary said:

1. "It is in the public interest . . . to make available the widest diversity of views and expressions, including those which are unorthodox or unpopular with the majority. . . ."

2. "Publishers and librarians do not need to endorse every idea or presentation contained in the books they make available. It would conflict with the public interest for them to establish their own political, moral, or esthetic views as the sole standard for determining what books should be published or circulated. . . ."

3. "It is contrary to the public interest for publishers or librarians to determine the acceptability of a book solely on the basis of the personal history or political affiliations of the author. . . ."

4. "The present laws dealing with obscenity should be vigorously enforced. Beyond that, there is no place in our society for extra legal efforts to coerce the taste of others, to confine adults to the reading matter deemed suitable for adolescents, to inhibit the efforts of writers to achieve artistic expression. . . ."

5. "It is not in the public interest to force a reader to accept with any book the prejudgment of a label characterizing the book or author as subversive or dangerous. . . ."

6. "It is the responsibility of publishers and librarians as guardians of the people's freedom to read, to contest encroachments upon that freedom by individuals or groups seeking to impose their own standards or tastes upon the community at large. . . ."

7. "It is the responsibility of publishers and librarians to . . . demonstrate that the answer to a bad book is a good one, the answer to a bad idea is a good one. . . ."

8. "We believe . . . that what people read is deeply important; that ideas can be dangerous; but that the suppression of ideas is fatal to a democratic society. Freedom itself is a dangerous way of life, but it is ours." (May 12.)

Books are indeed dangerous, for they are immortal, as Edna St. Vincent Millay movingly relates in *The Poet and His Book.*

Anyone who can establish a bridge over which people must pass and collect a toll from them for the privilege has a neat monopoly. And it seems that the more complex society becomes the greater the opportunity for the establishment of those toll bridges throughout the economy.

The way of the monopolist is ingenious. The patent system (August 13) has offered him many opportunities. A patent is itself a monopoly, authorized by the *Constitution* in order "to promote the Progress of Science and useful Arts." And the patent monopolist has often sought to enlarge it so as to include a larger territory than the patent itself.

That is often easy to do—if the law permits.

A phonograph manufacturer with a patent on the machine requires that it be used only with his records, which are unpatentable.

The owner of a patented heating unit requires that it be used only with his unpatented switch.

The owner of a patent for dropping salt tablets during the process of canning requires that it be used only with his salt.

It is stipulated that a patented stapling machine be used only with the owner's staples, which are not patented.

It is obvious that if a patent can be exploited in these ways, the monopoly is expanded to things that never could be patented.

The courts at first sustained this expansion, on the theory that since the patentee could withhold his patent from the market, he could allow it to be used on such conditions as he chose. The theory had the support of Holmes. But Brandeis, Hughes, and Stone were the other way; and their views eventually prevailed.

157

DECEMBER

"I believe in municipal ownership of all public service monopolies for the same reason that I believe in the municipal ownership of waterworks, of parks, of schools. I believe in the municipal ownership of these monopolies, because if you do not own them, they will in time own you. They will rule your politics, corrupt your institutions, and finally destroy your liberties."

These were not the words of a socialist or a communist. They were spoken by the capitalist Tom L. Johnson, who, beginning in 1901, became Cleveland's Mayor and served four terms.

Tom Johnson had made a fortune as an inventor and as an investor in street railway properties and in steel mills. He read *Progress and Poverty* by Henry George and became greatly influenced by it. He sought out George and came under his spell, all as related in Johnson's autobiography *My Story*.

The result was that Johnson entered politics. No one in American public life has left a greater mark on municipal government. He campaigned against monopoly in all its forms. His causes were, for that day, mostly unpopular—woman's suffrage, municipal ownership, public ownership of railroads. He brought high character and integrity to the office of Mayor and fought corruption, domination by vested interests, and inefficiency. He was a thoroughgoing democrat, who believed that municipal reforms could come only with an enlightened electorate. And so he moved about with a huge tent that would hold several thousand people, holding seminars on public affairs.

Municipal power plants have been in existence since 1882, and there were about 1,000 in the nation when Johnson acquired a small one for Cleveland in 1905. The municipal plant of which Cleveland today is proud was not Johnson's creation. It came later under Mayor Newton D. Baker, and has been an effective "yardstick" for the rates of competing public utilities ever since.

Tom Johnson of Cleveland (like Homer T. Bone of Tacoma and J. D. Ross of Seattle) became the symbol of the public interest in campaigns to control electric power. Johnson found private utilities "hostile to good government," and moved to contain them.

John Brown was hanged at Charlestown, Virginia, on December 2, 1859. He was convicted by a jury in a Virginia court of treason, of conspiring with slaves to rebel, and of murder. This gray-haired man of fifty-nine, whom Walt Whitman describes in *Year of Meteors*, headed a band of seventeen whites and five Negroes which seized a federal armory at Harper's Ferry. The plan apparently was to make the rugged Blue Ridge Mountains a base for guerrilla operations, to raid villages, release slaves, arm them and drill them, and use them in ever widening forages. The purpose was to frighten slave owners into emancipation of their slaves.

The raiders did not leave Harper's Ferry but holed up in the enginehouse with hostages they had seized. Two days later the marines, under Robert E. Lee, overpowered them. Five men had been killed by the raiders in the fracas. All but four of the raiders were shot in battle or hanged later.

Brown, when seized, talked freely about his own participation in the raid. "I will answer anything I can with honor but not about others." He took the whole blame. He was rendering, he said, "the greatest service a man can render to God." He added, "I pity the poor in bondage that have none to help them."

After the verdict he expressed satisfaction with the trial. "I believe that to have interfered as I have done . . . in behalf of His despised poor is no wrong, but right. Now if it is deemed necessary that I should forfeit my life . . . and mingle my blood further with the blood of my children and with the blood of millions in this slave country whose rights are disregarded by wicked, cruel, and unjust enactments, I say let it be done."

The next year, Lincoln summarized the episode: "An enthusiast broods over the oppression of a people till he fancies himself commissioned by Heaven to liberate them."

From the countryside came the folk song, "John Brown's body lies a-mould'ring in the grave."

And years later came *John Brown's Body* by Stephen Vincent Benét, which recited the epic in immortal verse.

Theodore Roosevelt, in his first message to the Congress on December 3, 1901, asserted that "The preservation of our forests is an imperative business necessity."

The destruction of forests causes streams and springs to dry up and topsoil to be washed to the ocean. Unless a seedling is planted when a commercial tree is cut, there will be no crop to fill the needs of the country a generation hence.

In 1901, Gifford Pinchot was already Chief of Forestry. His campaign to impress the American people with the importance of forest conservation now redoubled. Under Pinchot the Forest Service proclaimed that the small man had the first right to the natural resources of the West. "Better help a poor man make a living for his family than help a rich man get richer still."

The enthusiasm of the Roosevelt-Pinchot team kept the political crusade rolling. An effective administration rapidly developed. Regulations for the sale of timber went into effect. Livestock grazing was placed under permit. Fire protection was tightened. Even after his career in the Forest Service ended, Pinchot continued his crusade for the conservation of resources.

In 1911, Congress authorized federal purchase of forest lands for watershed-protection purposes, and in 1924, extended the purchase program to include lands chiefly valuable for timber production. Under these laws, the Forest Service now administers 181 million acres of federally owned land in 153 national forests, which amounts to about 29 per cent of America's forest lands. The Forest Service also co-operates with States and private owners in fire protection, tree planting, and forest management, and undertakes forest, range, and watershed research through regional forest and range experiment stations and a forest-products laboratory.

Some call the federal program "socialism." Under it the government owns, indeed, a vast acreage. But that policy was adopted for pragmatic, not ideological, reasons. It was aimed at protecting the public interest against those who treated forests merely as sources of *income*, not as *capital* assets that must serve every generation.

Acceptance by government of a dissident press is a measure of the maturity of a nation. Yet tolerance is sometimes pressed to the limits. In the Civil War many papers vented their spleen on Lincoln, trying to hold him in ridicule and contempt. Worse, they often printed stories that gave aid, comfort, and valuable information to the enemy, e.g., data concerning the movement of troops and the placement of guns. Spies were operating, and whole areas behind the lines were filled with disaffected people.

As a result, there was great anxiety among the military concerning the activities of the press. Lincoln said in 1864 that the question was "between what was due to the military service on the one hand and the liberty of the press on the other." Some twenty newspapers were suppressed, but only for short periods. Circulation was sometimes restricted. A few editors were jailed. Communities sometimes took matters into their own hands and attacked or destroyed a press. But on the whole, the Civil War period was marked by a degree of tolerance for the press somewhat surprising in view of the fact that the enemy was at the gates and secret societies were operating from within. Suppression was not carried so far as to force adjudication of the issue by the courts. The administration learned that an editor who was jailed had a more powerful platform than the editor when free.

Tolerance for the opposition press grew steadily with the country, so that Woodrow Wilson was able to say on December 4, 1917, in the midst of another war:

"I hear the criticism and the clamour of the noisily thoughtless and troublesome. I also see men here and there fling themselves in impotent disloyalty against the calm, indomitable power of the nation. I hear men debate peace who understand neither its nature nor the way in which we may attain it with uplifted eyes and unbroken spirits. But I know that none of these speaks for the nation. They do not touch the heart of anything. They may safely be left to strut their uneasy hour and be forgotten."

163

We think of Hamilton as the champion of a powerful national government. And so he was. He thought monarchy was preferable to republicanism. Failing to obtain a chief executive who was hereditary, he turned to other devices designed to rescue the nation from democracy. He believed that "the people is a great beast," not to be trusted. Therefore a coercive state was essential.

His philosophy was bottomed on a class conflict in society. He thought that the propertied class should dominate government. He lured that class by his proposal for the Bank (December 23). The debts assumed by the federal government would be funded, interest rates lowered, and the public credit supported by taxation. Taxation, he argued, would be "a spur to industry." He did more than lure the propertied class; he favored it. A tariff would be enacted, which would give a chance for the infant American industries to grow and develop.

Beyond these proposals lay Hamilton's vision of the great prospects which industrialization offered America. He analyzed these in his historic *Report on Manufactures,* December 5, 1791. He proposed a factory economy for America and full exploitation of our natural resources through the machine. Full exploitation of labor, with encouragement of immigration, was also part of his plan. He pointed with pride to the fact that nearly four sevenths of the laborers in England's textile mills were women and children, "of whom the greatest proportion are children, and many of them of a tender age." He saw opportunities for profits in that labor supply: ". . . women and children are rendered more useful, and the latter more early useful, by manufacturing establishments, than they would otherwise be."

The adoption of Hamilton's philosophy resulted in great good; but it also gave rise to grave abuses, which it took over a century to eradicate. Yet certain it is that Hamilton, more than any other, gave impetus to the transformation of an agrarian economy into an industrial one. He, as much as anyone, was responsible for a national government which in its relations to capitalism was paternalistic and protective.

On December 6, 1937, the Supreme Court upheld in a case from Georgia the constitutionality of a poll tax exacted as a prerequisite to voting. "Privilege of voting," said the Court, "is not derived from the United States but is conferred by the State and, save as restrained by the Fifteenth and Nineteenth Amendments and other provisions of the Federal Constitution, the State may condition suffrage as it deems appropriate."

But by 1954, there were only five States in the South with a poll tax—Alabama, Arkansas, Mississippi, Virginia, and Texas. North Carolina got rid of it in 1920, Louisiana in 1940, Florida in 1941, Georgia in 1945, and South Carolina and Tennessee in 1951.

Even those which still retain the poll tax usually exempt war veterans.

In the 1830's, some States had laws that made it a crime to circulate anti-slavery literature. Andrew Jackson proposed a law which would prohibit a postmaster from delivering "any pamphlet, newspaper, handbill, or other printed paper or pictorial representation, touching the subject of slavery," if the circulation of such material was prohibited by the State where it was sent.

Buchanan, speaking in the Senate in favor of the measure, said that the post office, by distributing those "incendiary publications," had become "the instrument of exciting insurrection." No abridgement of freedom of the press was involved, he argued; people could write and print what they pleased, but the government was under no obligation to distribute what the press produced. Jackson had, indeed, said in his message that this literature was calculated to stimulate the slaves to insurrection, and therefore that its circulation was "destructive of the harmony and peace of the country," and "repugnant to the principles of our national compact and to the dictates of humanity and religion." Calhoun, in support of the bill, argued that since the States had the right to bar these incendiary publications, the federal government had the right to abstain from aiding in their violation.

Webster argued that the law was so vague it would bar from the mails literature in favor of slavery, distributed in the North. He maintained that to make the postmaster censor of what went through the mails was an unconstitutional restraint on the press. Clay argued that there was no constitutional authority for the law, that if the law passed it would establish the right of the government to designate "who should have the benefit of the mails, excluding all others."

This law, proposed by Jackson in his message of December 7, 1835, was defeated in the Senate by a vote of 25 to 19.

On December 8, 1953, Eisenhower, in an address before the General Assembly of the United Nations, made a proposal for dealing with the problems of atomic energy:

"The governments principally involved, to the extent permitted by elementary prudence, to begin now and continue to make joint contributions from their stock piles of normal uranium and fissionable materials to an international atomic energy agency. We would expect that such an agency would be set up under the aegis of the United Nations.

"Undoubtedly initial and early contributions to this plan would be small in quantity. However, the proposal has the great virtue that it can be undertaken without irritations and mutual suspicions incident to any attempt to set up a completely acceptable system of world-wide inspection and control.

"The atomic energy agency could be made responsible for the impounding, storage and protection of the contributed fissionable and other materials. The ingenuity of our scientists will provide special, safe conditions under which such a bank of fissionable material can be made essentially immune to surprise seizure.

"The more important responsibility of this atomic energy agency would be to devise methods whereby this fissionable material would be allocated to serve the peaceful pursuits of mankind.

"Experts would be mobilized to apply atomic energy to the needs of agriculture, medicine and other peaceful activities. A special purpose would be to provide abundant electrical energy in the power-starved areas of the world. Thus the contributing powers would be dedicating some of their strength to serve the needs rather than the fears of mankind."

167

Man has found in the secrets of the atom and in the hydrogen bomb methods for exterminating the race. The generation that invented these terrible instruments of destruction must also invent the political instruments which will control or contain them. It must be done at the international level.

The world community is made up of diverse groups with differing cultures, differing standards of justice, differing moral codes. But there is more social tissue binding the nations of the world together than the headlines indicate. There is a growing awareness the world over that management of the secrets of the atom will determine the fate of everyone in every land. We can either flourish together under the benefits of atomic energy, or live in constant peril under its appalling threats.

The community of interest that all peoples have in survival transcends ideologies, political theories, and all economic and social dogma. We must seek it out and cultivate it. We must by all possible means try to find the common denominators of policy and action.

Law is man's refuge from the jungle. We must control the new instruments of destruction through law at the international level. Eisenhower has shown the way. Albert Einstein stated the price of failure: ". . . human society will disappear in a new and terrible dark age of mankind—perhaps forever."

There have been two conventional ways of settling disputes between sovereign states. The first is diplomacy; the second is war. In our *Constitution* we provided a third way. Disputes between the States that historically would have been resolved through diplomatic channels, or failing that, through armed conflict, are now handled peacefully through law. This is one of the most notable political inventions of the ages.

The *Constitution* extends the judicial power to controversies between two or more States and gives the Supreme Court original jurisdiction over them. In 1799, that jurisdiction was first sought to be invoked by New York against Connecticut in a dispute over a tract of land. Since that time the conflicts between the States have been many. They have involved fishing rights, boundary disputes, and controversies over the waters of a stream. When New York City took its garbage to sea on barges and dumped it, the tides carried it to New Jersey's beaches. When Illinois reversed the flow of the Chicago River so as to send its sewage to the Mississippi, it lowered the water of Lake Michigan so as to damage the beaches in other States. These and numerous other controversies between the States were adjudicated in proceedings that started and ended in the Supreme Court.

This is the pattern that will eventually evolve to settle disputes between nations. The seeds of it are in the Eisenhower proposal for the international management of atomic energy.

Plessy, a Negro, entered a railroad coach reserved for the whites. There was a coach reserved for Negroes where he refused to go. He was arrested and tried under a Louisiana law making it a crime for a person to enter a coach reserved for a race to which he did not belong. In 1896, the Supreme Court held (over the dissent of Justice Harlan, "Our Constitution is color-blind, and neither knows nor tolerates classes among citizens") that this segregation law did not violate the Fourteenth Amendment. The Court applied to railroads the rule that Massachusetts and other States, north and south, had applied to public schools and held that segregation of the races was permissible, provided the facilities offered Negroes were substantially equal to those given the whites.

This "separate but equal" doctrine became embedded in the law and practices of many States.

Beginning in December 1938, the Court decided a series of cases involving its application to education in professional schools. Missouri had no Negro law school but provided for the education of Negro lawyers through payment of tuition fees in schools of law in adjacent States. Nevertheless Gaines, a Negro, was held entitled to admission into Missouri's law school. The same rule was applied in Oklahoma, where there was no separate law school for Negroes, and in Texas and Louisiana, where there were separate schools which did not have substantial equality with the one for white students. Moreover, in 1950, a graduate Negro student in education was held to be denied substantial equality of treatment with whites though admitted to the same classroom, library, and cafeteria as the others. In each he was put in a different row or set apart at a separate table. This was held to be discrimination based on race in the administration of a State's educational facilities.

Thus was the Equal Protection Clause applied to remove legal barriers that might prevent a student of one race from being accepted by his fellow students on his own merits (May 17).

December 12, 1905, was a significant date in the development
of our arid lands in the Far West. That day, the Secretary of the
Interior approved two of our earliest irrigation projects. Those
were in the Yakima Valley of eastern Washington. One was the
Tieton, which I saw come into being as a small boy. The federal
government advanced $3,600,000 to the Tieton Irrigation Dis-
trict for its construction. Dams were erected to impound the
snow water of the Cascade Mountains, and miles and miles of
flumes were built to carry the water to desert lands.

About 27,000 acres were brought under cultivation. Cereals,
hay, vegetables, and fruits were produced. Down to 1947, the
gross value of these crops amounted to $221,436,554, the annual
return from 1945 to 1953 being three times the amount of the
original advance for the entire project. On February 14, 1947,
the District repaid the federal government the last dollar owed,
and the project was turned over to the water users.

The lesson of the Tieton is one to remember in discussions of
"deficit financing" and "balancing the budget." The loan to the
Tieton created new values in desert land, put countless thousands
to work, and will make the community thrive throughout the
years. The Tieton project is a capital asset, working to raise the
standard of living. There must be many other Tietons in the
future if oncoming generations are to have full employment, if
our natural resources are to be preserved and exploited.

The Tieton project creates capital. Bursting shells and explod-
ing bombs (though often necessary) destroy capital. It is the
military items in the budget that create the fiscal dangers. Those
who worry about unbalanced budgets should worry first about
foreign policy and the road to peace. The military takes over 70
per cent of our national budget. If it were taken by Tieton projects, we would be building a healthy economy to take care of
our expanding needs. That cannot be done as long as most of
our wealth is committed to destruction. That is one reason why
foreign policy must be foremost on America's agenda.

The more one studies the religions of the world the more he comes to appreciate the wisdom of the First Amendment in accommodating all of them. They are in many ways distinctive. But they have many common threads, and even patterns. Each honors truth, justice, charity. Each has the Golden Rule. Each teaches that inward peace comes from surrender to something bigger than self.

On December 13, 1953, Dr. A. Powell Davies, Unitarian, delivered an enduring sermon on these matters in Washington, D.C.:

"A Christian missionary went from England to India . . . to save the heathen from their blindness and bring them into the light. One day, in the streets of a crowded city, he saw a beggar, seated on the pavement, his body covered with sores. He felt moved by the man's misery and went to speak to him. He told him that he had brought him a truth that could save him—the truth of salvation through Christ. The beggar listened for a long time. Finally, he said: 'You have spoken much of believing. Did your Christ say anything of how men should live?'

"'Yes,' said the missionary, 'he said that we should love one another, that we should love our neighbors as ourselves.'

"'So did all the great teachers,' replied the beggar, 'but which of their disciples acts upon it? You, yourself—do you do what your Christ commands?'

"'I try to,' replied the missionary.

"'Good,' said the beggar, 'then bring a bowl of water and wash my sores.'

"The missionary felt a little sick. He said he would come again, when he had more time. Which he never did. But wherever he went, the words went with him. 'You, yourself—do you do what your Christ commands?' 'I try to.' 'Good! Then bring a bowl of water and wash my sores.'

"That is what the whole world is asking—especially its destitute and forlorn, who live in desolate places. Do you believe your religion? Do you do what it commands? Then cleanse the world's sores; bind up its wounds and heal its miseries."

The *Reconstruction Acts* of 1867 placed ten southern States under military rule. The worst phase of the "carpetbag" rule of the South followed. Some good men from the North went down to take over the reins of government, but many rascals and scalawags went also. What happened seared itself deep in the memory of the South.

Four of the ten States—Georgia, North Carolina, Virginia, and Texas—soon got rid of the carpetbaggers. But in the other six the rule of the carpetbaggers lingered on and brought real suffering.

In South Carolina, the military regime lasted until June 25, 1868, when South Carolina with a new constitution and a Republican Governor—Robert K. Scott of Ohio—was readmitted into the Union. But the rule of the carpetbaggers continued, and northern troops remained quartered in the State House.

In 1876, D. H. Chamberlain of Massachusetts, a former officer in the Army of the North, ran for Governor of South Carolina on the Republican ticket. Wade Hampton of Lee's army was his Democrat opponent. Each claimed to have won.

Wade Hampton took his oath of office December 14, 1876. Grant, who was still President, refused to remove the federal troops. Wade Hampton went to Washington, D.C., in the spring of 1877 to persuade Hayes to remove the troops. Hayes did so, and Hampton and his Democratic slate took over the management of South Carolina. Though that was in April 1877, the real hold of the carpetbaggers all through the South was broken December 14, 1876, when Wade Hampton—the symbol of home rule —took office.

This is the anniversary of the *Bill of Rights*—the first ten Amendments to the *Constitution*. At the time of their adoption there were fourteen States in the Union. Three fourths of the States are necessary to effect an Amendment. Ratification of the *Bill of Rights* was completed December 15, 1791, when Virginia, the eleventh State, approved it.

There was a division of opinion in the Constitutional Convention as to the necessity or desirability of a *Bill of Rights*. Its omission became the chief object of attack on the *Constitution*. Madison, in proposing the *Bill of Rights* to the First Congress, said:

"I believe the great mass of the people who opposed it disliked it because it did not contain effectual provisions against the encroachment on particular rights and those safeguards which they have been long accustomed to have interposed between them and the magistrate who exercises the sovereign power."

The *Bill of Rights* has not always been construed generously. Sometimes it has been looked upon with alarm or suspicion. On many occasions, however, the *Bill of Rights* has served to reaffirm our belief in the dignity of man and our faith in freedom of the mind and of the conscience. In spite of the limitations that have been read into it, in spite of the niggardly way in which some of its provisions have been treated, the *Bill of Rights* has survived as our *Magna Carta*.

On December 16, 1689, the English *Bill of Rights* was enacted. It was passed after James II had been forced to abdicate and Mary and her husband, William of Orange, had been offered the throne. The *Bill of Rights* listed the complaints against James II. It then declared that

- —suspension of laws, the creation of exemptions to laws, and the creation of new ones without consent of Parliament are illegal
- —ecclesiastical courts are illegal and pernicious
- —the levying of money without grant of Parliament is illegal
- —British subjects have the right to petition the King
- —standing armies are illegal in times of peace without consent of Parliament
- —Protestants as well as Catholics are entitled to arms for their defense
- —the people are entitled to free elections, and legislators must have freedom of speech and debates in Parliament with immunity from accountability elsewhere
- —frequent meetings of Parliament are declared necessary
- —excessive bail and excessive fines are condemned and cruel and inhuman punishments outlawed
- —free jury trials are urged and other irregular procedures in criminal cases denounced.

Most of the grievances at which the *Bill of Rights* was aimed related to oppressive practices against the Puritans. But underneath was a major political issue on which the very existence of representative government rests. The King had been in the habit not only of creating new regulations but of dispensing with existing laws. As a British judge said in 1688, if the power of the King to dispense with a law were allowed, there would be no need of Parliament.

Experience shows that when an army rules a people, injustices flourish. The caprice of the man in power is then the measure of the law.

Our own history is marked by successive victories of civil over military government. One of the abuses against which the *Declaration of Independence* protested was the attempt of the King "to render the Military independent of and superior to the Civil power." Hence our *Constitution* makes the President—elected by the people—Commander-in-Chief of the Armed Forces. It also provides for trials of civilians in the civil courts and prescribes standards and safeguards for them, one of which is the right to trial by jury, unknown to military jurisprudence. Moreover, in the federal courts the prosecution must start with an indictment from a grand jury, another restraint not known to military law.

In 1864, Lambdin P. Milligan, a civilian, was arrested on a charge that he had conspired against the government, afforded aid and comfort to rebels, and incited the people to insurrection. Though the civil courts in Indiana were open and functioning at that time, Milligan was tried by a military commission. He was convicted and sentenced to hang.

He sought a writ of habeas corpus, contending that the military commission had no jurisdiction over the case and that the trial therefore was illegal.

On December 17, 1866, the Supreme Court held that the military commission had no power to try Milligan for that offense and that he therefore must be set free. The theory was that military commissions might try civilians in theaters of war where the government was disorganized and the courts unable to function. But in 1864, Indiana was not in such dire straits. Her courts were open; and Milligan, if tried there, would have had all the benefits of procedural due process of law.

The Court said that civil liberty and martial law could not endure together. "The antagonism is irreconcilable."

That decision, though much criticized by one school of thought, is an outstanding declaration of the rights of man.

The presence of large numbers of people of the Japanese race on the west coast at the outbreak of war between America and Japan led to drastic military measures. The Army feared sabotage; and with Pearl Harbor in wreckage, there was a possibility that the enemy would attempt to land on our shores. The Army thought that the ties of blood and race were so deep that the Japanese who lived here would give their basic loyalties to Japan, even though they had become American citizens, and, in case of invasion, help the enemy.

The experience with the loyalty of the Japanese in Hawaii casts grave doubts on that premise. But in 1942, the military view prevailed. Curfews were imposed along the west coast, prohibiting the movement of any person of Japanese ancestry out of home after 8:00 P.M. and before 6:00 A.M. Finally all the Japanese were evacuated from that coast to inland centers.

These measures were upheld by the Supreme Court, even when applied to citizens of Japanese stock. Certainly those decisions went to the verge of constitutional power, and many thoughtful students believed they exceeded the bounds. But though the Court bowed to the decision of the military as respects the requirements of security along the western seaboard, it drew the line sharply and went no further. On December 18, 1944, it held on the application of Mitsuye Endo that the government could not detain or hold in custody a citizen whose loyalty was not impugned, against whom no charge of unlawful conduct was made, and who was suspected only because she was of Japanese ancestry.

Loyalty is indeed a matter of the heart and mind, not of race, creed, or color.

Holmes said, in the case where he labeled wire tapping as "dirty business," (June 4) that he thought "it a less evil that some criminals should escape than that the government should play an ignoble part." That philosophy is at the root of some of our rules precluding the use by the government of certain evidence.

A federal prosecutor made a lawless search of a business firm, seized important documents, and photographed them. The seized documents were ordered returned by the court (February 25). Then the prosecutor, on the basis of knowledge acquired by his lawless search, filed an indictment against the proprietor of the business and subpoenaed the same documents. The Supreme Court denounced the practice, holding that the prosecution could get no advantage from the forbidden act. To sanction it would reduce the Fourth Amendment (February 24, 25) "to a form of words."

That is also the philosophy underlying the rule of entrapment. Entrapment is the conception and planning of an offense by an officer and his procurement of its commission by one who would not have perpetrated it except for the trickery, persuasion, or deceit of the officer. The leading federal case was decided by the Supreme Court in 1932. It involved a prohibition agent who, by representing to the defendant that he was overseas in his division during World War I, persuaded his "buddy" to get him some liquor. Having received the liquor and paid his "buddy," he then arrested him. Thus the agent lured an innocent man into committing a crime. The Court refused to fasten the consequences of such an unconscionable scheme on the victim.

Government is sometimes penalized when it plays "an ignoble part." The almanac of liberty for the free world is filled with episodes where the *means* are outlawed, though the *ends* sought are worthy. The greatest battles for liberty have indeed been fought over the *procedure* which police and prosecutors may use.

The emotions of an inflamed community may be a greater risk to one accused of a crime than the charges against him. It was true on December 20, 1792, when Thomas Erskine rose in a London courtroom to defend Thomas Paine.

The specter of the French Revolution had brought fear to the ruling classes in England. The French had passed a decree promising aid to any revolting nation. This was not a propitious time to criticize the British Government. But Thomas Paine (who had written *Common Sense*) now published the *Rights of Man* (October 6).

This book called the British Government corrupt, its leaders tyrants. "All hereditary government is in its nature tyranny," Paine wrote. He proposed many reforms, including old age pensions, a graduated income tax, a steep inheritance tax. The government charged Paine with seditious libel and tried him *in absentia,* while he was in France. The jury was a "special" one, chosen from the frightened upper classes.

Erskine defended vigorously, making clear that Paine had not advocated rebellions and uprisings. Erskine's plea for Paine was a plea for the right of citizens to criticize their government. "I do contend that it is lawful to address the English nation on these momentous subjects . . . Government in its own estimation has been at all times a system of perfection; but a free press has examined and detected its errors, and the people have from time to time reformed them."

Erskine, sensing the outcome from the prejudiced jury, concluded: "Although my arguments upon the liberty of the press may not today be honored with your or the court's approbation, I shall retire not at all disheartened, consoling myself with the reflection that a season may arrive for their reception."

The jury found Paine guilty without even waiting for the Attorney General to reply. But Erskine's departure from the courtroom presaged better days to come. A cheering crowd bore him on their shoulders.

In 1897, the Supreme Court sustained an Act of Congress dating back to 1790, which authorized justices of the peace to apprehend deserting seamen and forcefully return them to their vessels to finish out the terms of their contracts.

The argument was that the law violated the Thirteenth Amendment, which abolished "slavery" and "involuntary servitude." The Court held that "involuntary servitude" covered only engagements that were unlawful from the inception and that seamen's contracts were impliedly excepted. It said that historically the contract of a sailor was an "exceptional one," which involved to some extent "the surrender of his personal liberty during the life of the contract," and that detention and imprisonment of sailors for desertion had long been sanctioned.

To this conclusion Harlan dissented, saying that the holding of any person in custody against his will to compel him to render personal service to another was "involuntary servitude." As a result of the Court's decision, he said, "we may now look for advertisements, not for runaway servants as in the days of slavery, but for runaway seamen."

The Act was repealed December 21, 1898.

"It is too much the habit of prosecuting officers to assume beforehand that a defendant is guilty and then expect to have the established rules of evidence twisted, and all the features of a fair trial distorted, in order to secure a conviction." So spoke the California Supreme Court in an historic decision rendered December 22, 1893. The reason for this attitude of prosecutors was stated in 1937 by a special committee of the American Bar Association: "The Bar has always been regarded as the nursery of political careers. Lawyers have, therefore, yielded to the temptation to seek publicity for their professional efforts as a basis for careers which they hope to achieve either on the Bench or in executive or legislative office."

Over and again our courts have held that an accused is deprived of a fair trial when the prosecution undertakes "by a side wind, to get that in as proof which is merely conjecture"; or where, in his argument to the jury, the prosecutor makes insinuations of personal knowledge which imply that a witness is a liar or engages in undignified and intemperate talk calculated to mislead the jury. The prosecutor may "strike hard blows," but "he is not at liberty to strike foul ones." He is there not only to see that the guilty do not escape, but that the innocent do not suffer.

Lord Edward Coke, who prosecuted Sir Walter Raleigh (November 17) was by our standards guilty of gross misconduct.

COKE: Thou art the most vile and execrable Traitor that ever lived.

RALEIGH: You speak indiscreetly, barbarously, and uncivilly.

COKE: Thou art an odious fellow, thy name is hateful to all the realm of England for thy pride.

RALEIGH: It will go near to prove a measuring cast between you and me, Mr. Attorney.

COKE: Well, I will now make it appear to the world, that there never lived a viler viper upon the face of the earth than thou.

Coke made up "by the violence of his demeanor for the poverty of his case."

December 23, 1913, is the date of the creation of the Federal
Reserve System. Early in our history we had a central banking
system of a sort under the First Bank of the United States (1791–
1811) and the Second Bank (1816–1836). When Jackson ended
the Second Bank, a long era of decentralized banking was inaugurated. Laws were passed regulating banking practices, but no
central banking system appeared until 1913.

Decentralization resulted in inefficient management of bank
reserves during times of need. Credit was too inelastic for the
requirements of trade and commerce. Clearing house problems
were multiplied by the decentralized banking system. The federal government lacked an effective depository system.

The Federal Reserve System federated existing banks into a
unified system. Twelve Federal Reserve Districts were created,
each with its own Federal Reserve Bank, managed by nine di-
rectors—three representing the stockholders, three the business
community, three the public. National banks were required to be
members of the system; other banks were encouraged to do so.

The Board of Governors, appointed by the President and confirmed by the Senate, was placed above the Federal Reserve
Banks. It was granted broad powers of supervision over member
banks and given the responsibility for regulating the supply and
cost of money.

During the period when we had no central banking system,
many of its functions were performed by private groups. The
Pujo Report of 1913 showed an enormous concentration of control over money and credit in the hands of a few New York banks.
Indeed, three of them had 341 directorships in 112 corporations.
They commanded the key banks, insurance companies, and corporations of the country. When there was a panic, a small, select
Wall Street group, headed by John Pierpont Morgan, determined
which banks would be saved, which would be sacrificed. This
power of life or death over the economy was too great for private
hands. The year 1913 saw it transferred to a public agency. That
is the basic political significance of the Federal Reserve System.

In 1776 and the years immediately following, church and state were not separated in this country. Most of the new state constitutions provided for taxes to support the churches and contained discriminations against Catholics, Jews, and atheists. Moreover, from Maryland on south the Anglican Church was the established church. It was supported by taxation, and only its clergy could officiate at marriages and baptisms. Yet it represented only a minority of the people. Moreover, many of its clergy had opposed the Revolution, siding with England. During the time the Anglican Church was the established church, the other religious sects existed only as a matter of favor.

The Anglican Church was disestablished in 1779. Then an effort was made in Virginia to put all Christian churches on an equal footing by supporting all of them by taxation. This proposal was endorsed by George Washington and John Marshall.

Jefferson and Madison waged war against it and on December 24, 1784, got consideration of the bill postponed in the Virginia legislature. Thereupon Madison wrote the *Memorial and Remonstrance against Religious Assessments*, perhaps the most eloquent brief ever written for separation of church and state. It argued against the bill as follows:

—Those who do not believe are taxed for the support of those who do.
—An established clergy is always a convenient aid to rulers who want to subvert the liberties of the citizens.
—Centuries of the legal establishment of a church produced pride and indolence in the clergy, ignorance and servility in the people, superstition, bigotry, and persecution in both.
—If government can establish Christianity to the exclusion of all other religions, it can later establish one sect to the exclusion of the rest or force a citizen to support such sect as it may choose.

It was this *Remonstrance* which defeated the proposed Virginia law.

Some nations base their civil and criminal laws on a religious creed. Thus in Afghanistan the *Koran* is the law of the land. On my visit to Kabul in 1951, a man was on trial for sacrilege, the charge being that he advocated the use of public money to build schools, not mosques. The enforcement by civil courts of religious creeds is not unknown here. In the early days of the Massachusetts Colony, the General Court found people guilty of sedition for criticizing what the majority called the true faith, and banished Roger Williams, Anne Hutchinson, and many others. Moreover, Maryland, in 1649, made the denial that Jesus was the Son of God a capital offense.

But the teaching of Roger Williams, that "God requireth not a uniformity of religion to be enacted and enforced in any civil state," soon prevailed. Church and state were finally separated. William Penn's creed, that no man should be enthroned "as king over conscience," and Roger Williams' thesis, that the "sovereigne, originall and foundation of civill power lies in the People," won out.

Nevertheless, we are not a godless, atheistic society. Our system presupposes that there is what James Otis, in 1764, called the "higher authority," to which all laws are ultimately appealable. Laws that prick the conscience, that violate standards of decency and justice are laws that Presidents veto, that legislatures repeal or modify, that courts ameliorate or even strike down. Our civilization rests on the premise that there is a Supreme Being to whom not only man, but government, is accountable. The *Declaration of Independence,* indeed, so states (July 4).

Our concepts of equity and justice come from numerous ethical and religious sources. But they have been more greatly influenced by the teachings of Jesus of Nazareth than by any other. The Beatitudes and the Sermon on the Mount gave the West its *ethical* revolution. Christ's words, "Render to Caesar the things that are Caesar's, and to God the things that are God's," are a charter of *political* freedom. It separates church and state. Equally important, it makes the conscience inviolable.

One has only to read the *Book of Acts* to realize how many of our roots run to the Roman law.

Paul was a Roman citizen. He therefore could not be "examined by scourging." (22:24.)

We outlaw "the third degree."

A group of Jews to whom Paul's teachings were anathema demanded that he be turned over to them for execution. The local Governor refused, saying that the accused had the right to see "the accusers face to face, and have license to answer for himself concerning the crime laid against him." (25:16.)

We give an accused the right to be heard and to be confronted with the witnesses against him.

The Governor did not want to return Paul to Rome for trial without specific charges against him. "For it seemeth to me unreasonable to send a prisoner, and not withal to signify the crimes laid against him." (25:27.)

We require that an accused be informed of the nature and cause of the accusation against him.

Both the Roman Governor and the local King heard the charges against Paul and, learning that they related only to religious differences between Paul and the high priests, refused to entertain them (25:19; 26:31).

Free speech, disputation, argument and debate, religious thought—these are immune from prosecution under our system of law.

In 1688, England had an established church. It was Protestant, and Parliament had enacted laws for its support. Thus it was a penal offense not to go to church, not to receive the sacrament, etc. James II, a Catholic, issued a *Declaration for Liberty of Conscience,* which by our standards was a liberal document. It suspended the penal laws supporting the established church, proclaimed toleration for diverse religious views, and pardoned all those who had violated the ecclesiastical penal laws. James ordered the *Declaration* read in all the churches.

The Archbishop of Canterbury and six other Bishops wrote the King that they refused to have the *Declaration* read in their churches because, among other things, it suspended laws—a power that only Parliament had. James had the seven Bishops arrested and tried for seditious libel.

A jury was selected, counsel for the Bishops striking off all the Catholics. A majority of the judges ruled that the Bishops were guilty, if the jury believed that they were authors of the petition. The jury was told (Justice Powell dissenting) that the petition was a libel because its effect was to "disturb the government, or make mischief and a stir among the people."

The jury was locked up in the courthouse all night "without fire or candle." At six o'clock in the morning, they brought in a verdict of "not guilty." A roar went up that filled the courtroom for a half hour. The shouting spread to the streets. River boats whistled, bells clanged, guns were shot off. And that night bonfires were lighted all over London for the "joyful deliverance of the Church of England."

In the winter of 1913–1914 a Boston lawyer, Louis D. Brandeis, whom Wilson later appointed to the Supreme Court, wrote a series of articles for *Harper's Weekly* which pointed with alarm to certain trends in business and finance.

The "money trust" had a strategic hold on the nation (December 23).

Investment bankers were using directorships in industrial companies to line their own pockets.

Interlocking directorates had knitted companies together into vast cartel arrangements that stifled competition and promoted monopoly.

Company after company was swallowed up in mergers and consolidations. Small business was coming under the heel of an oligarchy of big business.

The "curse of bigness" was a blight on the industrial world. Companies were big not in the interest of efficiency but largely in the interest of monopoly. Companies grew so big they were beyond the competence of management to operate efficiently.

The fear of Brandeis was that the big corporate state would leave no room for newcomers. He believed with Wilson that "No country can afford to have its prosperity originated by a small controlling class. The treasury of America does not lie in the brains of the small body of men now in control of the great enterprises. . . . It depends upon the inventions of unknown men, upon the originations of unknown men, upon the ambitions of unknown men. Every country is renewed out of the ranks of the unknown, not out of the ranks of the already famous and powerful in control."

Brandeis did not want America to become a nation of clerks, all working for some overlord. He wanted avenues of free enterprise open to everyone. We would have a healthier political democracy, he claimed, if men were trained to be on their own and have a stake in a free enterprise system.

The lessons Brandeis taught have been largely forgotten. More and more of our best brains are retained to promote a new creed for the corporate state—"monopoly competition."

On December 29, 1950, the Celler *Anti-Merger Act* became the law. It provides, with exceptions, that no corporation (whether or not engaged in commerce) shall acquire, directly or indirectly, the whole or any part of the stock, or the whole or any part of the assets of a corporation engaged in commerce "where in any line of commerce in any section of the country" the effect of the acquisition or the use of the stock "may be substantially to lessen competition, or to tend to create a monopoly."

Congress gave as the reasons for the law the desire to keep alive the American competitive system against the continuing growth of monopoly. The long-term trend of concentration of industrial power in the hands of a few has been due in considerable part to mergers. One third of the long-term growth of one steel company was due to mergers, two thirds in case of a second. In the case of the three largest copper companies, 70 per cent of their growth was due to mergers.

Between 1940 and 1947, *at least* 2,500 independent manufacturing and mining companies disappeared in mergers. More acquisitions and mergers took place in the "small business" field than in any other. Typical of these were textiles, apparel, and food. Steel drums, tight cooperage, and wines were nearly all taken over by the large companies. The pattern was that of the big company buying up the little ones, not the little ones combining to resist the large ones. From 1940 to 1947 some 33 of the 200 largest corporations bought out an average of 5 companies each, and 13 purchased more than 10 concerns each.

The progress of the growth of big companies was shown by the 1946 figures: One tenth of 1 per cent of all American companies owned 49 per cent of all the corporate assets; 2 per cent owned 78 per cent; 8 per cent owned 89 per cent; 12 per cent owned 98 per cent.

The earlier laws had proved largely ineffective due to the hostility of the courts in their construction and application.

188

The Civil War rid us of human slavery. But by 1890, there was an uneasy feeling that we were about to become slaves of the corporate state. Wendell Phillips, Henry George, and Edward Bellamy helped awaken people to the dangers of the trusts. The Populist party undertook political action, getting some dozen States to pass anti-trust laws. Cleveland proclaimed against monopolies. In 1888, both the Republican and Democratic parties promised reforms. In 1890, the *Sherman Act* was passed, making monopolies in interstate commerce, and contracts, combinations, or conspiracies in restraint of interstate commerce illegal.

During the sixty-four years of its existence the Act has made some changes in corporate practices. It has, for example, fairly effectively outlawed price-fixing. But its total impact has been slight. From the beginning it has been applied by judges hostile to its purposes, friendly to the empire builders who wanted it emasculated. Theodore Roosevelt made gallant gestures in enforcement, and others emulated his example. But trusts that were dissolved reintegrated in new forms. When one monopolistic device was outlawed, a new one was invented. Trusts began to be classified as either "good" or as "bad," and most seemed to be labeled "good." The judiciary was not wholly responsible for emasculating the *Sherman Act*. But it deserves the greatest share of blame. Under its decisions monopoly and trusts have thrived and prospered and grown to an unprecedented extent. Their present strength makes the alarms sounded in 1890 seem feeble indeed.

It is ironic that the *Sherman Act* was truly effective only in one respect, and that was when it was applied to labor unions. Then the courts read it with a literalness that never appeared in their other decisions.

In December 1641, the Massachusetts Colony adopted *The Body of Liberties*—the code of laws to govern their affairs. These men were Puritans and their laws reflected their severity and their faith. For example, blasphemy was a capital offense; civil courts had the authority to enforce "the peace, ordinances and rules of Christ" in every church; foreigners "professing the true Christian religion" and fleeing from persecution were made welcome; churches could be established by those who were "orthodox in judgment" and who organized them in a "Christian way with due observation of the rules of Christ revealed in his word." But *The Body of Liberties* also contained many of the seeds of the civil liberties which today distinguish us from the totalitarian systems:

—equal justice under law for citizens and foreigners
—no punishment except by an express law
—compensation for private property taken for public use
—freedom of speech and publication at any town meeting
—freedom to leave the colony at any time
—right to bail and to a speedy criminal trial
—right to jury trial
—protection against being twice sentenced for the same offense
—prohibition of use of torture and the hated inquisitional oath to make an accused or any other person testify to things that might incriminate him
—right of the people to elect those who will govern them
—prohibition of slavery and of inhumane, barbarous, and cruel punishment
—free (as distinguished from feudal) land ownership.

Separation of church and state, and tolerance for diverse religious views, were yet to come. Moreover, *The Body of Liberties* provided that once a defendant had been convicted, he could be tortured in order to get evidence that might incriminate others. Yet *The Body of Liberties*, in its main emphasis, was a new *Magna Carta*.

JANUARY

On January 1, 1863, Abraham Lincoln issued the *Emancipation Proclamation*, freeing the slaves in those areas which then were "in rebellion against the United States."

". . . I do order and declare that all persons held as slaves within said designated States, and parts of States, are, and henceforward shall be free; and that the Executive government of the United States, including the military and naval authorities thereof, will recognize and maintain the freedom of said persons.

"And I hereby enjoin upon the people so declared to be free to abstain from all violence, unless in necessary self-defence; and I recommend to them that, in all cases when allowed, they labor faithfully for reasonable wages.

"And I further declare and make known, that such persons of suitable condition, will be received into the armed service of the United States to garrison forts, positions, stations, and other places, and to man vessels of all sorts in said service.

"And upon this act, sincerely believed to be an act of justice, warranted by the Constitution upon military necessity, I invoke the considerate judgment of mankind, and the gracious favor of Almighty God."

By this *Proclamation* about 3,120,000 slaves were freed. The final victory—the abolition of slavery by the Thirteenth Amendment to the *Constitution*—was realized late in 1865.

On the evening of January 2, 1920, the F.B.I., operating under A. Mitchell Palmer, conducted one of the most disgraceful raids in our history. At a zero hour, almost 500 agents and police in 20 New England towns raided homes, halls, and offices looking for aliens who were communists and therefore deportable. The disgrace was not in the purpose of the raid but in the manner of its execution.

From 800 to 1,200 people were arrested, many of whom were citizens, not aliens. Thus in Lynn, Massachusetts, 39 people were holding a meeting to discuss the formation of a co-operative bakery. About half were citizens. The police bundled all of them off to the police station, kept them overnight, docketed them as "suspects," and the next morning discharged 38 of them.

Men and women were arrested without warrants.

Houses, desks, files were ransacked from top to bottom without search warrants, and the literature and letters found impounded by the police.

Women were separated from their children.

Those arrested, in most instances quiet and harmless working people, were handcuffed in pairs, chained together, and marched to railroad stations, the federal agents taking pains to have them exposed to public photography.

About 400 people were transported to Deer Island, where there were inadequate sanitary appliances and little heat, and held *incommunicado* for several days.

George W. Anderson, a fearless federal judge of that era, condemned the procedure as "lawlessness" of law officials.

The words "whoever holds, arrests, returns, or causes to be held, arrested, or returned . . . any person to a condition of peonage, shall be fined . . . or imprisoned" do not make a sentence that is sound by grammatical standards. One does not "arrest" a person "to" peonage; he arrests him so as to place him in or return him to peonage. But the Supreme Court on January 3, 1944, held the law sufficiently clear to sustain a criminal prosecution against one who was charged with arresting a laborer who was indebted to him for the purpose of making the laborer work for him (January 31).

This is the *Anti-Peonage Act* of 1867. It was passed for the protection of Indians in the Southwest. Peonage was an institution among the Indians and the Mexicans of the Southwest. In the 1860's a healthy, intelligent Navajo girl, eight years old, would sell for $400 or more. Over 2,000 Navajos were held in slavery. The whites took up the practice of raiding Indian villages and selling the captives. When one of these peons escaped, the U. S. Army would often go in pursuit and return him to his owner.

This condition aroused the Congress. It led to the passage of the *Anti-Peonage Act*.

The right of the people "peaceably to assemble" has roots deep in our society. Town meetings, forums, club activities, political conventions, rallies—these are all manifestations of the fundamental constitutional right to meet together for the discussion of problems and for the management of affairs which people have in common. The right attaches to the obscure, the unpopular, the unorthodox, as well as to the dominant groups. It is, indeed, this right that the police state seeks to control and curb. For meetings where people come together to discuss matters of mutual concern are breeding grounds for dissension and revolution against an oppressive government.

There have not been many instances in our history where government has interfered with this right. One famous incident was in the 1930's when Oregon convicted one De Jonge for participating in a public meeting called under the auspices of the communist party, and sentenced him to seven years. The meeting (which was broken up by the police) was orderly, and no one advocated the overthrow of the government. The speakers discussed a bitter maritime strike then in progress in Oregon, raids on communist headquarters, and other activities of the police; and in addition, De Jonge urged people to get members for the communist party and to buy communist literature.

On January 4, 1937, the Supreme Court reversed the conviction, holding that even the despised communists had the right "peaceably to assemble" for lawful purposes. Chief Justice Hughes emphasized the importance in our democratic society of "the opportunity for free political discussion." It is necessary, he maintained, so that government "may be responsive to the will of the people and that changes, if desired, may be obtained by lawful means."

And we can add that the opportunity to meet and "blow off steam" is healthy for everyone, including the malcontents, as Hyde Park in London eloquently demonstrates. When a cause is driven underground, it usually acquires a virulence it would not otherwise have.

In January 1941, Franklin D. Roosevelt appealed to Congress for support of the "four freedoms"—freedom of speech, freedom of religion, freedom from want, freedom from fear—and for support of peoples the world around who were fighting for those freedoms. A good treatment of the relationship of these needs, one to the other, in the world community is by Harrison Brown in *The Challenge of Man's Future,* published in 1954.

Freedom from want is the product of a complicated equation, involving food, population, birth control, scientific agriculture, industrialization, and the channels of trade between surplus and deficit areas. Freedom from want begins, of course, with water and topsoil. Given them, sunlight works its magic in the production of the green leaf. Without them, there is hunger.

The tragedy of erosion has been experienced by many nations. Parts of the Middle East have seen at least three feet of topsoil go into the ocean. When our rivers run thick with silt, they fairly shout that more farms are being swallowed up by the ocean.

Franklin D. Roosevelt made no more enduring contribution to liberty than the program he designed to save our water and topsoil. It began with the Civilian Conservation Corps, which brought a vast forest acreage under protection and built over 6 million small dams. Roosevelt's program entailed the construction of numerous flood control and power dams, big and small. More important, for the long run, were the tightening of controls over grazing and the cutting of timber, the bringing of new lands under federal supervision for protection against abusive practices, the cleaning up of rivers, the construction of fish, game, and bird sanctuaries, the education of farmers in contour plowing and crop rotation (August 19), the withdrawal of marginal land from cultivation, and finally the erection of a shelter belt of trees, running east and west, on the Northern Great Plains.

Water and topsoil—these will be the mainstay of man long after the other wealth of the earth has been extracted and consumed.

Harlan Fiske Stone was a heavy-set man with a twinkle in his eyes and a warm heart for every racial or religious minority. He was as tenacious in his beliefs as the granite of New Hampshire where he was born. He had been professor and Dean of the Law School at Columbia, and a practicing lawyer in New York City since his admission to the Bar in 1898. Coolidge named him Attorney General in 1924 to take the place of Harry M. Daugherty, discredited in the Tea Pot Dome scandal. In 1925 Coolidge nominated him as Justice of the Supreme Court, where he served until his death in 1946.

He and his wife went to New York City to spend the Christmas holidays of 1935 with their sons. While there he received a copy of the majority opinion of the Court (announced January 6, 1936) declaring unconstitutional the *Agricultural Adjustment Act,* which, in order to increase farm prices, authorized payment to farmers who decreased their crops (August 16). This Act was one of the planks in the New Deal program of Franklin D. Roosevelt, Democrat. Stone, a Republican, was not overly sympathetic with that program. But he did not think that a Justice's personal opinions as to the wisdom of a law had anything to do with the determination of its constitutionality. Stone was convinced that this law was being struck down because it did not jibe with the political philosophy of a majority of the Court. He cut short his holiday to write a dissent that became famous overnight: "Courts are concerned only with the power to enact statutes, not with their wisdom . . . For the removal of unwise laws from the statute books appeal lies not to the courts but to the ballot and to the processes of democratic government."

When Coolidge nominated Stone to the Court, Senator George Norris of Nebraska strenuously opposed his confirmation. When Roosevelt nominated Stone as Chief Justice in 1941, Norris retracted and praised him for the philosophy reflected in this famous dissent.

The House of Commons voted that William Scroggs, Chief Justice of the King's Bench, should be impeached; and on January 7, 1681, it referred the matter to the House of Lords. The House of Lords did not try Scroggs, but instead managed to have him retired on a pension for life. He was charged with the administration of justice with an uneven hand, with the suppression of literature favorable to the Protestants, and with treasonable participation in "the Popish Plot" to kill the King. One other charge has a bearing on our liberties today. It related to his denial of bail in prosecutions coming before his court.

The House of Commons reported that Scroggs over and again denied bail to prisoners pending trial, though the offenses with which they were charged were not such as to make it prudent to detain them in custody. One was a constable who had arrested some of Scroggs' servants "for great disorders," and was in turn arrested and held in jail. Another was a bookseller who offered for sale a pamphlet called *Observations on Sir George Wakeman's Trial,* and, for the offense, was hailed before Scroggs, who committed him to jail, saying he would "pile him and all the booksellers and printers up in prison like faggots." Another bookseller was committed for selling a book called *A Satire Against Injustice,* which Scroggs said was a libel against him. Scroggs said he would show these booksellers "no more mercy than they could expect from a wolf that came to devour them." These and others in disfavor with Scroggs were denied release on bail pending their trials. They were all eventually released on applications for habeas corpus, meanwhile spending months in jail.

The tyranny of Scroggs is part of the history behind the provision of the Eighth Amendment that "Excessive bail shall not be required." (November 10.)

Can government require a person to register before making a public speech? The question was answered in the negative on January 8, 1945, by a closely divided Supreme Court in a decision from Texas. Texas required labor organizers to register. One Thomas went to Texas to speak at a labor rally, urging workers to become unionized. He refused to register. The Attorney General of Texas got a restraining order from a court enjoining Thomas from speaking without registering. Thomas spoke anyway and was fined and jailed for contempt.

Thomas won in the Supreme Court in a five to four decision, Wiley Rutledge writing for the majority. The right of free speech was held as applicable to labor problems as it is to religious, political, or other issues. The *Constitution* promotes free trade in ideas. If government were to regulate speech, it would assume a guardianship of the mind. Registration is a form of regulation —a burden on the right to speak freely, a restraint on the right to speak when and where one chooses. Government can license those who pursue various callings. But it cannot exact a license from anyone who would proclaim from a platform or soapbox the rights of man, the rights of business, or the rights of labor.

On January 7, 1920, five Socialists took their seats in the New York Assembly. In a few hours they were advised by the Speaker that they had been elected "on a platform that is absolutely inimicable to the best interests" of New York and the nation. Thereupon a resolution was passed denying them seats pending an investigation, the charge being not that these men had violated any law but that they were Socialists. They were, in other words, outlawed because of their political beliefs and social philosophy.

Two days later, Charles Evans Hughes, then a private citizen, wrote the Speaker a letter which will live forever in our chronicles:

"If there was anything against these men as individuals, if they were deemed to be guilty of criminal offenses, they should have been charged accordingly. But I understand that the action is not directed against these five elected members as individuals but that the proceeding is virtually an attempt to indict a political party and to deny it representation in the Legislature. This is not, in my judgment, American government.

". . . If public officers or private citizens have any evidence that any individuals, or group of individuals, are plotting revolution and seeking by violent measures to change our Government, let the evidence be laid before the proper authorities and swift action be taken for the protection of the community. Let every resource of inquiry, of pursuit, of prosecution be employed to ferret out and punish the guilty according to our laws. But I count it a most serious mistake to proceed, not against individuals charged with violation of law, but against masses of our citizens combined for political action, by denying them the only resource of peaceful government; that is, action by the ballot box and through duly elected representatives in legislative bodies."

This letter rallied public opinion. The press denounced the tactics. So did the Bar Association. But the Assembly would not be turned back. It expelled the five Socialists. Hughes' protest, however, quickened the conscience of America in a dark day of intolerance.

Earl Grey became Prime Minister of England in 1830 and installed a cabinet of landowners. Rioting among agricultural laborers followed, the disturbances being directed against working conditions and pay on the farms. Nearly 1,000 persons were tried and punished, some by hanging.

Richard Carlile wrote a piece in his weekly paper, the *Prompter,* congratulating the agricultural workers for claiming their rights, and urging them to persevere. His strongest statements were, "In war all destructions of property are counted lawful . . . Yours is a state of warfare and your ground of quarrel is the want of the necessary of life in the midst of an abundance . . . Your demands have been so far moderate and just and any attempt to stifle them by the threatened severity of the new Administration will be so wicked as to justify your resistance even to death and to life for life." He added that if an effort were made to suppress their discontent, they would be justified in suppressing the Prime Minister.

Carlile was indicted for seditious libel and on January 10, 1831, was tried at Old Bailey. The jury did not want to convict. But the judge kept them without food, fire, or drink or anything comfortable to sit or lie down on and threatened all-night confinement. Finally at 1:45 A.M. the jury capitulated and found Carlile guilty. He was sentenced to 2 years' imprisonment. The judge also imposed a fine of £200, security of £1,000 for good behavior for 10 years, and imprisonment until the fine was paid and the security given. Those sums were never paid, and Carlile was released from prison after serving 8 months.

The *Times* commented, "The truth is . . . that if men expect to live free from mischievous excitement wherever printing is known and exercised as an art, they expect that which cannot take place."

The Fifth Amendment provides that "No person . . . shall be compelled in any criminal case to be a witness against himself." In 1868, Congress passed an *immunity statute* for the protection of witnesses. The Act provided that no "evidence obtained from any . . . witness by means of a judicial proceeding . . . shall be given in evidence, or in any manner used against him, or his property or estate, in any court of the United States . . . in any criminal proceeding, or for the enforcement of any penalty or forfeiture."

A grand jury was investigating violations of a federal Act making it a crime for carriers to grant and for shippers to receive freight rates lower than the tariffs. A shipper of grain refused to answer, on grounds of self-incrimination, whether he had received rates lower than the lawful ones. He was held in contempt for his refusal, the judge concluding that since the statute gave him *immunity* for the consequences of his answer, he could not invoke the Fifth Amendment.

On January 11, 1892, the Supreme Court ruled on the case. It held unanimously that the Fifth Amendment covered testimony given in any investigation concerning violations of federal laws as well as that given in a trial of the accused. The Court also held that the *immunity statute* of 1868 did not deprive the witness of the privilege of retreating behind the Fifth Amendment. True, the answers he gave could not be used against him. But the *immunity statute* would not prevent those answers from being used to search out other testimony which might be used against him. In other words the *immunity statute* did not provide "complete protection" to the witness. Therefore he could rest on the Fifth Amendment. "Legislation cannot detract from the privilege afforded by the Constitution."

It was once the practice of some employers to require each employee to sign a contract, whereby it was agreed that if the employee was at any time injured, he would execute a release of all claims against his employer. Some courts refused to enforce those contracts; others, including the Supreme Court, held they were valid, and barred all recovery by the employee against his employer.

Many state laws were passed outlawing these contracts. In 1908, Congress also acted, declaring unenforceable any "contract" or "device" which in purpose or intent enabled a common carrier by railroad "to exempt itself from liability." How about contracts made after the injury? What about releases signed at the instance of claim agents?

One such contract provided that the carrier would advance the injured workman $600 "for living and other expenses" with a proviso that if he elected to bring suit, he would "first return" the $600. He sued without returning the $600, and was not allowed to recover. Was this agreement made after the injury a lawful one?

On January 12, 1942, the Supreme Court ruled that it was not. Compromises of claims can be made after injuries have been suffered. But this contract, the Court held, was one which in practical effect exempted the carrier from liability. To sue, the employee would have to repay the $600; and his "straitened circumstances" would probably make that impossible.

Thus have Congress and the Court reduced the power of claim agents, who, operating in the sickrooms and hospitals, often got ignorant people to sign unconscionable agreements that deprived them of their legal rights.

It has been the theory of the law, since the beginning, that the King could do no wrong. The King was the state and the source of all law. He therefore could not be sued without his consent. This is the doctrine of sovereign immunity, which we adopted in this country, governing suits by a citizen against the government.

It had interesting consequences. For example, the Fifth Amendment provides that private property shall not be taken for public use "without just compensation." Congress could condemn land and the owner could whistle for his money. His only remedy was to get a private bill through Congress reimbursing him. As a result of this and other embarrassments, Congress, beginning in 1855, passed laws granting jurisdiction to federal courts to entertain suits against the United States on contracts, express or implied. In 1910, the United States submitted itself to suits for patent infringement, and in 1920 and 1925, to suits for injuries arising from the operation of its vessels.

But if a mail truck, operated negligently by a postal clerk, injured a person, there was no recovery. After 1922, there was a remedy if the truck caused property damage not exceeding $1,000. For in that year Congress authorized department heads to settle such claims. But claims for personal injuries and for death could not be enforced.

One bill granting relief was vetoed by Coolidge in 1929. After prolonged effort, a law was finally enacted in 1946 under Roosevelt's aegis. It allows department heads to settle claims for $1,000 or less for property damage, personal injury, or death. And it gives claimants a right to sue on such tort claims, whatever their amount. Certain claims are excepted. Apart from them, the law makes the United States liable for the negligent or wrongful act of an employee where a private person would be liable.

The sovereign has often done wrong. At long last the citizen can do something about it.

204

Cummings—a Catholic priest—was indicted under a Missouri law for teaching and preaching without first having taken an oath that he had not been in sympathy with the South in the Civil War and had not aided its forces, etc. In an historic decision on January 14, 1867, the Supreme Court reversed the conviction, holding the Missouri law unconstitutional.

To begin with the law was a bill of attainder (October 8), i.e., a legislative act which inflicted punishment without a judicial trial. English history is replete with instances where Parliament, by legislative fiat, convicted men of treason or subjected them to other penalties and punishments. The fathers of the *Constitution*, knowing that history, abolished the bill of attainder. Missouri's law did not put a teacher or preacher in jail because he had sympathized with the South. But it deprived him of his calling, and was in a real sense punishment for his conduct. The expurgatory oath was merely a means to that end.

Moreover, the Missouri law was an *ex post facto* law and therefore in violation of another constitutional mandate. An *ex post facto* law is one which punishes an act which was not punishable when it was committed. It was not against Missouri's law to sympathize with the South during the Civil War, therefore Missouri could not punish that conduct after the war by passing a law with retroactive effect.

During the 1940's and '50's, legislatures, courts, and educational institutions in America forgot the lesson of the *Cummings* case. People were removed from government posts and from faculties of schools and colleges, not because they were communists, not because they were using their positions to serve the communist party or to advance the communist cause, but because at some prior time they had been members of "subversive" organizations. The cause of their punishment was not present unfitness for the work, but some prior act, lawful when done—and often innocent. They were not given a judicial trial with all of its safeguards; they were cast into the outer darkness by legislative fiat or administrative order.

Samuel Swartwout wrote in 1829 after the election of Andrew Jackson that "No—— rascal who made use of his office or its profits for the purpose of keeping Mr. Adams in and General Jackson out of power, is entitled to the least lenity or mercy, save that of hanging. . . . Whether or not I shall get anything in the general scramble for plunder, remains to be proven; but I rather guess I will." (Swartwout was appointed Collector of the Port in New York, stole $1,125,000, and fled the country.)

"To the victor belongs the spoils" had been the policy since the beginning, though Andrew Jackson is credited with having established it. The charge against Jackson has been greatly overstated, for he dismissed during his eight years no more than one fifth of all federal officeholders, and probably fewer. Jackson did maintain that "office is considered as a species of property." His political formula was to give the people the feeling that the government was in truth theirs. One of his first acts, therefore, was to redistribute many of the federal offices. This was part of his demonstration that the government was no longer "an engine for the support of the few at the expense of the many."

The "spoils system" was thus conceived as a reform measure. It brought to power a fresh, militant group to displace a regime that had a monopoly of the offices and yet did not have the confidence of the country.

The "spoils system" was not to survive for long, as it brought many evils in its train. The civil service became the pay roll of the party leader and helped "make politics pay." But historically, the "spoils system" served the function of breaking the hold on government that an aristocracy of wealth might have acquired, and of giving the people more direct participation in the actual workings of a democracy.

On January 16, 1883, a federal civil service was authorized, Arthur signing the *Pendleton Act* that day. A Commission of three members was created, which was to provide for open, competitive examinations for the classified public service. Provision was made that no person should be removed from the public service for refusing to contribute to any political fund or to render political service, and that no person in the service should use his office to coerce political action. No recommendation of a Senator or Congressman should be considered, except as it bore on "the character or residence" of the applicant; and all Senators, Congressmen, and other officers of government were barred from soliciting or receiving any contribution for a political purpose from a person on the government pay roll.

The tragic death of Garfield at the hands of a disappointed office seeker gave great impetus to a demand for reform. The *Pendleton Act* marked the beginning of the end of the "spoils system." Yet the reform was not soon completed. When the new civil service rules were extended to a new class of offices, the incumbents were ensconced without having to undergo an examination. A retiring administration which took that course was accused of inaugurating a policy more vicious than the "spoils system"—"to the vanquished belongs the spoils."

The federal civil service grew slowly. Theodore Roosevelt, Chairman of the Commission under Harrison, gave it character and prestige. And of all the arguments made in favor of the system, the most powerful was that government to be efficient must be "business-like."

In 1925, the Tennessee legislature passed a statute making it unlawful for any teacher "to teach any theory that denies the story of the Divine creation of man, as taught in the *Bible*, and to teach instead, that man has descended from a lower order of animals." Tom Scopes, a high school teacher in the hill town of Dayton, was indicted for telling his students approvingly about Darwin's theory of evolution. His case became famous overnight, when prominent lawyers volunteered their services—William Jennings Bryan for the prosecution, Clarence Darrow for the defense. For Bryan, this was a battle between religion and atheism. He was deeply convinced that evolution conflicted with the *Bible*, and that religion would fail if the literal words of the *Bible* were not believed. To Darrow, evolution was a scientific fact like the earth's being round. In his view the Tennessee law not only infringed Scopes' academic freedom, but also violated the First Amendment, by favoring the Fundamentalist religion.

Darrow stood in his shirt sleeves and lavender suspenders to condemn the statute: "If today you can take a thing like evolution and make it a crime to teach it in the public school . . . at the next session you may ban books and newspapers." When the defense introduced a letter from Woodrow Wilson subscribing to evolution, there were whispers in the courtroom, "Must be a forgery. Woodrow Wilson was a Democrat." The jury found Scopes guilty and the judge fined him $100.

On January 17, 1927, the Tennessee Supreme Court, though sustaining the law, set aside the verdict, because under Tennessee law, the jury rather than the judge should have imposed the fine. The case was never tried again, the Court directing the prosecution to drop the matter. But the year and a half in which the Scopes case was in the news awakened the country to the danger of making teachers trim their instruction to meet the requirements of any one religious creed.

One religious controversy that, in end result, gave powerful impetus to liberal thought and social reform in this country was loosened by the great Unitarian, William E. Channing. Beginning about 1815, he undertook to attack orthodox Calvinism in New England. He rejected the thesis that man was base and ruled over by a God of wrath. To Channing, God was love, man was His child, made in His image, and the object of His compassion. "The adoration of goodness—this is religion," preached Channing.

The thesis had broad implications that did not end with theology. These Unitarian tenets began to be translated into political terms. A humanitarian philosophy, flavored with the idealism both of New England and of France emerged, which Theodore Parker, another Unitarian preacher, was to renew a generation later. "It is because I have learned the essential quality of man before the common Father," Channing wrote, "that I cannot endure to see one man establishing his arbitrary will over another by fraud, or force, or wealth, or rank, or superstitious claims. . . . It is because I've seen in him a great nature, the divine image, and vast capacities, that I demand for him means of self-development, spheres for free action—that I call society not to fetter, but to aid his growth."

It was this idea that quickened the social conscience of the country. Some immediate effects were the bizarre adventures in utopianism. At the Oneida Community and Brook Farm, a few Americans dabbled in communism and found it alien to American thought and hostile to American individualism. But the social conscience, which Channing helped awaken, had profound effects. It set in motion great impulses for reform. In 1830, there were many abolition societies in America, but none in New England. Channing's preachings helped awaken New England to the evils of slavery. Once the tenacious Yankee became seized with such a cause, sparks were certain to fly.

"No man shall be compelled to frequent or support any religious worship, place, or ministry whatsoever, nor shall be enforced, restrained, molested, or burthened in his body or goods, nor shall otherwise suffer, on account of his religious opinions or belief; but that all men shall be free to profess, and by argument to maintain, their opinion in matters of religion, and that the same shall in no wise diminish, enlarge, or affect their civil capacities." This is the heart of *A Bill for Establishing Religious Freedom* drafted by James Madison and Thomas Jefferson and enacted by Virginia, January 19, 1786.

This philosophy has become part of the American ideal:

—The community will tolerate every religion.
—The state will establish, favor, or support no religion.
—Each man's religion is his own affair.
—Religious freedom and sanctity of rights of conscience go hand in hand.

This is the philosophy of the First Amendment: "Congress shall make no law respecting an establishment of religion, or prohibiting the free exercise thereof."

"This Constitution, and the Laws of the United States which shall be made in Pursuance thereof; and all Treaties made, or which shall be made, under the Authority of the United States, shall be the supreme Law of the Land; and the Judges in every State shall be bound thereby, any Thing in the Constitution or Laws of any State to the Contrary notwithstanding."

This is the famous Supremacy Clause which has been the object of much debate. On January 20, 1941, the Supreme Court applied it to override a Pennsylvania law requiring the registration of aliens. There was a federal law which had the same basic purpose, but which contained somewhat different provisions. Foreign affairs, however, is the exclusive domain of the federal government; and registration of aliens touches on a sensitive field because it involves our relations with other governments.

At times, the States may legislate concurrently with Congress, so long as their regulations are not inconsistent with the federal law. But in this case, the Court concluded that the federal registration law was designed as a single, integrated, and exclusive system of control over aliens, leaving them "free from the possibility of inquisitional practices and police surveillance" that might affect our international relations.

The treatment of aliens in this country has often had serious repercussions abroad. As Madison said, "If we are to be one nation in any respect, it clearly ought to be in respect of other nations."

It took from 1790 to 1952 to eliminate race and color as barriers to citizenship in this country. The decision in the *Dred Scott* case (March 6), that Negro slaves born here were not citizens, was overruled by the Fourteenth Amendment (July 28). So it came to pass that children born here of aliens who were ineligible for naturalization (e.g. Chinese and Japanese) were American citizens. But even though the Amendment provided that "All persons born" here were citizens, the Supreme Court in 1894 held that American Indians were not included. It took an Act of Congress in 1924 to make them citizens.

Congress in 1790 provided for the naturalization of aliens. But it extended the privilege only to free whites. In 1870, aliens of African descent were made eligible for naturalization; in 1940, "descendants of races indigenous to the Western Hemisphere"; in 1943, Chinese; in 1946, Filipinos and persons indigenous to India. The *McCarran-Walter Act* of 1952 provided: "The right of a person to become a naturalized citizen of the United States shall not be denied or abridged because of race."

Thus America has become a member of the world community slowly and sometimes hesitatingly, but definitely and completely.

On January 22, 1851, Thomas R. Hazard, prominent Rhode Island philanthropist and reformer, who had made his fortune in sheep, submitted an historic report to the General Assembly on the treatment of the poor (and the insane). He condemned the lack of segregation in almshouses—the poor, the insane, and children all being housed together. He denounced the almshouses that kept paupers in chains, or that put them in dungeons on bread and water for such offenses as swearing, quarreling, and defacing walls. He recommended "outdoor relief" for those who had homes, and almshouses for the poor who were friendless or homeless. He condemned the practice of some towns in contracting with individuals to keep the poor.

Hazard was even more vehement against auctioning off ("venduing") the poor to the lowest bidder. He asked if any farmer would "offer his cattle at auction to be kept by the lowest bidder, and depend solely for their good treatment on such security as is taken for that of their pauper poor." He ridiculed the idea, saying, "Bog hay would be substituted for English." He pleaded that "venduing," which was "revolting alike to common humanity and to every precept of the Christian religion," be abolished.

Hazard gave some lurid case histories. The poor were assigned to places unfit "for the use of the most degraded of savages." They lived on porridge or "unripe, watery potatoes." One Chapman bid for Joshua Babcock and got him. Joshua told how the poor at Chapman's place froze to death "on account of the pooreness of the bed and clothes which were not fit to put over a hog and the windows being out for 3 or 4 nights in as cold weather as any in the winter."

Some of Hazard's reforms were immediately adopted. Others came later. The ideas germinated by his report spread. But it was not until the turn of the century that reform reached full tide.

On January 23, 1920, Kansas established a Court of Industrial Relations with jurisdiction over businesses "directly affecting the living conditions of the people," viz., those involving food, clothing, and fuel, in which continuity of supply was essential. The court was given authority to enter orders fixing working and living conditions, hours of work, and "a reasonable minimum wage."

Violence had long marked American industrial relations as labor fought for its place in the sun. The Haymarket riots (June 26) and the great railway strike of the '90's, in which Eugene V. Debs played the tragic role (October 9), were still fresh in mind. During World War I, there were more than 6,000 strikes in the United States. In 1919, over 4 million employees were involved in strikes and lockouts in this country. Railroad shop workers struck in August, steel workers in September, coal miners in November. Even the police struck (September 11). In the four years ending in 1919, there were 705 strikes in the coal mines of Kansas. The "right to strike" and the "right of property" were locked in bitter battle.

Kansas thought that "this gingham-dog and calico-cat business of eating each other up" was getting so serious that government should step in to protect the public interest. The right of employees to quit work was preserved. But once the Industrial Court took jurisdiction, employees were barred from striking and employers were compelled to pay the wages fixed.

In 1916, Wilson got Congress to pass the *Adamson Act* and so staved off a railroad strike that threatened to paralyze the nation. That Act, which established an eight-hour day and fixed the wages for a temporary period pending report of a commission, was sustained in the Supreme Court by five votes to four, Chief Justice White writing for the majority.

A meat packer challenged a wage order issued under the Kansas law; and in 1923 a unanimous Supreme Court, speaking through Taft, held the law invalid as involving a taking of property without due process of law. The Court indicated that compulsory arbitration was outlawed, except possibly for common carriers in times of great emergency.

214

The power of Congress to conduct investigations is one of the great powers of government. Historically, it has been chiefly utilized for one of three purposes: to ascertain the eligibility of its own members to sit; to probe into matters for the purpose of determining what laws, if any, should be passed; to look into the administration of the laws by the executive department, in order to find out if the will of Congress has been executed faithfully or efficiently.

On January 24, 1881, the Supreme Court handed down a decision curtailing that power. The House had voted an inquiry into the operations of a real estate pool, the amount of indebtedness of the bankrupt Jay Cooke & Co., and the deposit made by the Secretary of the Navy of public money in the London branch of that bank. A member of the real estate pool refused to answer questions propounded by the committee. He was arrested by the House to answer for contempt. He sued for false imprisonment and was allowed to recover against the Sergeant-at-Arms. The Court ruled that the investigation was "into the private affairs of individuals who hold no office under the government," and as respects which Congress could pass "no valid legislation."

That limit on the power of Congress to investigate has never been removed. But in practical operation the authority of Congress to make investigations has seldom been curbed for absence of constitutional power.

Times were hard in 1786. A postwar depression had hit the country. The state legislatures were swept by agrarian influences. Debtors wanted relief. There was no strong central government. Only Congress under the feeble *Articles of Confederation* had national authority; and it was not in position to act decisively.

Up at Northampton, Massachusetts, in August 1786, Daniel Shays moved into action. His armed group seized the courthouse in order to put an end to legal proceedings for the collection of debts. The example at Northampton was followed in other parts of the State, about 1,200 armed men joining Shays. Courts were paralyzed. In September, Shays' men moved on Springfield and overawed the court with their claims that their leaders should not be indicted, and that there should be a moratorium on the collection of debts. They also insisted that the militia be disbanded. The stakes now were high, because at Springfield there was a federal arsenal filled with artillery, guns, and ammunition which Shays planned to take.

The decisive engagement took place on January 25, 1787, Shays being routed by state militia equipped with federal cannon. Congress had acted, but its efforts to raise and finance an army were ineffective. The troops that had saved the day were state, not federal, troops.

Shays' Rebellion, more than any other incident, was responsible for the decision at Philadelphia to create a powerful central government: a strong executive; the grant of a broad war power to Congress; the power in the national government to make laws that would override state action; the guarantee to each State of a republican form of government and of protection against invasion; the promise of the national government, on the request of a State, to come to its aid in case of domestic violence.

Shays' Rebellion gave impetus not only to a strong central government, but also to checks and restraints on populism. The mercantile, financial, and large landed interests were getting tired of talk of the rights of man; they were becoming much concerned with the protection of their property. Too much democracy in the state governments, it was argued, was bringing bad times on the country. Massachusetts, New Hampshire, and Rhode Island were said to be disintegrating. General Knox wrote Washington from Massachusetts in the fall of 1786:

"This dreadful situation, for which our government has made no adequate provision, has alarmed every man of principle and property in New England."

Though Shays' Rebellion was shortly put down, the populist or agrarian forces remained in control of some state legislatures, and repudiation of debts remained a threat. Majorities in state legislatures ruled without restraint. The commercial, financial, and landed interests moved to Philadelphia in an anti-democratic mood. A *republican* form of government emerged which, to use the words of Madison, was designed "to protect the minority of the opulent against the majority."

The House was to be elected for a short term by the people. Barriers, however, were erected against majorities. Senators were selected for a longer term by the state legislatures; the President for a fixed term by electors chosen by the people. Thus, a large measure of assurance was granted that majority groups would not be able to unite against the minority propertied interests.

Moreover, amendment of the *Constitution* was made laborious: two thirds of both the Senate and the House were to propose amendments; three fourths of the States were to ratify them.

A final check or balance was an independent judiciary named by the President, approved by the Senate, and serving for life.

The test of a strong government was soon to come. The First Congress imposed excise taxes on domestic distilled liquors. These taxes excited the farmers beyond the Alleghenies. Whisky was a valuable farm product, and the farmers found it more profitable to market the whisky than the grain that went into it. Moreover, the revenue officers who came to enforce the laws ran smack into American ideas of privacy, liberty, and rugged individualism that flourished along the frontier. Protest meetings were held and revenue officers were mobbed.

Congress passed a law providing that when a federal judge should certify that federal laws were obstructed "by combinations too powerful to be suppressed by the ordinary course of judicial proceedings," the President was empowered to call out the militia to suppress the combination.

In 1794, Justice James Wilson of the Supreme Court notified Washington that such condition prevailed in two counties of western Pennsylvania. Washington acted at once. He ordered the insurgents to disperse; he raised 15,000 troops and marched against them. There was no opposition to the military expedition; the ringleaders were arrested and turned over to the civilian courts for trial; the malcontents went back to their farms.

The Whisky Rebellion of 1794 served to demonstrate the strength of the new central government. Washington reported to Congress that the people were "now as ready to maintain the authority of the laws against licentious invasions, as they were to defend their rights against usurpation."

Both Cleveland and Taft vetoed bills imposing literacy tests on immigrants seeking admission here. On January 28, 1915, Wilson also vetoed such a bill. What Wilson said about the bill in his veto message was a moving appeal for respect of the American tradition of political asylum:

". . . It seeks to all but close entirely the gates of asylum which have always been open to those who could find nowhere else the right and opportunity of constitutional agitation for what they conceived to be the natural and inalienable rights of men; and it excludes those to whom the opportunities of elementary education have been denied, without regard to their character, their purposes, or their natural capacity.

"Restrictions like these, adopted earlier in our history as a Nation, would very materially have altered the course and cooled the humane ardors of our politics. The right of political asylum has brought to this country many a man of noble character and elevated purpose who was marked as an outlaw in his own less fortunate land, and who has yet become an ornament to our citizenship and to our public councils. . . . the laws here embodied are not tests of quality or of character or of personal fitness, but tests of opportunity. Those who come seeking opportunity are not to be admitted unless they have already had one of the chief of the opportunities they seek, the opportunity of education. The object of such provision is restriction, not selection."

The course which Cleveland, Taft, and Wilson espoused was lost in 1917, when a literacy test was imposed on all immigrants. This was followed in 1921 by the quota system, which represents a severe phase of our immigration policy.

The veto had an odious history in the American Colonies, because the Royal Governors had used it oppressively. As a result only three States—Massachusetts, New York, South Carolina—granted their Governors a veto power. The other States left the legislatures uncurbed. By the time of the Convention many felt with Madison that a veto power was needed "to check Legislative injustice and encroachments."

Hamilton wanted the President to have an absolute veto, not subject to being overridden. Mason protested, saying that would create "a more dangerous monarchy" than England had. Randolph proposed that the judiciary share the veto power with the President. Wilson favored the idea, saying that judges should have the power to defeat not only unconstitutional laws but laws that were "unjust," "unwise," "dangerous," or "destructive." Mason agreed. So did Madison, who said that the proposal would "enable the Judiciary Department the better to defend itself against Legislative encroachments."

The proposal to implicate the judiciary on the veto was voted down. The philosophy that prevailed was that the grant of a veto to the judges "involved an improper mixture of powers" and would cause them to "give a previous tincture of their opinions."

The proposal to give the President an absolute veto was defeated, as was the suggestion that the President have the power to suspend an Act of Congress for a while. The present provision, granting the President power to defeat a law unless overruled by two thirds vote of both Houses, was adopted by a divided vote, Connecticut and Massachusetts dissenting.

From Washington through Truman 2,011 bills were vetoed. Of these, 71 were passed over the veto, 15 in Johnson's administration, 9 in Franklin D. Roosevelt's, 12 in Truman's. The first four Presidents had no veto that was overridden. Neither did Buchanan, Lincoln, McKinley, nor Harding.

Franklin D. Roosevelt will be remembered for many reforms. But perhaps more basic than any others to a free enterprise system were the efforts he made to restore honesty and fair dealing to the financial markets.

In the decade following World War I, some 50 billion of new securities were floated in this nation, half of which were worthless. Each State was powerless to give effective regulation, as it could not reach the out-of-state promoter. The law said, "Let the buyer beware." Roosevelt said, "Let the seller also beware." So, in 1933, the *Securities Act* was passed, requiring full disclosure of the character of securities offered.

Speculation in securities, stock market pools, and other ways of manipulating security prices were forces behind the creation of the bubble that burst in 1929. Between September 1929 and July 1932, the market value of all stocks on the New York Stock Exchange fell from 89 to 15 billion dollars. As a preventive against recurrence of that kind of disaster, Roosevelt got through the *Securities Exchange Act* of 1934. Stock exchanges were placed under government supervision, methods of manipulating stock market prices were outlawed, purchase of securities on borrowed money was sharply curtailed.

Public utility holding companies had built sprawling empires across the country. By 1932, thirteen of them controlled three fourths of the private utility industry, and three controlled over 40 per cent. Their financial transactions were concealed in a maze of corporations, which often seemed to have the fertility of a rabbit warren. Values were distorted, consumers and investors were mulcted, insiders made fortunes. The political power of the corporate dynasties was too great for the feeble regulatory agencies of the States. The remedy was the *Public Utility Act* of 1935, which had two main requirements: simplification of holding company structures and geographical restriction of holding company systems to appropriate units.

These three measures marked official acceptance of the Brandeis thesis of an earlier generation that those who manage "other people's money" are trustees (December 28).

On January 31, 1865, Congress proposed the Thirteenth Amendment to the *Constitution:*

"Neither slavery nor involuntary servitude, except as a punishment for crime whereof the party shall have been duly convicted, shall exist within the United States, or any place subject to their jurisdiction."

This Amendment became a part of the *Constitution* in December of the same year.

In 1867, Congress made it a crime to hold a person in peonage (January 3). Peonage is compulsory service in payment of debt.

Over the years various States have passed laws making it a crime fraudulently to procure money on a promise to perform labor. In operation those laws often worked as follows:

A man would obtain, say, $15 from an employer on a written agreement to work for a year at $12 a month. He was to be paid $10.75 a month and $1.25 a month was to be applied to his debt. If he quit before working out the contract, he would be arrested and tried for fraudulently procuring money. At the trial he would be *presumed* to have acted fraudulently. If he did not pay the fine and costs, he would be sentenced to hard labor. Then the employer would take the convict as a laborer, for so much a month. Soon the man would quit, and would be convicted again; and so under recurring prosecutions, the employer would get his labor supply at a very small cost. The Supreme Court in a series of decisions, the last in 1944, set aside convictions obtained in that manner, because they violated the Thirteenth Amendment and the *Anti-Peonage Act.*

FEBRUARY

In February 1913, Charles A. Beard gave his publisher the provocative book *An Economic Interpretation of the Constitution of the United States.*

Beard showed that the movement for the *Constitution* was promoted and carried through by people whose interests in public securities, money, manufacturing, and trade and shipping had been adversely affected under the *Articles of Confederation*—a group truly national in scope and drawn from the several States. Beard's thesis was that the *Constitution* was essentially a document designed to put private rights in property beyond the reach of popular majorities. Under Beard's thesis the system of checks and balances was designed as a protection of property interests against democratic forces. The *Constitution,* therefore, was a safeguard which an opulent minority erected against populism that had got out of hand during the Revolution (January 25).

This thesis exploded many preconceptions. The operation of the system to protect the *status quo* was not, as many had claimed, a repudiation of constitutional principles. An equalitarian democracy was not envisaged by the *Constitution.* Its rejection was a fulfillment of constitutional principles, not their subversion.

Realization of this fact had severe repercussions on liberal thought in America. Radicalism followed on the heels of the discovery, some searching Marxism, others socialism for cures. Caustic critics of American business and economics appeared. The tide of reform under Woodrow Wilson was greatly influenced by the discovery.

When the virgin land west of the Mississippi opened to settlers, the competition between the freeholder and the slave owner was on. Small farmers were staking out homestead claims. The large plantation owners with their slaves coveted the land. The freeholders, who were there first, stood across their path. With those freeholders stood Lincoln. In that posture the issue of slavery was one of *property* rights. But an *ethical principle* was also involved. In 1860, Lincoln stated the conflict:

"Any policy to be permanent must have public opinion at the bottom—something in accordance with the philosophy of the human mind as it is. The property basis will have its weight. The love of property and a consciousness of right or wrong have conflicting places in our organization."

The conflict between *property* and *conscience* was further complicated by the problem of saving the Union. Lincoln knew that "A house divided against itself cannot stand."

Lincoln did not compromise on the *ethical principle* that condemned slavery. But he did compromise on ways and means of solving the problem. He rejected the extremists on either side and sought a middle course. When war was thrust on him, he did not wage it vindictively. And when it was won, he counseled conciliation, not revenge (May 16).

Lincoln knew that a coercive government does not long endure, that the consent of the governed and their good will are essential. He knew that the cement which binds the body politic together is tolerance, compassion, and compromise. A coercive government, designed to exploit one class for the benefit of another, has been offered us over and again. Lincoln's greatness was his rejection of it. Lincoln considered *good will* the best sovereignty: "With malice toward none, with charity for all."

That is the antithesis of the class warfare which sweeps the world.

That is the antithesis of the intolerance that almost overwhelmed us in the 1940's and 1950's, when the hunt for communists became a hunt for the unorthodox.

On February 3, 1908, the Supreme Court decided the *Danbury Hatters* case. The United Hatters were trying to organize the industry and were boycotting shops which hired non-union labor. The owner of a factory at Danbury, Connecticut, sued the union for damages to the business suffered as a result of the boycott. Treble damages were asked under the *Sherman Act,* a law passed by Congress in 1890 making illegal "every . . . combination . . . or conspiracy, in restraint of trade or commerce among the several States." (December 30.)

The defense argued that the purpose of the *Sherman Act* was to safeguard the public against the social and economic evils of massed capital. But the Court ruled that combinations of labor as well as combinations of capital were covered and that the sanctions of the Act applied where, as here, the trade restrained was interstate commerce.

The legal battle impoverished both sides. It cost the union over $400,000. The employer ended in poverty. In 1947, his grandson was a member of the Hatters' Union, employed in a factory in New York.

226

The power of the federal courts to declare legislation unconstitutional is not expressly provided for in the *Constitution*. Yet the power of the Supreme Court to hold that state laws conflict with the federal *Constitution* is essential. If the States had the final say on whether their regulations conformed to federal law, the tendency over the years would probably be toward a disintegration of the Union. State legislatures, with an eye to local problems, would likely lose sight of larger national interests as respects foreign affairs, interstate commerce, and perhaps even civil rights.

The need for judicial review of Acts of Congress is not as clear. But the power has been asserted from the earliest days.

Marshall took his seat on the Court February 4, 1801, near the end of John Adams' administration. His nomination was perhaps calculated to embarrass Jefferson, the incoming President, by preserving for the Federalists some control of the courts. The issue soon came to a head. Marbury had been another of Adams' "midnight" appointments. Since his commission had not been delivered when Jefferson was inaugurated, it was withheld. Thereupon, Marbury sought a writ of mandamus in the Supreme Court to force its delivery.

Marshall ruled that Marbury was entitled to the commission. But he finessed the chance of an open fight with Jefferson by holding that the Supreme Court could not exercise jurisdiction, because the Act of Congress empowering the Court to grant the writ of mandamus in this type of case was unconstitutional.

The decision was denounced as a "deliberate partisan coup." Some contended that Marshall should have disqualified himself, since he, as Secretary of State, had failed to give Marbury his commission. Others insisted that Marshall manufactured an opportunity to declare an Act of Congress void. No one, however, missed the immense import of the opinion. Although the Court did not again declare an Act of Congress unconstitutional until the *Dred Scott* decision (half a century later), Marshall's opinion established the precedent that courts could determine when Congress overstepped the bounds. Thus, another of the "checks and balances" was introduced into our federal system.

The doctrine of judicial supremacy has deep roots in this country. An illustration is the action of the Supreme Court of New York sitting in 1733 with Lewis Morris as Chief Justice. William Cosby was the Royal Governor. During his absence in England, Lieutenant Governor Van Dam drew all the Governor's salary. Cosby, on his return, demanded one half of the salary from Van Dam, who refused to pay.

If Cosby sued for the money, there would be a trial before a jury. Cosby feared juries. So, as Governor, he established a special court—a "Court of Exchequer with an equity side." In such a court there would be no jury; judges who held office at the pleasure of the Governor and the King would determine both the law and the facts.

The new court being established, Cosby had the Attorney General sue there for his salary claims. A question as to the validity of the new court was raised, and the matter finally came before the Supreme Court of New York. Chief Justice Morris ruled that the creation of a new court "without Assent of the Legislature" was unlawful.

Cosby immediately dismissed Morris, appointed a new Chief Justice, who rendered a "hansome" opinion in Cosby's favor.

The episode was one of the grievances listed in the *Declaration of Independence:*

"He has made Judges dependent on his Will alone, for the tenure of their offices."

What Morris said and did had a lasting influence. It helped make firm the American maxim that courts cannot be made a tool of executive power, that they can be established only by a Legislature representative of the popular will.

On February 6, 1933, the "lame duck" session of Congress passed into history. The terms of all Congressmen and some Senators had ended every second year on March 4. The second session of every Congress had begun on the first Monday in December. Those elected in November could not take office until March 4. Meanwhile the defeated candidates held their posts and often bargained for political favors.

The Twentieth Amendment ended this condition: the terms of the President and Vice-President begin at noon on January 20, those of Senators and Representatives on January 3; and Congress convenes January 3.

George W. Norris of Nebraska, who served ten years in the House and thirty years in the Senate, sponsored this Amendment. Norris had other historic political battles. He led the revolt against Uncle Joe Cannon and obtained liberalized rules for the House. He fought long for public power (May 18). He helped write a charter of freedom for labor (March 23, October 23). He was partly responsible for exposure of the Teapot Dome scandals. He promoted a federal law outlawing the poll tax. But he opposed a federal law outlawing lynching, for fear it would "raise again that slumbering monster which came into being as a result of the Civil War."

Norris was plain, honest, sincere. He voted his conscience, whatever might be the consequences. He was one of the few liberals of this century who remained true to his principles. He believed that "economic slavery" was as cruel as "political slavery." He spent his life fighting "special interests" who used monopoly power to benefit a few.

I remember him as he stood in my office one winter afternoon. He seemed bent and broken, and there was deep sadness in his voice. "I have fought the good fight with all that was in me," he said. "Now there is no strength left. Other hands must take up the burden. Remember, the battle against injustice is never won."

Norris had not come to know the forces at loose in the world. But he had come to grips with the most powerful ones at home, and he never once surrendered to them.

The Tenth Amendment reserves to the States the powers not delegated to the United States nor prohibited to the States by the *Constitution*. That Amendment is the one in mind when "states' rights" are mentioned. It has sometimes been invoked to support extreme positions.

In 1932, Wisconsin enacted an unemployment insurance law. Few, however, followed her lead, because industries in such a State would be handicapped in their competition. *A national law was needed.*

Pressure for protection against this hazard of the industrial age mounted. From 1922 to 1929, an average of 8 per cent of the industrial workers of the country were unemployed. From 1930 to 1933, the rate had risen to 25 per cent, with a peak of over 16 million unemployed people. Roosevelt urged a *federal* plan as "a measure of prevention" of depressions and as "a method of alleviation" of economic distress.

The *Social Security Act* of 1935 placed a tax on employers for unemployment benefits but allowed them a credit up to 90 per cent of the tax for any contributions made by them to unemployment programs established by the States. The fund, managed by the federal government, was paid to the States for distribution under their laws only if those laws met certain standards. For example, a State could not deny compensation to a man who refused to work, where to be employed he would have to join a company union.

It was argued that the law violated the Tenth Amendment. Since the moneys paid under state plans were supervised by a federal agency and the 90 per cent credit denied unless the state law met federal standards, four Justices thought the independence of the States was impaired. Cardozo, speaking for the majority, held otherwise. The law encouraged States to enact compensation laws, but it did not coerce them. Administration of the fund by a federal agency was only a scheme for efficient administration, undertaken with the consent of a participating State.

By the narrowest of margins the nation finally won its battle for unemployment insurance.

The *Constitution* grants Congress the power "to regulate commerce . . . among the several States." Great controversies have raged around the meaning of that clause. Some maintain that it has no force of its own, that it is a mere source of national power, that until Congress acts the States may legislate as they will. Others have thought that it created a zone from which the States are excluded, even though Congress has passed no law conflicting with the state regulation.

The latter view prevails. The Commerce Clause, by its own force, creates an area of free trade, where the States may not interpose barriers or restraints. The cases that illustrate it are legion. One decided February 8, 1954, by the Supreme Court shows the problem in its simplest terms. Texas imposed a tax on the "gathering" of gas, but it so defined the term as to make the tax applicable to a pipe-line company that did nothing but transport the gas from Texas to other States. The tax was, therefore, imposed on the privilege of sending the gas out of state. It had the vice of another Texas law, condemned by the Supreme Court in 1882, which placed a tax on each telegraph message sent out of Texas.

The area of free trade, created by the Commerce Clause, has had a powerful unifying effect. It has made it easy for our industries to become truly national. It has prevented a "Balkanization" of the country through the erection of custom and trade barriers.

Madison wrote in 1786, "Most of our political evils may be traced to our commercial ones, as most of our moral may to our political." The commercial evils that Madison referred to were the duties imposed, and trade barriers erected, by the States under the *Articles of Confederation.* Under the Confederation, Congress had no power to regulate commerce. Virginia imposed duties upon articles manufactured in the northern States and imported into Virginia. New York imposed entrance and clearance fees for vessels coming from or sailing to not only foreign ports but to other ports in this country as well. The interior States thus suffered.

Yet the South, with indigo, rice, and tobacco as its mainstay feared the transfer of the power to tax and the power to regulate commerce to the Congress. Future revenues of the national government, it was thought, would come chiefly from taxes on imports and exports. Since the South was largely dependent on profits from exportation of crops raised by slaves, it feared that a Congress, dominated by the North and hostile to slavery, would lay discriminatory taxes on southern exports. By a vote of seven States to four, Congress was prohibited from laying a tax or duty on articles exported from any State. It was likewise denied power to prefer one port over another. Vessels bound from one State to another were made immune from duties. And no State was allowed to lay duties on imports or exports without the consent of Congress.

The South's fear of the mercantile and shipping interests of the North was not allayed. Charles Pinckney worked hard to get a provision in the *Constitution* that Congress could make no regulation of commerce without the assent of two thirds of each House. He thought the North would use its political power to perpetuate its monopoly. He marshaled four States for his proposal, seven voting against it (September 16).

The Huey Long regime of Louisiana enacted a law which imposed a tax of 2 per cent on the gross receipts derived from advertisements carried in newspapers when, and only when, the newspaper circulation was more than 20,000 copies per week. The tax was one imposed on newspapers exclusively. It apparently was aimed at a group which was politically opposed to the Huey Long regime. Huey Long was reported as saying that "these big Louisiana newspapers tell a lie every time they make a dollar. This tax should be called a tax on lying, 2 cents per lie."

On February 10, 1936, the Supreme Court struck the tax down as one which abridged the freedom of the press.

Taxation, as an instrument aimed at the press, could be as devastating as censorship. If approved in principle, it could be used to destroy both advertising and circulation. The Court said this tax was "a deliberate and calculated device" to limit circulation and curtail the dissemination of news. Justice Sutherland summarized several centuries of experience when he said, "A free press stands as one of the great interpreters between the government and the people. To allow it to be fettered is to fetter ourselves."

Taxes on papers, periodicals, and books go back to 1711, when Queen Anne got Parliament to pass such a measure in order to suppress comments and criticisms which Her Majesty found objectionable. They continued in existence until 1855. They included taxes on every piece of paper used in a newspaper, on every advertisement, on every pamphlet or book. News agents and street vendors could be fined and imprisoned for selling unstamped publications. The effect was to reduce the size of papers, keep the price high, and restrict the circulation. The effect on the cheaper papers—the ones that usually reached the masses of the people—was pronounced. They were indeed the hardest hit.

In this way the Crown defended itself against criticism. The tax not only lessened the number of readers of the "radical" papers but made it difficult, if not impossible, for an editor to launch a new publication. The taxes restrained publication as effectively as censorship.

That is one reason why these taxes were so odious on this side of the ocean. The *Stamp Act* of 1765 was applicable to many documents, including newspapers, pamphlets, and books. A duty of two pounds was imposed on every degree conferred by institutions of learning. There was resistance to the law on several grounds. The effect of the taxes on freedom of the press was denounced. They were condemned as "taxes on knowledge." When the stamps for newspapers arrived in 1765, the American Revolution began in earnest.

William Bradford, who brought the first press to Pennsylvania, ran afoul of the laws regulating it. He was charged with printing the *Charter* without permission and in February 1689, was hailed before the Governor and the Council. The transcript of the hearing gives life both to the First and Fifth Amendments:

GOVERNOUR: . . . I desire to know from you, whether you did print the *Charter* or not . . . ? . . . if you were so ingenuous as to confess, it should go the better with you.

BRADFORD: Governour, I desire to know my accusers; I think it very hard to be put upon accusing myself. . . . Let me know my accusers, and I shall know the better how to make my defence . . .

  . . .

GOVERNOUR: . . . I will search your house, look after your press, and make you give in £500 security to print nothing but what I allow, or I'll lay you fast.

  . . .

BRADFORD: . . . Printing is a manufacture of the nation, and therefore ought rather to be encouraged than suppressed.

GOVERNOUR: I know printing is a great benefit to a country if it be rightly managed, but otherwise as great a mischief. . . .

BRADFORD: . . . I would willingly ask one question, if I may, without offence, and that is, whether the people ought not to know their privileges and the laws they are under?

  . . .

GOVERNOUR: It is a thing that ought not to be made publick to all the world; and therefore is intrusted in a particular person's hand whom the people confide in. . . . There is that in this *Charter* which overthrows all your laws and privileges. Governour Penn hath granted more power and privileges than he hath himself.

BRADFORD: That is not my business to judge of or determine; but if any thing be laid to my charge, let me know my accusers. I am not bound to accuse myself.

At one time in England, the oath which one takes to tell the truth was used against the accused with devastating effect. If he refused to take the oath, he was held in contempt and punished. If he took the oath and then refused to answer a question, the refusal was taken as a confession of the thing charged in the question. Thus were men compelled to testify against themselves.

A widely heralded defiance of this practice was made by John Lilburne who was charged with sending scandalous books into England. He refused to be examined under oath, saying that the oath was "both against the law of God and the law of the land." He announced that he would never take it, "though I be pulled in pieces by wild horses." (August 2.)

Lilburne was held in contempt, publicly whipped, fined, and placed in solitary confinement. That was in 1638. On February 13, 1645, the House of Lords set aside that judgment as "against the liberty of the subject and law of the land and *Magna Carta.*" And in 1648, Lilburne was granted damages for his imprisonment.

Lilburne was willing to testify as to matters of which he was accused. His refusal related to questions "concerning other men, to ensnare me, and get further matter against me." At that time an accused had no immunity from testifying against himself at his own trial. Lilburne's protest, therefore, was against being compelled to testify on matters not properly charged against him. In other words, he objected to furnishing evidence to be used as the basis for future prosecutions against him.

Before the seventeenth century ended, the immunity claimed by Lilburne had been broadly extended in England. It protected the person who was charged with a crime from testifying against himself at his trial. It also protected any witness from testifying to anything that might incriminate the witness in future proceedings.

The idea spread to this country. The Puritans who came here knew of the detested oath, which Lilburne refused to take. They too had been its victims. *The Body of Liberties,* adopted in 1641 by Massachusetts, afforded protection against self-incrimination either through torture or through the oath (December 31). The highhanded practices of the Royal Governors who sought to compel citizens to accuse themselves of crimes also whipped up sentiment for the immunity. A majority of the Colonies, therefore, as part of their programs for independence, adopted bills of right, which included the immunity against self-incrimination. Later it was written into the Fifth Amendment and into most state constitutions.

The immunity has been broadly interpreted. It extends to all manner of proceedings in which testimony is taken, including legislative committees. It was early held by the Supreme Court to give immunity from testifying not only to acts or events which themselves constitute a crime or which are elements of a crime, but also to things which "will tend to criminate him" or subject him to fines, penalties, or forfeitures. As Marshall put it at the beginning, immunity protects the witness from supplying any link in a chain of testimony that would convict him.

Madison originally proposed that the Fifth Amendment provide immunity broad enough to protect a person from being "a witness against himself," whether in a civil or a criminal case. But at the suggestion of John Lawrence of New York it was restricted to the latter.

It was the law in the time of Queen Elizabeth that any one who converted a person from the Protestant to the Catholic religion, or any Protestant who became a Catholic, should suffer the same penalty as those guilty of high treason.

In 1696, John Freind was tried for treason. He desired to know whether George Porter, a witness, was a Catholic. The prosecutor objected, saying, "He was bred a Protestant, no doubt, and then turning Roman Catholic, he subjects himself to a very severe penalty." The court sustained the objection, holding that Porter was under no obligation to answer the question, "because it may tend to accuse himself of a crime for which he may be prosecuted."

In 1950, the Supreme Court had before it a case where Patricia Blau refused to answer before the grand jury questions concerning her employment by the communist party and her knowledge of its books and records, on the ground that the answers might tend to incriminate her. At that time, Congress had made it a crime to advocate the desirability of the overthrow of the government by force or violence, or to organize or help to organize any such group. Mrs. Blau was convicted of contempt for refusing to answer the questions. The Court set aside her conviction, holding that the provision of the Fifth Amendment, that no person "shall be compelled in any criminal case to be a witness against himself," protected her. The reason was that the answers to the question would have furnished "a link in the chain of evidence," needed to establish a violation of the Act of Congress.

The Fifth Amendment is an old friend, and a good friend. It is one of the great landmarks in man's struggle to be free of tyranny, to be decent and civilized. It is our way of escape from the use of torture. It protects man against any form of the Inquisition. It is part of our respect for the dignity of man. It reflects our ideas of the worth of rugged individualism.

A person who refuses to answer a question on the ground that it might incriminate him may ruin his reputation, though he saves his neck. The protection of the Fifth Amendment does not extend to condemnations which his neighbors or his employer may make because of his refusal to testify. The immunity does not afford a witness a certificate of good character. In an election fraud case, a Kentucky court said:

"Here were police officers being interrogated as to existence of crimes they were paid to prevent, if possible, if not, to expose and punish afterwards; and yet they one and all refused to answer 'under advice of counsel.' Suppose a secret murder had been committed, and the police on that beat, when asked about it, should say, 'I decline to answer for fear of incriminating myself.' This, under the rule invoked, would protect the witness from answering; but how long would it justify his retention on the roll of the police?"

Yet that conclusion does not justify the easy use of the term "Fifth Amendment communists." Some who claim the privilege may have had remote relationships to communism in bygone days, but relationships that never involved espionage nor any overt act against this nation. Yet even innocent and unguarded associations may involve a person in the web of the law.

The Fifth Amendment, it should be remembered, was written for the protection of the innocent and guilty alike, as Reverend John Fearon wrote in the *Commonweal*, February 19, 1954. An act that in fact is wholly innocent may fit logically into a pattern of evidence, indicating guilt. Hence, if the innocent witness testifies, he may be furnishing the prosecution with a case against himself and be forced to depend on a jury to clear him. That is one reason we cannot fairly assume that everyone who invokes the Fifth Amendment during investigations of communism is another agent of the Kremlin boring from within.

The police have always been less inclined to use their wits than their fists. From the beginning, confessions were exacted from suspects by use of every conceivable form of torture. Men were stretched on the rack, their thumbs twisted off, their fingernails pulled out. They faced blinding lights while relays of police questioned them for hours. Hitler introduced a devilish device of drilling a hole straight through a tooth. Every person has a breaking point, beyond which he will, though innocent, confess to any crime in order to get respite from pain.

That history is one reason for the provision in the Fifth Amendment that no person can be compelled to testify against himself. The Fifth Amendment, however, applies only to *federal* courts. The Fourteenth Amendment prohibits the *States* from depriving any person of life, liberty, or property "without due process of law." Can a *state* court convict a man on a confession exacted by force? The answer is no. But it was not until February 17, 1936, that the Supreme Court so held.

In that case the police obtained one confession by hanging the accused from a tree and beating him and another by laying the victims across chairs and whipping them with a strap and a buckle until they bled. This was the "third degree"—a dishonorable instrument of tyranny.

The "third degree," extensively used in communist lands both in crude and in subtle forms, still has an ugly hold here. No section of the country is completely rid of it. Criminals must be detected and punished. But due process of law is a mockery when the torture chamber is substituted for a public trial before a calm and dispassionate tribunal.

In 1933, when Roosevelt came to the Presidency, domestic affairs were in a serious crisis. A dollar would purchase on average about one and a half times as much in 1933 as during the 1921–1929 period. Our national income, which was over 80 billion in 1929, had shrunk 50 per cent. Though incomes diminished and property values dropped, debt and interest remained fixed. A paralyzing deflation had come, and runs on the banks were beginning.

Roosevelt, in his first inaugural, told the nation that "the only thing we have to fear is fear itself." And then he undertook bold measures. He closed the banks for a brief period, and obtained from Congress a program for devaluating the dollar. Many obligations contained promises to pay in gold. Those obligations were estimated to amount to 100 billion dollars. But the gold reserves of the country were only about 4 billion. Gold, being scarce, rose in value. There was much hoarding and much exporting of gold.

One part of Roosevelt's program was a law declaring payment in gold unlawful and making obligations dischargeable, dollar for dollar, in any legal tender currency.

Suits were brought on bonds, some creditors demanding payment in gold, some demanding dollars equal to the value of the old gold dollars. If the latter claims were valid, creditors having a $1,000 bond would collect $1,690.

On February 18, 1935, the Supreme Court in a five to four decision upheld the devaluation program, speaking through Chief Justice Hughes. In the case of private obligations, it held that the power of Congress over the currency was sufficient to make old debts payable in new money. As respects obligations of the United States, it said that the action of Congress in changing the basis of payment was invalid, but that the creditors could not recover damages because they had failed to show that they had sustained any loss on the buying power of the new dollar.

William Lloyd Garrison, the militant abolitionist, was the product of a poor and broken home in Newburyport. The temperance movement was his first "cause"; abolition of slavery the next. In 1831, he started in Boston publication of the *Liberator,* a paper that was to stir the nation. He fought slavery through its pages and on the public platform. His meetings were broken up; he was in and out of jail; his shop was mobbed; he was more roundly cursed than perhaps anyone in American life.

There was good reason for the violence directed toward him. He used every tactic known to agitators to promote what to him was a religious cause. He urged the North to secede from the South, so as to avoid any "compromise with sin." He not only denounced the *Constitution;* he burned it in the course of his speeches. He called it "A Covenant with Death and an Agreement with Hell." These extremes, which caused men like Whittier to break with him, were part of the passion of the man. "Slavery," he said, "will not be overthrown without excitement, a most tremendous excitement." And he devoted his life to providing that excitement.

His first blow at slavery was struck in Baltimore, where he started a paper in 1829. New England fortunes had been made in the slave trade. In those days traffic in slaves was a lawful enterprise. But Garrison, who rated slave-runners no higher than slave owners, printed the name of a Newburyport merchant who owned a ship engaged in coastwise slave traffic, which recently had carried slaves from Annapolis to New Orleans. Garrison claimed that such a merchant should be "sentenced to solitary confinement for life," that he deserved "the lowest depths of perdition." On February 19, 1830, Garrison was indicted for libel; and although the facts stated were true, he was found guilty and fined. Unable to pay the fine, he was sentenced to jail for seven weeks, from which place he wrote, "Of all injustice, that is the greatest which goes under the name of law."

One of the remedies recommended by Roosevelt was the provision of the *Banking Act* of 1933, which created the Federal Deposit Insurance Corporation, a federal instrumentality. Congress authorized it to guarantee bank deposits of closed banks—100 per cent where the deposits did not exceed $10,000, 75 per cent if the deposit was between $10,000 and $50,000, and 50 per cent where the deposits were in excess of $50,000.

In 1931, there were about 2,300 bank failures. During 1931 and the first two months of 1933, there were about 1,850 more. In December 1932, 153 banks had closed with deposits of over 83 million, in January 1934, 237 with nearly 143 million of deposits, in February 1933, 148 with over 72 million deposits.

As the House committee report stated, "More than 90 per cent of the business of the Nation is conducted with bank credit or check currency. The use of bank credit has declined to the vanishing point. The public is afraid to deposit their money in the banks, and the banks are afraid to employ their deposits in the extension of bank credit for the support of trade and commerce."

Some were opposed to federal insurance of bank deposits, because the law would "tax the good bankers" to pay the losses of the inefficient. But the House committee concluded, "Now's the time of all times for this great reform."

The insurance of deposits was later extended to solvent banks. Provision was made whereby both state and federal banks could join the insurance program. First the maximum amount of the insured deposit of any depositor was $5,000. In 1950 it was increased to $10,000.

From 1934 to 1952, the law protected depositors of 420 banks in distress. These depositors received 99.6 per cent of their deposits.

On February 21, 1682, the Royal Governor of the Colony of Virginia and his Council called John Buckner before them. His offense was printing the laws of 1680 "without his Excellency's licence." Buckner and the printer were ordered "to enter into bond in 100 pounds *not to print anything* thereafter, until His Majesty's pleasure should be known."

The new Governor, in 1683, promulgated an order that no person should be allowed to use a printing press "on any occasion whatsoever."

This has been called the "sad period of Virginian annals." No printing was done in Virginia for fifty years. The heavy hand that was laid on Virginia's presses gave leadership to the North in the pamphleteering that preceded the Revolution.

The design behind the prohibition of presses in Virginia was stated frankly by Berkeley, one of the Royal Governors:

"I thank God, there are no free schools nor printing; and I hope we shall not have these hundred years; for learning has brought disobedience and heresy and sects into the world and printing has divulged them and libels against the best Government. God keep us from both."

On February 22, 1634, ten ships were at anchor in the Thames, bound for New England, "fraighted with passengers and provision." On that day, the Privy Council barred their departure because they were filled with people "ill affected and discontented as well with civil as ecclesiasticall government," who would add to the "confusion and disorder" in the Colonies, "especially in poynt of religion." Then the Council ordered that during the voyage the book of Common Prayers of the Church of England be read morning and night, and that before departure each passenger should produce a certificate from the port authorities that "he hath taken both the oaths of allegiance and supremacie."

In 1647, Oliver Cromwell's army made a *Declaration* insisting that courts be deprived of their power to make a person answer questions "against himself in any criminal cause." The same year came *The Humble Petition of Many Thousands,* which prayed:

". . . that you permit no authority whatsoever to compell any person or persons, to answer to any questions against themselves or neerest relations, except in cases of private interest between party and party in a legall way, and to release such as suffer by imprisonment, or otherwise, for refusing to answer to such interrogatories."

The Fathers well knew the various devices used to make men testify against themselves (August 2, February 13). Before 1776, it was common to find in the penal laws of the Colonies the oath of purgation. That is to say, the accused was asked to swear that he had not committed the crime. Refusal to take the oath was treated as a confession that he was guilty.

The history of oaths has burned itself deep in men's minds. It helps explain why all oaths—whether loyalty oaths or oaths designed to exact a pledge of conformity to some orthodox creed—are so obnoxious to our people. They help explain why the Methodists and the Unitarians instantly contested the California law, passed in 1953, requiring them to give a loyalty oath before their church property could be exempt from taxation.

The navigable rivers of the country, such as the Columbia, the Mississippi, the Tennessee, and the Ohio, are arteries of commerce over which the federal government, not the States, has paramount authority. It is the federal government that can control their use, build locks in them, determine the height of bridges, etc. The legal battles that resolved those disputes raged over the years and involved projects for improving navigation for flood control and for the development of hydroelectric power. While the federal government has exclusive control over navigation of these streams, in some States the State itself has title to the river bed, in other States the riparian owner owns to the thread of the stream. But who owns the power which is in the flow of the stream?

The answer to that question turns on who has the dominant control over the land below the ordinary high-water mark. A series of decisions recognized the paramount authority of the federal government. They held that the land below ordinary high-water mark in a navigable stream could be used and controlled by the federal government without the necessity of paying compensation to persons having structures or other property interests there. Then came a setback. On February 23, 1903, the Supreme Court decided a case where a dam on the Savannah River caused the flooding of a plantation that lay between high and low water. The Court held that the federal government had to pay the plantation owner for the damages. Three Justices, headed by Justice Edward D. White, dissented. Their dissent finally became the law in a unanimous decision made in 1941. Thus, at long last, it was firmly established that the dam sites on navigable rivers are federal property.

That is the principle on which the T.V.A., Grand Coulee, and the other great dams built across our navigable streams rest.

"A man's house is his castle" is a principle deep in our traditions. The home is a place of privacy, a sanctuary from the world. The police may not come night or day to search the premises as they desire. This was not always so. In colonial days, writs of assistance were issued authorizing officers to search places of business and homes from top to bottom, and to seize property and papers of every nature. They were used principally by custom inspectors seeking to find violations of the revenue laws. No showing was required that there were reasons to believe the person whose place was searched had violated any law. They were fishing expeditions, whereby officers ransacked houses looking for violations of the law.

On February 24, 1761, James Otis made an historic argument to the Boston court, urging that applications for these writs be denied. Otis reminded the judges that "the freedom of one's house" is an essential liberty, that a man in his home must be as secure "as a prince in his castle," that a law which violates that privacy is an instrument of "slavery" and "villany." He showed how easy it was to get a writ: "Bare suspicion without oath is sufficient. . . . Every man, prompted by revenge, ill-humor, or wantonness, to inspect the inside of his neighbor's house, may get a writ of assistance." Otis proved that the writs were negotiable, passing from one officer to another. He showed that the writs, once granted, "live forever" and that no one could be called to account for their use.

Otis lost. The writs he opposed were issued. But his speech—one of the first public denunciations of Britain—rallied public opinion. "Then and there," wrote John Adams, "the child Independence was born."

Experience with the writs of assistance produced the Fourth Amendment:

—the right of the people to be secure in their persons, houses, papers, and effects, against unreasonable searches and seizures

—a requirement that no search warrant issue except on a showing under oath that some law has probably been violated

—a specification in the warrant of the place to be searched and the things to be seized.

Thus was the weight of the *Constitution* placed behind the right of privacy—the right which Justice Brandeis once described as "the right to be let alone."

In 1914, the Fourth Amendment was given a powerful sanction by a holding of the Supreme Court that evidence obtained through an unlawful search could not be used in a federal prosecution of the person whose privacy was invaded. But in 1949, the Court held that the state courts were not debarred from using, in their criminal trials, evidence obtained in violation of the Fourth Amendment.

Frank Murphy wrote an eloquent dissent. He pointed out that there were three possible ways to enforce the search and seizure clause.

One would be to prosecute the violators—a theoretical remedy since it would require the District Attorney to prosecute himself and his staff.

Another would be a suit for damages against the police by the person whose privacy was invaded—a remedy also illusory.

The only real sanction, he maintained, was exclusion of evidence obtained in violation of the Fourth Amendment.

". . . Only by exclusion can we impress upon the zealous prosecutor that violation of the Constitution will do him no good. And only when that point is driven home can the prosecutor be expected to emphasize the importance of observing constitutional demands in his instructions to the police."

February 26, 1704, the House of Lords submitted a resolution to which the House of Commons subsequently agreed. The resolution stated an important point in legal procedure: "That every Englishman, who is imprisoned by any authority whatsoever, has an undoubted right, by his agents, *or friends,* to apply for, and obtain a writ of habeas corpus, in order to procure his liberty by due course of law."

The federal Act regulating the use of habeas corpus in this country provides that the application must be signed by the prisoner "or by someone acting in his behalf." The right of "a next friend" to file for habeas corpus often serves an important function. The prisoner may be held *incommunicado,* unable to hire a lawyer or to authorize anyone to act on his behalf. He may be an alien, unable to read or write our language. He may be *non compos mentis* or temporarily deranged or unconscious.

It was this procedure that was used in the application for habeas corpus, which obtained a stay of execution in the case of Julius and Ethel Rosenberg in June 1953. The "next friend" who made application was not an agent or attorney for the Rosenbergs. But he had a substantial and serious legal point to tender on their behalf, a point which their counsel had never raised.

Not every volunteer has standing to act as "a next friend." The matter rests in the sound discretion of the judge.

The Twenty-second Amendment to the *Constitution,* limiting the President to two terms, was ratified on February 27, 1951.

Thus, there was laid at rest much of the argument revolving around the third term for Franklin D. Roosevelt.

The idea of rotation in office is old in this country. William Penn's *Frame of Government* of 1683 provided that, after the first seven years of operation of the government, every councilor, having served three years, must retire for one year so that "all may be fitted for government, and have experience of the care and burden of it." In pre-Revolutionary days, some of the Colonies had like provisions. Rotation in office was one of the principles in the Virginia *Declaration of Rights* of 1776. In the Revolutionary period the idea of rotation grew, the purpose being not to educate the people in government so much as to guard the public against overbearing officers.

Those most feared during the early years were the sheriffs, on account of the role they played in selection of juries, and the justices of the peace. Soon the idea of rotation became regarded as essentially democratic. And so other offices, not carrying dangerous powers, were given short, limited terms. Today the principle of rotation finds a wide variety of expression in many federal and state offices, both elective and appointive. Ineligibility for re-election is not common. Frequent elections and short-term appointments are the usual method of restraining the power of public offices.

In 1787, Jefferson was strongly of the view that the President should be restricted to one term. Washington thought otherwise, saying, "When a people shall have become incapable of governing themselves and fit for a master, it is of little consequence from what quarter he comes." Hamilton and the weight of the Convention were aligned with Washington. Jefferson's view more nearly prevailed in 1951.

When the Roman Emperor Caligula published a law, he would have it written "in a very small hand, and posted up in a corner, so that no one could make a copy of it."

Some of our laws have been as obscure, not by reason of being hidden from view, but because they were written so vaguely as to be a trap for the unwary.

In 1917, Congress made it a crime for a person to make "any unjust or unreasonable rate or charge" in handling or dealing in food. On February 28, 1921, the Supreme Court struck down the law because it did not provide an ascertainable standard of guilt, there being no way of determining in advance what price a court and a jury might eventually hold to be "unjust" or "unreasonable." Thus the law was held to violate due process of law.

Oklahoma passed a law which punished contractors with the State who paid their workmen less than the "current rate of per diem wages in the locality where the work is performed." The Supreme Court also held that law to be so vague and uncertain as to violate due process of law.

The Oklahoma law was declared unconstitutional for two reasons:

—the word "locality" was too obscure
—"current rate of wages" indicated a range from minimum to maximum without indicating which rate was meant.

During 1935 and 1936, the Supreme Court nullified many phases of Roosevelt's domestic program. A code to govern the petroleum industry, a compulsory pension law for railroad employees, an Act for the relief of farmer-debtors, removal by the President of a member of the Federal Trade Commission, the *National Industrial Recovery Act*, the *Agricultural Adjustment Act*, an Act regulating the bituminous coal industry, and a municipal bankruptcy Act—these were all invalidated. Moreover, in the lower federal courts, 1,600 injunctions were issued restraining federal officers from carrying out Acts of Congress. And, as Jackson, in *The Struggle For Judicial Supremacy*, relates, the judges who issued them often gave vent to their spleen, throwing the federal courts into the conflict of politics.

It was against this background that Roosevelt in February 1937 proposed a reorganization of the federal judiciary. "Court packing" was what the opposition called it. Roosevelt asked authority to appoint a new justice or judge to any federal court where an incumbent had reached seventy years of age. To encourage retirement of older judges, he proposed that those who reached seventy should be able to retire on full salary for life. There were then six Justices on the Supreme Court over seventy.

The retirement provision, but not the main feature of the plan, was enacted. The Court, under the leadership of Hughes, slowly swung away from some of its conservative positions, and retirements of the older Justices soon started.

Roosevelt, people said, had lost a battle, but won a war.

MARCH

The Fourteenth Amendment prohibits a State from depriving a person of property without due process of law. With the increasing complexity of modern life have come a host of measures regulating business, many of which affect the value of property. Zoning ordinances, price control, rate fixing, laws limiting the amount of oil produced from a well—regulations of this character often make a business less profitable. Do they deprive the owner of property without due process of law?

The issue was presented in connection with the political program of the Granger movement that swept the Middle West in the 1870's. Farmers were suffering from 10 per cent interest and 10 cent corn. They were incensed at the practices of the railroads which gave secret rebates to large customers, corrupted legislatures, controlled grain elevators and warehouses, and charged excessive rates. The Grangers campaigned for legislation to curb these evils. The constitutionality of Illinois laws fixing maximum freight and passenger rates and maximum charges for storage of grain in elevators and warehouses was presented to the Supreme Court.

On one side, it was argued that the law reduced the value of the properties and interfered with the freedom implicit in a free enterprise system; on the other, that government must have the power to regulate in the public interest oppressive business and financial practices.

On March 1, 1877, the Court upheld these Granger laws, saying that legislatures could regulate any private business that was "affected with a public interest" and that a business was so affected "when used in a manner to make it of public consequence and affect the community at large." This decision gave legislatures broad powers over social legislation. If unwise legislation was passed, the remedy was at the polls, not in the courts.

The tide was soon to turn. It was not long before the category of businesses "affected with a public interest" was greatly narrowed by new Justices who were named to the Court. Reasonableness of state regulation of business was first fought out in the legislatures, and if the battle was lost there, it was transferred to the courts. The Supreme Court became a "super-legislature," sitting in judgment on the wisdom of laws.

Over the next sixty years a host of legislation was declared unconstitutional under the Fourteenth Amendment. Thus a ten-hour day for bakers was struck down. So were laws fixing minimum wages and regulating the fees of employment agencies and the prices at which theater tickets could be resold.

Mark Twain's quip that "Solomon's justice depends on how Solomon is raised" became a guiding principle. It was during this period that Holmes and Brandeis developed their reputations as dissenters. They maintained that if social legislation had any reasonable basis in fact, it should be sustained. They urged the importance of allowing the States to experiment, of leaving the removal of unwise laws to the voters.

The tide began to turn in favor of that view in the 1930's. By the 1940's, new Justices had adopted the earlier dissents and in large measure had restored this branch of constitutional law as it was in 1877. Typical was the ruling on laws from Arizona, Nebraska, and North Carolina forbidding "closed shop" agreements, i.e., contracts under which only union members could be employed in a particular factory or shop. In earlier decades, employers used the Fourteenth Amendment to challenge social legislation. Now the unions claimed that outlawing the "closed shop" would be fatal to their survival and hence unconstitutional. The Court upheld the laws, saying that the legislatures had power to protect non-union as well as union members, and that a judge's notion as to the wisdom of a law was no measure of its constitutionality.

In 1920, a bill passed the New York legislature authorizing a New York Court, on petition of the Attorney General, to determine whether a political party supports or advocates principles or policies which, if carried into effect, would violate the state or federal Constitution and unlawfully imperil or destroy the government of the nation and the State. Governor Alfred E. Smith, in vetoing the bill, said:

". . . If unpopular minorities are to be deprived by any such device as this of their basic rights to representation upon the ballot, they will, indeed, have conferred upon them a just claim to political martyrdom. The very evils of ultraradicalism which are feared by the proponents of this measure would, in my opinion, be infinitely enhanced if the bill became law.

"The voters of this State are entitled as of right to the privilege of choosing their own candidates and their own officials and to enunciate their own platform, and no majority should have the right to exclude any minority from its just participation in the functions of government.

"This country has lived and thrived from its inception until today, when it is recognized as the leading world power, upon the fundamental principles set forth in the Declaration of Independence, one of which was the declaration that all men are created equal. No matter to what extent we may disagree with our neighbor, he is entitled to his own opinion, and, until the time arrives when he seeks by violation of law to urge his opinion upon his neighbor, he must be left free not only to have it but to express it. In a State, just as in a legislative body, the majority needs no protection, for they can protect themselves. Law, in a democracy, means the protection of the rights and liberties of the minority. Their rights, when properly exercised, and their liberties, when not abused, should be safeguarded. It is a confession of the weakness of our own faith in the righteousness of our cause when we attempt to suppress by law those who do not agree with us. . . ."

Jefferson's *First Inaugural Address,* delivered March 4, 1801, contains one of the most enduring statements of the democratic ideal contained in our political annals:

". . . having banished from our land that religious intolerance under which mankind so long bled and suffered, we have yet gained little if we countenance a political intolerance as despotic, as wicked, and capable of as bitter and bloody persecutions. During the throes and convulsions of the ancient world, during the agonizing spasms of infuriated man, seeking through blood and slaughter his long-lost liberty, it was not wonderful that the agitation of the billows should reach even this distant and peaceful shore; that this should be more felt and feared by some and less by others, and should divide opinions as to measures of safety. But every difference of opinion is not a difference of principle. We have called by different names brethren of the same principle. We are all Republicans, we are all Federalists. If there be any among us who would wish to dissolve this Union or to change its republican form, let them stand undisturbed as monuments of the safety with which error of opinion may be tolerated where reason is left free to combat it. . . ."

Men have never been willing to collaborate in the parliamentary tradition when political contests have become wars of extermination. In 1953, Walter Lippmann described how in the Old World great nations declined and fell when the people became irreconcilably divided among themelves, when politicians became enemies and, instead of trying to win elections by open debates, devised schemes to destroy one another. Mr. Lippmann added:

"In the democracies that are foundering, and there are many of them, the underlying bonds have been ruptured which hold men together through all their differences in one community. The parties deny the good faith and loyalty of the opposition. Partisanship is a license to outlaw and ruin political opponents. When such a rupture of faith and confidence has occurred, democratic government and free institutions are no longer workable."

Free men have found no alternative to tolerance for opposing political ideas. There is the beginning of the end of liberty when a difference of opinion becomes confused with treason or disloyalty. The strength of the parliamentary method is in the contest for men's hearts and minds, with both majority and minority content to abide the result. Once the power of government is used to defame the character of public men and so crush the opposition, the parliamentary system begins to crumble and the seeds of dictatorship are sown.

In 1846, Dred Scott, a Negro, asked the courts for his freedom. He based his claim on the *Missouri Compromise Act* of 1820, by which Congress banished slavery from certain territory, including Illinois. Since Scott had been taken by his owner to that free territory, he claimed he was still free when he returned to Missouri.

The case was twice argued before the Supreme Court. On March 6, 1857, the Court rendered probably the most unworthy, ill-advised opinion in its long history. Dred Scott was denied his freedom. The Court held *first* that Negroes, by reason of their inferior status when the *Constitution* was adopted, could not be citizens of the United States, and *second* that the *Missouri Compromise Act* was unconstitutional, since Congress had no power to exclude slavery from the territories.

The Court may have thought that the great political issue of slavery could be settled by judicial decision. That was a grievous miscalculation.

Moreover, Taney, in his opinion, summarized the attitude toward the Negroes that prevailed when the *Constitution* was adopted: ". . . that they had no rights which the white man was bound to respect." That dictum cut to the quick. It helped awaken the conscience of the nation to the teaching that all men are created equal.

A bitter war and two constitutional Amendments shortly outlawed the *Dred Scott* decision. The Thirteenth Amendment, adopted in 1865, abolished slavery. The Fourteenth Amendment, adopted in 1868, made all persons born or naturalized in the United States citizens.

In 1790, Alexander Hamilton proposed the chartering of a Bank of the United States. Debates in Congress over the proposal were acid and animated. The "strict constructionist" Republicans opposed it as unconstitutional; the "broad constructionist" Federalists favored it. Jefferson argued that since the *Constitution* granted no express power to create a bank, it should be strictly construed to limit Congress to those powers indispensable for the conduct of the national government. He thought the Bank was a device for exploiting farmers and laborers for the benefit of capitalists and manufacturers.

The Bank continued to be a controversial issue even after its creation. It drew customers away from the state banks. Accordingly Maryland brought the issue to a head. She tried to curtail the Baltimore branch of the Bank by taxing its notes. The Bank refused to pay on the ground that a State could not tax a federal instrumentality. Thus the resolution of the historic controversy fell to the Supreme Court.

On March 7, 1819, Marshall delivered the opinion which sustained the chartering of the Bank and struck down the state tax. He asserted the "broad" construction theory of the Federalists- that Congress has "implied powers" that can be used to carry out its express powers. The *Constitution* does not expressly grant to Congress the power to create a bank. But it does grant Congress power to raise revenues, coin money, pay debts, and borrow money. Marshall held that the creation of the Bank was convenient, if not necessary, for the exercise of these currency and fiscal powers. State taxation could not be permitted to impede that federal undertaking.

The North and the East supported the decision; the South and the West opposed it on the ground that it prostrated state sovereignty. Marshall's formula did mark out broad federal authority against the claim of States' rights. It is one of the cornerstones on which the pervasive power of the national government over domestic affairs presently rests.

The separation of church and state has had a long history filled with acrimonious argument (December 24, 25; April 11, 12, 13). One of the most recent chapters was closed by a Supreme Court decision rendered March 8, 1948.

Early in the century, a movement for religious training got under way which had as its premise that the public schools took too much of the child's time, the churches too little. It was proposed that children be released from classes in order that they might receive religious instruction. The "released time" program was first inaugurated at Gary, Indiana, in 1914, the religious instruction being held on church premises and the public schools having no hand in it.

The "released time" program spread until in 1947 it was in vogue in some 2,200 communities. The case reaching the Court involved Champaign, Illinois. Parents who desired religious instruction for their children notified the public school, which in turn provided classrooms for the purpose. The teachers of religion were selected and paid by the churches, subject to the approval of the superintendent of schools. A child not enrolled in a religious class attended a regular class or a study period. The churches and the public schools co-operated to see that the enrolled children attended the classes on religion.

This program was held unconstitutional by a divided Court, as "a utilization of the tax-established and tax-supported public school system to aid religious groups to spread their faith." The use of the public school rooms and of the public school machinery to help sectarian groups in their religious instruction was the fatal feature of the scheme.

The United States is a constant, eternal threat to any political oligarchy, to any totalitarian regime in the world. It is a threat because it is founded on "the consent of the governed" and because it grants civil rights to all people, regardless of race or creed. Our very existence is therefore a more potent threat than any stock pile of bombs.

Ideas are indeed the most dangerous weapons in the world. Our ideas of freedom are the most powerful political weapons man has ever forged. If we remember that, we will never have much to fear from communism. The force we generate with our ideas of liberty can give powerful impetus to freedom on other continents, as well as at home; in another century, as well as today.

We have not always remembered that, and forgetting, have given the words un-American strange meanings. Communism is, of course, un-American, because it is a way of life that denies man his unalienable rights. But un-American has other meanings equally important, but commonly forgotten by the proponents of un-American investigations. Un-American means:

—discrimination against racial, religious, or other minorities
—denial to anyone of the right of free speech
—denial to a person under investigation of the benefit of counsel
—making the accusation the substitute for proof
—using guilt by association as the standard of proof
—using faceless informers as witnesses against men
—using communism as the label to denounce any opponent
—condemning a person for all work because he may not be fit for some.

These too are un-American activities. The failure to recognize them as such leads to humorous as well as tragic results. I heard a speech on the *Bill of Rights* at a meeting of lawyers in the Far West. There was little more in it than a description of some of the roots of our civil liberties. As the speaker was leaving, I heard one lawyer say to another, "There goes a communist if I ever saw one."

In 1777, William Goddard published in Baltimore a paper called the *Maryland Journal*. His journalism encountered a severe and powerful censorship—the censorship of the community. He had several encounters with the mob, his first growing out of a piece signed, Tom Tell Truth. The British had offered to discuss terms of peace with the rebellious colonists. Tom Tell Truth wrote in Goddard's paper that it might be advisable to accept the British terms. In the same paper was a piece by Caveto urging rejection of the British offer. Caveto was ignored; Tom Tell Truth became the talk of the town.

A delegation from the Whig Club waited on Goddard, insisting he disclose the identity of Tom Tell Truth (Samuel Chase apparently was author of both pieces). Goddard refused. He was ordered to attend a meeting of the Club the next night. He ridiculed the idea in the pages of his paper. The next night Goddard was taken by force to the meeting and given twenty-four hours to leave Baltimore and three days to leave the county.

Goddard went straight to Annapolis and petitioned the Assembly. He said he was "bound in honour not to suffer the secrets of his press to be extorted" in a "tumultuous way," that the Whig Club was a "self-created court," acting in a way not patiently to be endured "by a freeman possessed with a spark of honour or sensibility."

On March 10, 1777, the Assembly censored the Whig Club for action in "manifest violation" of the *Constitution* and "directly contrary" to the *Declaration of Rights*. Goddard visited Annapolis at least two more times for protection from the mob. Whatever may have been the merits of the views of this hotheaded, doughty publisher, his fortitude helped give character to the office of publisher in America.

The *Pennsylvania Constitution* of 1776 required each legislator to swear:

"I do believe in one God, the creator and governor of the Universe, the rewarder of the good and the punisher of the wicked. And I do acknowledge the Scriptures of the Old and New Testament to be given by Divine inspiration."

The *Delaware Constitution* of 1776 required public officials to swear:

"I, A.B., do profess faith in God the Father, and in Jesus Christ His only Son, and in the Holy Ghost, one God, blessed for evermore; and I do acknowledge the holy scriptures of the Old and New Testament to be given by divine inspiration."

The *Massachusetts Constitution* of 1780 required state officials to swear:

"I believe the Christian religion and have a firm persuasion of its truth."

In contrast to these religious oaths is the constitutional oath of the President:

"I do solemnly swear (or affirm) that I will faithfully execute the Office of President of the United States, and will to the best of my ability, preserve, protect and defend the Constitution of the United States."

In the Colonies, there were some religious qualifications for public office. The *Georgia Constitution* of 1777 required legislators to be "of the Protestant religion."

Our *Constitution* provides that "no religious test shall ever be required as a qualification to any office or public trust under the United States."

Queen Elizabeth sent word to the House of Commons in 1572 that "no bills concerning religion" should be considered unless they were first approved by the clergy. Peter Wentworth, a Member who in the previous Parliament had urged that free speech was one of the great liberties of the House of Commons, took the floor against the Queen. He called her instructions "a doleful message." He condemned the spreading of rumors in the House to "take heed what you do, the Queen's Majesty liketh no such a matter; whosoever prefereth it, she will be offended on him." He also condemned orders to the House from the Queen to do this or not to do that as "very injurious to the freedom of speech and consultation." He pleaded for "free speech and conscience in this place" as necessary for the preservation of the state. He argued that the Queen was "under God and under the law."

For these utterances Wentworth was sent to prison for a few weeks, ending March 12, 1573.

Wentworth was to go to prison again for maintaining on the floor of the House that it was a place where "any of the griefs of this Commonwealth" may be discussed without restraint or danger of punishment.

Many others were likewise punished in England before the immunity of Members of Parliament for words spoken in debate was established.

In 1629, during the reign of Charles I, John Elliot and other Members of Parliament were charged with raising sedition between the King, his nobles, and the people. It appears that the King ordered the House of Commons to adjourn. John Elliot and his associates did not want an adjournment until they had made their speeches. So they held the Speaker in the chair until they had finished. The gist of their speeches was that the government had "conspired to trample under foot the liberties of the subjects."

Elliot and the other defendants protested the jurisdiction of any court to try them, saying that if they were to be punished Parliament alone had the power. The judges ruled against them, holding that a court had jurisdiction to try them for what they had done in Parliament after Parliament had adjourned. Elliot and the others were fined and imprisoned.

Elliot died in prison. In 1641, the House of Commons voted awards to these men as damages suffered by reason of their service to their country. In 1668, the House of Lords voted that the judgment against Elliot and his associates was illegal and against the freedom and privileges of Parliament.

In 1689, the privilege of Members of Parliament to be free from arrest or suits for damages for what they said or did in Parliament was established by a provision in the English *Bill of Rights:* "That the Freedom of Speech, and Debates or Proceedings in Parliament, ought not to be impeached or questioned in any Court or Place out of Parliament."

Our *Constitution* makes specific the privilege of Senators and Representatives: " . . . for any Speech or Debate in either House, they shall not be questioned in any other Place."

The provision was included so that Congressmen would enjoy the fullest liberty of speech without fear of civil or criminal prosecutions for what they said or did.

Some, like Jefferson, feared the tyranny of the legislatures. Yet it was decided to trust the self-discipline of the members of Congress and the wisdom of the voters to correct any abuses that might arise from the immunity granted Congressmen.

When litigation arises which involves the immunity, courts do not look into the motives of the legislator who is sued. Whether the intent behind a particular speech is honorable or venal, the immunity obtains. The value to society is in the maintenance of a legislative body where men can speak or act without fear of punishment or reprisals.

The immunity extends to the activities of standing or special committees of either House so long as they act within the bounds of legislative authority, including the reports of those committees. It also extends to the resolutions offered and to the voting, as well as to the debates themselves.

And so the Supreme Court held in 1881 that Congressmen were not liable in damages for false imprisonment, though they acted beyond their authority in having a witness before a committee arrested for contempt because of his refusal to answer a question. But the Sergeant-at-Arms of the House, who made the arrest, stood responsible, as the immunity was deemed personal to the legislators.

At times Congressional investigations so far exceeded the bounds of fair play that it seemed the Inquisition had come to America. People's reputations were ruined or soiled by indecent tactics. Hearsay and innuendo, even the accusation itself, became the substitute for proof. In March 1954, Dean Erwin N. Griswold of Harvard suggested reforms:

1. Only the committee, not the chairman or staff, should issue a subpoena.
2. When a witness is summoned, he should have the right to counsel and counsel should be entitled not only to advise him, but to speak on his behalf.
3. No testimony should be taken in executive session (secretly), unless the witness is willing. If so taken, it should not be used or referred to in open hearings unless the full evidence is produced.
4. Witnesses should not be required to testify before cameras, on the radio, or on television. "Legislative investigations are not a part of show business."
5. Legislative investigation is "improper" when its purpose is to "expose" people or evidence for use in criminal prosecutions.
6. A witness should be entitled to rebut evidence against him.
7. A witness need not testify if a committee violates the rules.

In 1949, the Supreme Court, speaking through Frank Murphy, enforced one check against irresponsible minority action of committees. Under the House Rules a committee could act only by majority vote. The Court, therefore, ruled that a witness could not be held in contempt if there was no quorum present when he was asked the questions leading to the perjury charges.

In March 1954, the National Council of the Churches of Christ also demanded reforms. It condemned, among other things, "the forcing of citizens, under pretext of investigation of subversive activities, to testify concerning their personal, economic and political beliefs," saying that it is not "within the competence of the state to determine what is and what is not American."

The problem of security in government is a real one because of the international nature of the communist conspiracy. While the British have been as fully aware of that fact as we, they have gone about finding a solution in a fair way.

Their civil service includes over 1 million employees. They applied their loyalty procedure only in areas "vital to the security of the State," which, down to 1954, had covered only 17,000 civil posts. The British used the loyalty procedure to test the qualifications of an employee for a particular job, not to condemn him for all public employment. Down to 1954, 198 civil servants had been suspended. Of that number, 78 were reinstated, 69 were transferred to non-secret work, 23 were dismissed, 19 resigned, and 9 were on leave pending decision on their cases. A lively sense of decency and fair play has been evident throughout the administration of the program.

There has been no such meticulous regard for the rights of employees in this country. Men and women have been officially condemned and ruined for life as a result of a procedure which someday the bright conscience of America will denounce as unworthy of our libertarian philosophy.

In 1954, Bishop Bernard J. Sheil of the Roman Catholic Church denounced the use of lies, calumny, and calculated deceit, so often present in our loyalty investigations. "These things are wrong," he said, "even if they are mistakenly thought of as means to a good end. They are morally evil and to call them good or to act as if they were permissible under certain circumstances is itself a monstrous perversion of morality. They are not justified by any cause—least of all by the cause of anticommunism, which should unite rather than divide all of us in these difficult times."

There are three functions in the law—investigation, prosecution, adjudication. Traditionally these functions have been separated. The grand jury investigates, an attorney for the government prosecutes, a judge makes his decision after a trial that is conducted publicly. In 1917, Michigan passed a law which blended the functions of the judge and the grand jury. A judge could summon witnesses before him and if he felt that a witness was evasive or not telling the truth, he could hold him in contempt of court, fine him $100, and put him in jail for sixty days. At the end of that time, the judge could call the witness before him once more and once more convict him. If at any time after sentence, the witness would talk freely, the judge could commute the sentence or suspend it.

This one-man grand jury was known in Michigan as the "portable grand jury," since the hearings could be held anywhere and at any time; they could be secret or public, as the judge chose

In March 1948, the Supreme Court struck down the law as applied to a witness in a secret hearing before a judge who, in the midst of the secret investigation, charged him with contempt, sentenced him, and sent him off to jail. The Court ruled that the secrecy of the contempt trial violated due process of law (July 22). It also held that an investigating officer could not in one breath transform himself into a judicial officer and in the next breath make a criminal out of a witness. Traditional grand juries never punished witnesses who testified falsely or evasively. Punishment under our system requires notice of the offense and an opportunity to defend, the right of the accused to examine the witnesses, and the right to counsel.

Reformers often have a cause which makes a short cut seem justified. But one of the main objects of our *Constitution* is to see that short cuts are not taken. Experience showed that once one man's rights could be tampered with, all men's rights were in jeopardy.

The manner in which committees have trenched on the liberties of citizens is shown by a March 1954 hearing before the McCarthy committee investigating government operations. Roy M. Cohn was cross-examining Annie Lee Moss, a widowed colored woman, unskilled and with little education, who "transmitted" messages for the Army but never worked in the code room. She had an attorney, but McCarthy refused to allow him to speak. Mrs. Moss was now unemployed, for when the investigation started she had been suspended. It appeared that there were three Annie Lee Mosses in Washington, D.C. *This* Mrs. Moss hotly denied she was or ever had been a communist or attended any communist meetings. No testimony was offered against her.

Mr. Cohn adopted the tactic of smearing by innuendo, "We have the testimony of Mrs. Markward, the undercover agent for the F.B.I., stating that an Annie Lee Moss was a member, a dues-paying member of the communist party, the Northeast Club of the communist party. We have corroboration of that testimony by another witness who . . . gave a sworn statement to the effect that she also knew Mrs. Moss was a member of the Northeast Club of the communist party." But those witnesses were not called to confront the accused and to establish that *this* Mrs. Moss was *the* Mrs. Moss to whom Cohn referred and to give *this* Mrs. Moss the opportunity to defend against the charge.

McClellan protested, saying that if there was evidence against Mrs. Moss, she was entitled "to have it produced here in her presence." Mundt ruled that the statement of Cohn be stricken.

McClellan's protest took up the earlier challenge by Eisenhower:

"In this country, if someone dislikes you or accuses you, he must come up in front. He cannot hide behind the shadows, he cannot assassinate you or your character from behind without suffering the penalties an outraged citizenry will inflict. . . . If we are going to continue to be proud that we are Americans, there must be no weakening of the codes by which we have lived. By the right to meet your accuser face to face, if you have one . . ."

The historic remedy of an employee for injuries suffered in his employment was a suit against the employer for damages. This remedy was wholly inadequate. It was, to begin with, a speculative venture, whose outcome turned on the skill of lawyers and the vagaries of a jury. Moreover, recoveries were long delayed, during which time the family was often on charity. The basis of the liability of the employer was negligence. Yet from studies made, it appeared that probably not more than one fourth of the industrial accidents could be credited to the negligence of the employer. At least a half were traceable to risks inherent in the job. In the majority of accidents, the injured workman and his family received no substantial recovery. Workmen, as a practical matter, could not take out sufficient accident insurance to protect themselves. The result was untold misery and suffering.

The feeling grew that industrial accidents were part of the overhead of business, that the breaking of a leg or the loss of a life was as legitimate a cost of doing business as the loss of a drill or the explosion of a boiler, that those costs should be paid for by those who enjoyed the product.

Ideas were borrowed from Europe, particularly Germany; and shortly after the turn of the century drives were made in the States. The main impetus came from New York as a result of the Wainwright Commission, which submitted its first report on March 19, 1910. On the basis of that report, a compulsory compensation law was enacted by New York in 1910, only to be declared unconstitutional by the courts. Thereupon the Wainwright Commission proposed a constitutional amendment, which was adopted and under which, in 1913, a New York law was passed. Today, there are compensation laws in all of the States and Territories and in the District of Columbia. Moreover, the federal government has compensation Acts for civil service employees and longshoremen. Today industrial accidents are part of the *human overhead* of doing business.

On March 20, 1924, a Virginia statute was enacted which provided for the sexual sterilization of inmates of institutions supported by the State who were found to be afflicted with a hereditary form of insanity or imbecility. In 1927, this law was sustained by the Supreme Court (June 1).

"It is better for all the world, if instead of waiting to execute degenerate offspring for crime, or to let them starve for their imbecility, society can prevent those who are manifestly unfit from continuing their kind. The principle that sustains compulsory vaccination is broad enough to cover cutting the Fallopian tubes. . . . Three generations of imbeciles are enough."

The suit was brought by Carrie Buck, a feeble-minded white woman, who was the daughter of a feeble-minded mother and who in turn had an illegitimate feeble-minded daughter.

The program to eliminate communists from the executive branch began in 1939. Under Roosevelt and the first year or so of Truman, various committees or boards were appointed to screen employees against whom charges of disloyalty were made. Dismissals were to be made in clear cases only, not on the basis of "mere suspicion unauthenticated by credible evidence."

On March 21, 1947, Truman instituted a more rigorous system. Loyalty boards were established to ascertain not only the "disloyal" but also the "potentially disloyal" employees. Appeals were allowed to a review board, but none to the courts.

Charges against employees had to be only as specific "as security considerations will permit." The parties could introduce only such evidence as the board "may deem proper." The employee could appear by counsel and cross-examine, but he could not cross-examine the informants. Nor could he force his accusers to confront him. The employee testified under oath. But the testimony of the informants was not sworn. There were two records of the proceedings—one for the employee, one for the government. The employee was not entitled to see the latter, which commonly contained the most damaging evidence against him.

In 1951, Truman took sterner measures. The standard for refusal of employment or dismissal had been that of "reasonable grounds" for believing that the person was disloyal. In 1951, the government dismissed employees on a finding "that, on all the evidence, there is a reasonable doubt as to the loyalty" of the person.

Down to June 30, 1953, 16,503 employees had been cleared, 557 removed or denied employment on loyalty grounds, and 6,382 had left the service or withdrawn their applications after reference of their cases to the loyalty boards.

Removal of communist agents from government was essential. But the *procedures* by which it was done marked a break with tradition. Men and women were cast into the outer darkness by *procedures* that would never be tolerated, even in a case where, say, a cow was killed by a train.

The Truman order could not compare in severity to the one promulgated by Eisenhower in 1953. Herb Block ridiculed it in a cartoon entitled, "Gosh, It Isn't Even Safe to Resign Any More." An innocent employee was shown tipping his hat as he left a government building. Unknown to him, a sign was being placed on his back, "Security Risk ✗2201."

Under the Eisenhower order a person suspected was at once suspended "in the interests of national security." One could be suspended for a wide variety of reasons—not only for evidence of sedition, espionage, communism, or affiliations or associations with subversive people or groups, but for "any immoral" conduct or "sexual perversion" or "any behavior" which tends to show that he is "not reliable or trustworthy."

The determination was commonly made by an officer whose identity was unknown to the employee and before whom he could not plead his case.

Once suspended, his salary stopped immediately. He could hire a lawyer and get a hearing. But even so, his accusers were never known to him. He would in effect have to prove that he was *not* a subversive, *not* dangerous, *not* unreliable, *not* a homosexual, *not* a communist.

Even if he took the full blast of publicity and proved that he was an honorable person, he would not automatically be reinstated. The head of his agency would still have to find that his re-employment was "clearly consistent with the interests of the national security."

Under this order men and women were discharged because they were liberals or Jews or opposed to the policy of the department head. Most dared not fight, because they would be smeared by the charges and ruined, no matter if they disproved the accusation.

The boast in Washington, D.C., was that under the Eisenhower order anyone could be got rid of at any time for any reason. Joseph and Stewart Alsop, writing in January 1954, denounced the procedure, which resulted in "306 State Department security firings," as "palpably dishonest."

By the early 1930's, government by injunction was a blight on the nation. The courts had undertaken to control strikes and their attendant conflicts and tumult. They were alert to move swiftly in aid of employers against mounting union agitation. They policed industrial disputes, using their power to hold recalcitrant laborers in contempt of court as a means of punishing misdeeds that normally would be prosecuted before juries in criminal or civil suits. The injunctions that were issued often went so far as to forbid labor from telling anyone that a strike was in progress or from paying benefits to laborers on strike. They were broad and devastating in their scope. In the 1922 railroad strike, some 300 were issued.

Earlier efforts to correct the abuses had largely failed (October 18). The Republican and Democratic platforms in 1928 both promised relief. Norris in the Senate and La Guardia in the House led the reforms.

On March 23, 1932, a law was enacted sharply curtailing the power of federal courts to issue injunctions. Certain acts, e.g., striking and paying strike benefits, were made immune from injunctions. Yellow dog contracts (October 23) were made unenforceable. A strict procedure was established for those cases where the federal courts were permitted to issue injunctions. People charged with disobedience of court orders were granted jury trials.

Thus, at last, the federal courts were neutralized in industrial conflicts, no longer being allowed to throw their weight against the efforts of labor to organize. The *Norris-La Guardia Act* indeed marked the commencement of an era when the peaceful, collective activities of labor were freed from interference by government.

On March 24, 1765, the *Quartering Act* was passed. The idea came from General Gage, whose troops here were trying to enforce tax laws obnoxious to our people. The law provided that troops could be quartered in inns, eating houses, and other public establishments or in uninhabited houses or buildings. The host was obliged to furnish the soldiers, quartered in his place, "with diet, and small beer, cyder, or rum mixed with water" at rates fixed by the Army. If an owner was willing to furnish the soldiers quartered with him "candles, vinegar, and salt, and with small beer or cyder, not exceeding five pints, or half a pint of rum mixed with a quart of water for each man *per diem,* gratis," and to allow the soldiers the use of fire and the necessary utensils for dressing and eating their meat, then the owner need not feed the soldiers. For soldiers quartered in barracks or in uninhabited houses or buildings, the local government was to provide each man free of charge fire, candles, vinegar, salt, bedding, cooking utensils, beer or cider (not exceeding five pints a day) or half a pint of rum mixed with a quart of water.

The dispute between the Army and the Colonies over the quartering of troops went back many years. The Army had seldom forced people to evacuate their homes. The dispute was a legal contest—whether the King and Parliament could quarter troops, or whether the power was in the colonial legislatures. The Colonies, after much strife and bickering, had managed the matter. The *Quartering Act* of 1765 challenged their authority. That was the cause of the violent reaction. That was the emphasis in the complaint registered by the *Declaration of Independence:* "He [the King] has kept among us, in times of peace, Standing Armies without the Consent of our legislatures."

J. S. Coxey of Ohio proposed to end the 1893 depression by a nationwide public works program. A county road system was to be constructed under the supervision of the Secretary of War. A minimum wage of $1.50 per day for common labor and $3.50 per day for teams and labor, together with an eight-hour day, were part of the proposal. These public works were to be financed by the issuance of Treasury notes against non-interest-bearing, twenty-five-year bonds issued by the States, counties, or other local authorities, and deposited with the Secretary of the Treasury.

Coxey led one "army" out of Massillon, Ohio, on March 25, 1894. All told twenty-five "armies" moved on Washington. They came from all regions of the country singing:

> *"After the march is over*
> *After the first of May*
> *After these bills have passed*
> *Then we will have fair play."*

They came on foot and horseback, by wagons and freight trains. There was a great deal of lawlessness, some twenty trains being stolen by these "armies." There were many arrests. Of the 100,000 who, according to Coxey, were scheduled to arrive in Washington, D.C., by May 1, only 1,000 or so appeared.

This "petition in boots" soon fizzled out. But it left definite marks:

—It showed the reaction of the frontier to an industrialism that produced unemployment.
—It emphasized the right to work.
—It dinned into consciousness the responsibility of government to provide employment through public works.

It took years for the public school system to evolve in this country. It was the product of many battles, and the obstacles were great. One was the rate bill. This was a practice brought over from England and used to supplement school revenues. It amounted to an assessment on the parents for each child in school. The fee was small, New York charging 25 cents per quarter for the first three classes, 50 cents per quarter for the next three, and $1.00 per quarter for grades 7, 8, and 9. But the charge, though small, had a serious effect on the school system, for it put a premium on non-attendance. The proof was clear that the charge, though small, was enough to keep many poor children away from school.

The abolition of the rate bill and the establishment of a free common school were proposed in an Act passed by the New York legislature March 26, 1849, which by its terms was submitted to a referendum of the people, who voted almost three to one for the measure. Its opponents got the 1850 legislature to resubmit the measure to the people. Forty-two counties voted against free schools, seventeen for free schools. But the seventeen counties were the populous ones. The city vote won out in a close election.

The rate bill was not abolished in all the northern or the southern states until after the Civil War, New Jersey ridding herself of it in 1871. But the fight in New York was the crucial one. It created the climate of opinion that rid the country of a practice which had no place in a democratic society. The victory traveled on the wings of a slogan coined in New York, "Free as air should knowledge be."

On this day in 1868, Congress took action which in 1954 was the basis for a resolution proposing an Amendment to the *Constitution*.

William H. McCardle, a Mississippi editor, was jailed by the Army for libel, disturbing the peace, inciting insurrection, and for impeding reconstruction in the South. The charges were based on certain newspaper articles McCardle printed. The military claimed the right to try him under the odious *Reconstruction Acts*. McCardle, a civilian, claimed that the military had no right to try him, that only civil courts had jurisdiction. He asked the federal court in Mississippi to discharge him from custody by habeas corpus. That court denied him relief, and he appealed to the Supreme Court.

While the appeal was pending, Congress passed the Act of March 27, 1868, taking away from the Supreme Court jurisdiction over appeals in habeas corpus cases, whether future or pending. The Act, which was aimed at McCardle's case, was passed (over Andrew Johnson's vigorous veto) as part of the harsh policy which Thaddeus Stevens was imposing on the South (May 16).

The Supreme Court unanimously held that Congress had power to deny it jurisdiction over the appeal. The *Constitution* qualifies the appellate jurisdiction of the Court—granting it "with such Exceptions, and under such Regulations as the Congress shall make." Congress, therefore, has the power to deny, as well as to grant, appellate jurisdiction; to withdraw it, as well as to confer it.

Never before or since has Congress undertaken to interfere with cases pending before the Court. In 1954 the Senate Judiciary Committee, however, recommended an Amendment to the *Constitution* which would take from Congress any power to deny the Supreme Court appellate jurisdiction "in all cases arising under this Constitution."

March 28, 1841 is a date of great significance in the history of our insane asylums. On that day, Dorothea Lynde Dix visited a House of Correction in Massachusetts. The appalling conditions she found led her to make, on her own, a two-year investigation of the treatment of the insane in Massachusetts. The memorial she then presented to the legislature is one of the most moving ones in our annals. The insane were confined "in cages, closets, cellars, stalls, and pens." They were "chained, naked, beaten with rods, and lashed into obedience." In that day, the insane were condemned as people of a depraved nature who had fallen to the level of brutes. They were accordingly treated as beasts. The plea of Miss Dix was for a transfer of the insane from almhouses and jails to asylums supported by taxation and manned by intelligent personnel.

She proceeded from State to State, making in each a thorough investigation of the treatment of the insane. She got reforms in sixteen of the States. Her memorial to Congress in 1848 summarized her findings as respects the 9,000 patients she had personally seen. She did not win in her effort to get 5 million acres of public land set aside for treatment of the insane. But she inaugurated a regime of sanity toward the problems of the insane. She brought to public consciousness the realization that there is a spiritual quality in every human being; that no one is beyond redemption; that often those who have been cast into the outer darkness of "insanity" can be reclaimed and restored to health and good citizenship.

The right of employees to organize and bargain collectively was the product of a slow and gradual growth. Many milestones mark its evolution (July 12). But it was not until the 1930's that the power of government to guarantee those rights on a national scale was definitely put at rest.

When unions grew in size and strength, some employers started "company unions," i.e., organizations of employees which were under the domination and control of the employer. Congress in the *Railway Labor Act* of 1926 provided that in a railway labor dispute each side should be allowed to designate its representatives, without interference or coercion by the other. This was held by the Supreme Court in 1930 to justify a federal court in ordering a railroad to disestablish its company union. The employers, said Chief Justice Hughes, have "no constitutional right to interfere with the freedom of the employees" in organizing.

On March 29, 1937, the Court, speaking through Stone, held that a railroad company could be required by a court to "treat with" the employees' union. This did not mean that the employer was required to enter into an agreement with the employees; it merely meant that the employer was to negotiate in good faith. The elimination of the company union and "the meeting of employers and employees at the conference table" were thus approved as constitutional means to avoid industrial strife and promote amicable settlements of disputes.

Those rulings were capped by the 1937 decision (October 23) which upheld the provisions of the *Wagner Act* guaranteeing collective bargaining and granting employees unions of their own choice, in a host of industries subject to regulation under the Commerce Clause.

On March 30, 1870, the Secretary of State certified that the Fifteenth Amendment had become a part of the *Constitution.* Its chief provision reads:

"The right of citizens of the United States to vote shall not be denied or abridged by the United States or by any State on account of race, color, or previous condition of servitude."

This Amendment, conferring political rights on Negroes, completed the trilogy of constitutional Amendments (January 31, July 28) deemed necessary as a result of the emancipation of Negroes following the Civil War.

The Fifteenth Amendment was rejected, and not subsequently ratified, by California, Kentucky, Maryland, Oregon, and Tennessee.

On March 31, 1949, the Maryland legislature enacted a law which (as construed) provided that no person could become a candidate for election unless he took an oath that he was not a person engaged "in one way or another in the attempt to overthrow the government by force or violence" and that he was not "knowingly" a member of an organization engaged in such an attempt. That law was sustained by a unanimous Supreme Court.

Prior to January 19, 1918, the Constituent Assembly in Soviet Russia was composed of several parties. On that date Lenin dissolved the Assembly, putting an end to parliamentary government. From that time on Russia reverted to a police state, governed by a small select group called the communist party. Lenin formulated a program of political action to foment world revolution. The instrument was the Comintern (Third International), formed in 1919. It was merely an agent of the communist party, subordinate to it and doing its will. It was, moreover, completely Russian; and in its long history no alien ever became more than a figurehead in the organization.

The Comintern furnished the link between Russian and communist revolutionaries in every country. All communist parties came under its orders and changed their tune and tactics to conform with Russia's strategy. Moreover, the Comintern did not believe in persuasion, debate, and control by majorities. Its political instruments were force and violence; it believed in seizure of control by a minority and the liquidation of any opposition; it made plain that the loyalty of every communist in the world must be to Moscow.

The Comintern was dissolved by Stalin in 1943 to make alliance with Russia for prosecution of the war against Germany more palatable. Probably the Comintern never died. In any event, by 1947 the Cominform had taken its place and renewed class warfare throughout the world.

Those political aims and tactics are at war with American political traditions. That is the reason why those who profess and practice the communist cause can be barred from the ballot in this country.

284

APRIL

In the 1940's and '50's, people charged with being communists or subversives sometimes had difficulty in getting good lawyers to represent them. There was first the fear that the defendants might try to interfere with the defense and use the trial for propaganda purposes. Second was the feeling of reluctance among lawyers to act by reason of the temper of public opinion.

Some bar associations took action, most notable of which was Maryland. The Maryland Bar recognized the menace of communism. It also recognized that even a communist should receive a "fair trial," which includes representation "by competent and reputable counsel." Counsel does not always share the philosophy of his client; in fact he may be quite opposed to it. But the public and his other clients "may gravely misinterpret his action" and conclude that if he represents a "subversive," he must also be one. Therefore, the Maryland Bar concluded that the wise way was for defense lawyers to be appointed. Accordingly, it made an historic resolution in 1952:

"We recommend that on the request of any person charged with being a communist or subversive person in criminal or in disbarment or in other proceedings, this Association shall appoint one or more lawyers to represent such a person and that such appointment and the reason therefore be made public. Any such appointment would be subject to the condition that the lawyer be free to defend the case in such manner as to him seems proper as an officer of the court."

Stephen Colledge was tried in England for treason in 1681. While confined in the Tower, counsel had visited him and he had made notes on some points of law. At the trial he asked the return of those papers, which was denied. He asked for a copy of the indictment, the names of the jury, and a lawyer to defend him. These were denied him. He was told by the court that if during the trial any question of law was raised on which he needed legal advice, the court would appoint a lawyer.

"Are you guilty or not guilty?"

"I cannot plead first. I must lose my life, if I must. I neither know who accuses me, nor what it is they accuse me of."

Colledge, forced to plead without benefit of counsel, pleaded not guilty and stood trial alone. He cross-examined witnesses of the King and called witnesses of his own. He groped in the darkness of ignorance for the nice points of the law of treason— whether two witnesses were needed, whether carrying a pistol was levying war. He fought the judges throughout the trial, and his plea to the jury could not match the thundering of the prosecutor. The trial today reads like a mockery.

The judges betrayed "their poor client," the defendant, for "their better client," the King.

The jury found him guilty. He was sentenced to be hanged by the neck, cut down alive, his privy members cut off, his bowels taken out and burned before his face, his head cut off, and his body divided into four quarters.

In case of minor crimes (misdemeanors) the accused had the right to counsel from the days of Henry I. But he was denied counsel when he needed counsel most. In 1695, Parliament finally gave a person accused of treason the right to counsel and the right to compel the attendance of witnesses (November 7).

The Fifteenth Amendment forbids both the federal government and the States from denying citizens the right to vote "on account of race, color, or previous condition of servitude"; and the Fourteenth Amendment forbids the States from denying any person "the equal protection of the laws." When Texas passed a statute making Negroes ineligible to vote in the Democratic primary, the Supreme Court held that action was denial of equal protection.

The Texas legislature then gave each political party power to prescribe the voting qualifications for primary elections. The Democratic party in Texas limited the primaries to white people only. That action was also condemned by the Supreme Court, which held that it was a "state" action within the meaning of the Fourteenth and Fifteenth Amendments (June 21).

Once more the Texas procedure was altered. This time the Texas legislature passed no law. But the Texas Democratic convention ruled that Negroes were ineligible to vote in the primaries. The Supreme Court in 1935 held that action to be private action, not "state" action, within the meaning of the *Constitution*. Thus the "white primary" became constitutional.

In 1944, a new Court reconsidered the question. On April 3, 1944, it reversed the 1935 decision and outlawed the "white primary." Primaries, the Court held, are conducted under state authority and regulation and are an integral part of the election machinery of the States. In the South, the Democratic primary has indeed been the decisive contest, for the winner of that election has almost invariably won the general election.

In 1952, there were 1,213,472 registered voters in Florida, of whom 120,913 were Negroes.

In 1952, there were 1,009,655 registered voters in Louisiana, of whom 97,101 were Negroes.

A liberal estimate is that in 1952, 1,100,000 Negroes were registered voters in the twelve southern states.

On April 4, 1800, our first *Bankruptcy Act* was passed. The panic of 1792 had been followed by the crash of 1797 as a result of land speculation. Robert Morris, who financed the Revolution, owed 12 million dollars and was in a debtors' prison. A Justice of the Supreme Court, James Wilson, moved from Pennsylvania to North Carolina to avoid a like fate. The debtor interests got the law passed. It covered only traders, not farmers or manufacturers. It was used by Robert Morris to get out of jail and it relieved several hundred other speculators. It was short-lived, being repealed in 1803.

The panic of 1837 produced the *Bankruptcy Act* of 1841. That Act was in force only a little over a year, some 33,000 debtors taking advantage of it. The panic of 1857 produced new demands for a *Bankruptcy Act*. Then came the war, after which the northern creditors of southern debtors pressed for a new law by which they could cut under local stay laws and collect their debts. This led to the 1867 Act, which lasted only until 1878. It came into considerable disrepute as a result of defective administration and charges of its fraudulent use. The panic of 1893 renewed the demand for relief. Our present Act dates from 1898. Though frequently amended, it has survived.

Panics and depressions have always been associated with agitation for bankruptcy legislation. Prior to the 1898 Act, each *Bankruptcy Act* was repealed when business conditions improved. Since 1898, a *Bankruptcy Act* has ceased being a temporary, emergency measure. Since then it has applied to non-traders as well as to traders; it can be invoked by the debtor as well as by creditors; it provides for creditor participation and for discharge of the debtor.

Underlying all of our bankruptcy laws is the philosophy expressed by Henry Clay in 1840:

"I maintain that the public right of the State in all the faculties of its members, moral and physical, is paramount to any supposed rights which appertain to a private creditor."

The bankruptcy power of Congress historically was used to liquidate the assets of a debtor, distribute the proceeds among the creditors, and discharge the debtor from any further responsibility for his obligations. In modern times it has also been used to rehabilitate or reorganize the debtor, scaling down his debts and continuing him in business.

In the '20's and '30's, farmers were in great distress. Farm prices fell, while manufactured prices remained high. Farmers found it impossible to pay the charges accruing under existing mortgages. Wholesale foreclosures were imminent. Congress in 1933 wrote a farmer-debtor relief provision into the *Bankruptcy Act*. In substance it stayed foreclosure, kept the debtor in possession for five years, required him to pay a reasonable rental while in possession, and allowed him to acquire the property by paying the appraised value.

In 1935, the Supreme Court held the law unconstitutional because it took away from the creditor the right to retain his lien and the right to a judicial sale. That was held to be a taking of private property in violation of the Fifth Amendment. After Congress restored those rights, the Court sustained the law. That was in 1937.

Then started a period of construction of the law which was friendly to the debtor. While the creditor could foreclose, the debtor could get an extension of time in which to redeem the property. Moreover, he could have the property appraised and redeem it at that price before it was sold. Thus the right to foreclose was cut down drastically. But the creditor was protected to the extent of the value of the property. "There is no constitutional claim of the creditor to more than that."

In 1934, Congress amended the *Bankruptcy Act* so as to allow municipalities and public corporations, such as water improvement districts, to work out plans of readjustment in the federal courts.

At the time of the passage of the law between 2,000 and 4,000 municipal corporations in 41 States had defaulted on bonds amounting to nearly 3 billion dollars.

Many communities were demoralized by their financial problems; bondholders had no effective remedy. Communities which could pay 50 per cent, if the debts were pared down, were paying nothing. State laws could not cut the debts down because the *Constitution* says no State shall pass any law "impairing the Obligation of Contracts." So it was that creditors and debtors alike turned to Congress for relief under the *Bankruptcy Act.*

The Supreme Court in 1936, by a five to four decision, struck down the law. Even though the municipal corporation had voluntarily sought relief in bankruptcy, the Court held it could not obtain it. To allow relief, the Court said, would be to permit the federal government to exercise control over the "fiscal affairs" of municipalities and thus infringe state sovereignty!

In 1938, the Court changed its position. Chief Justice Hughes, who dissented earlier, now had a majority with him. Voluntary plans of readjustment filed under the federal *Bankruptcy Act* by municipal corporations, with the consent of the State, were held not to infringe state sovereignty. "The State acts in aid, and not in derogation, of its sovereign powers," when it asks the federal court "to save its agency," which the State is powerless to save.

Near the beginning of the nineteenth century, agitation mounted for removal of property qualifications for voters which the Colonies had taken over from England. Massachusetts led the way with a constitutional amendment ratified and adopted, April 1821. New York shortly followed, lifting the requirement for property qualifications from all except colored people. These were the beginnings of the movement that eventually swept most of the States.

The movement met powerful opposition. Chancellor James Kent of New York referred to universal suffrage as an "extreme democratic principle" that has been regarded "with terror, by the wise men of every age." Universal suffrage, he argued, was "too mighty an excitement for the moral constitution of men to endure"; and it had the tendency "to jeopardize the rights of property, and the principles of liberty."

Up in Massachusetts, Daniel Webster led the fight against the people. "In the nature of things, those who have not property and see their neighbors possess much more than they think them to need, cannot be favorable to laws made for the protection of property. When this class becomes numerous, it grows clamorous. It looks on property as its prey and plunder, and is naturally ready, at times, for violence and revolution. It would seem then to be the part of political wisdom to found government on property."

The opponents of universal suffrage forgot (or chose not to remember) the teaching of the *Declaration of Independence,* "That to secure these rights, Governments are instituted among Men, deriving their just powers from the consent of the governed."

In 1951 and 1952, there was a serious dispute in the steel industry over the terms and conditions to be included in new collective bargaining agreements. The unions and the employers could not agree. Federal mediation agencies failed to settle the controversy. On April 4, 1952, the United Steel Workers of America, C.I.O., gave notice of a nationwide strike beginning April 9. On April 8, 1952, a few hours before the strike was to begin, Truman issued an executive order directing the Secretary of Commerce to take possession of most of the steel mills and keep them running.

Truman gave as his principal reasons for the seizure the necessity of keeping American troops in Korea and elsewhere supplied with weapons and materials, and the importance of a continuing supply of steel to defense efforts at home and to the maintenance of the economy.

The Secretary of Commerce issued orders directing the steel companies to carry on their activities in accordance with his directions. Suits were brought to enjoin the Secretary of Commerce from carrying out the seizure program. The Supreme Court ruled that Truman's action was unauthorized. There were Acts of Congress which permitted seizure of plants under certain conditions. But those conditions had not been met. If the President had authority to act, it was to be found in the *Constitution*. The Court rejected the argument that the *Constitution* granted the seizure power to the President. The Court held that the seizure was an act of lawmaking which under the *Constitution* is a function of Congress, not the Chief Executive.

The decision is probably the most important one in our history concerning the separation of powers between the President and the Congress, and the role of the Court in enforcing the separation.

On April 9, 1919, shortly after the end of World War I, Nebraska passed a law making it a crime for any person in any school, public or private, to teach any subject in any language other than English. One Meyer was convicted under that law for teaching a collection of Bible stories in German at a Lutheran parochial school. The Supreme Court reversed that conviction, holding that "liberty" within the meaning of the Fourteenth Amendment includes the right of a student to acquire useful knowledge and the right of a teacher to teach in his medium. The Court recognized the interest of the States in making sure that all students receive a solid understanding of the English language. But in the interests of academic freedom, it refused to close doors that might be opened only with another language.

294

The public school system, which today is firmly a part of the American tradition, did not arrive full blown. It is indeed the result of many battles of almost innumerable political campaigns. New England led the way (plus New York and later Ohio) with its Colonial colleges, academies, and grammar schools. The middle and southern colonies lagged behind. Jefferson's program for a complete public school system for Virginia failed. In this region the main educational effort was left to private schools and to parochial schools. For the most part, the State stepped in only in case of paupers, for whom it created separate schools. Moreover, Rhode Island, New Jersey, North Carolina, and other States to the south and west operated on the theory that education was no business of government.

The pauper school came from English rule. It belonged to a society built along class lines. It had friends among aristocrats, big taxpayers, and supporters of church and private schools. Those imbued with Jefferson's ideas were opposed to the segregation of the children of the poor for purposes of education. The intellect, they maintained, bore no mark of rich or poor; pauper schools were incompatible with the democratic ideal. It was along these lines that the battle was waged.

The major campaign was waged in Pennsylvania. The victory over the pauper school forces was won by Thaddeus Stevens, then in the Pennsylvania legislature. This fiery man, later to vent his spleen on the South and on Andrew Johnson in the Reconstruction days (May 16), prevented repeal of a law which provided for a public school system. Opponents of the law had the votes and carried the Senate. On April 10, 1835, Stevens spoke in the House against the pauper school law, which he derisively labeled "An Act for Branding and Marking the Poor." His eloquence turned defeat of a public school system into victory. What Pennsylvania did was the beginning of the end of the pauper school, both north and south.

"No school . . . in which any religious sectarian doctrine shall be taught . . . shall receive any portion of the school moneys." This provision of a New York law passed April 11, 1842 was a significant victory in the battle to eliminate sectarianism from public schools. Like provisions were later put into the constitutions of the several States.

In our earliest days, education of the young was left to the church. The state, indeed, looked to the church to provide the necessary education and assisted it through donations of land and money. It took a long and bitter struggle to change that pattern. The reasons for the change were numerous: The flow of immigration and the development of cities resulted in the intermingling of peoples of many different faiths. This led to the necessity of respecting rights of minorities and of tolerating their religious freedom as well as the majority's. Moreover, independence and the growing responsibilities of the new nation created a new political motive for education. It was realized that the ideals of the *Declaration of Independence*—liberty and equality—could not be preserved without general education for all the people.

The fight of religious groups for a continuing share of school funds was one of the most acrimonious in our history. It tore communities apart and promised to build strife and bitterness out of religious differences. There was, however, a growing awareness of the full meaning of the constitutional command that the state should establish no religion. State financial support was an establishment of religion wholly at war with the First Amendment (December 24). New York's victory in 1842 was an eloquent testimonial to faith in that democratic ideal.

The Gideons work "to win men and women for the Lord Jesus Christ" through various means, which include "placing the *Bible* —God's Holy word . . . or portions thereof in hotels, hospitals, schools, institutions, and also through distribution of same for personal use." The *Bible* they distribute is the King James version. The Board of Education of Rutherford, New Jersey, authorized the Gideons to distribute copies of the *Bible* in its public schools to all children who wished a copy.

Two parents—one of the Jewish faith, one of the Catholic— brought suit, challenging the constitutionality of the action of the Board of Education. In 1953, the Supreme Court of New Jersey held that the introduction of the *Bible* into the public schools would violate the principle of separation of church and state embodied in the First Amendment to the federal *Constitution*. It would, the court ruled, establish one religious sect in preference to another. Judaism does not accept the *New Testament* as a sacred book. The *Bible* of Judaism is the *Old Testament*. Catholics bar the King James version, using instead the Douay version. The court held, therefore, that the King James version is a sectarian book.

To put the weight of the State behind one sectarian book would, in the eyes of the New Jersey court, renew "the ancient struggles among the various religious faiths to the detriment of all."

The fact that the *Bible*, so much a part of our heritage, is involved has made many people disagree with the New Jersey court. Would they not feel differently if the school board had introduced into the public schools the *Koran* or the *Bhagavad-Gita* instead of the *Bible*?

A board of education in New Jersey reimbursed parents for money expended by them for the transportation of their children to school on public busses. Included were parents who sent their children to Catholic parochial schools. It was claimed that this was in substance the levying of a tax to support religious activities. In 1947, a sharply divided Court held that it was not, that it was no more forbidden than the furnishing of police and fire protection to all schools, public and religious alike, or requiring local transit companies to carry all school children at reduced rates.

In 1952, another closely divided Court upheld a "released time" program for New York City schools. This program, unlike an earlier one that was condemned (March 8), involved neither religious instruction in the classroom of public schools nor expenditure of public funds for the purpose. The religious instruction was off the public premises; no child was forced to attend; no coercion was employed by the public schools to get the children into religious classes.

The First Amendment does not require the state and the churches to be aliens to each other. Policemen can help parishioners into their churches, prayers can be said in legislatures, Thanksgiving Day can be proclaimed, "So help me God" can be used in the courtroom without violating the First Amendment.

"When the state encourages religious instruction or cooperates with religious authorities by adjusting the schedule of public events to sectarian needs, it follows the best of our traditions. For it then respects the religious nature of our people and accommodates the public service to their spiritual needs."

"We are a religious people whose institutions presuppose a Supreme Being."

Walter M. Pierce, schoolteacher, farmer, lawyer, and politician, was long a stormy influence in Oregon's affairs. As Governor he strengthened the initiative and referendum, defeated a sales tax, and created a climate of opinion for a graduated income tax. Due in large measure to his activities, Oregon today has one of the fairest tax systems in the nation. At the age of seventy-one he started a second public career by running for Congress, where he served for ten years ending in 1943 after a defeat. In Congress he sponsored chiefly conservation measures and public power. His bill on the Bonneville Dam, introduced April 14, 1937, granted a preference and priority to public bodies and co-operatives in the electric energy generated at Bonneville—a provision that was included in the legislation finally enacted (May 11).

The construction of Bonneville and the inclusion of this preference and priority provision were in a real sense the culmination of a long crusade. For years he had campaigned for public power in Oregon. During most of this time he operated wheat ranches heavily mortgaged under loans of 8 per cent interest. In the early 1930's, a stranger came to his ranch near La Grande, Oregon, and said, "You are heavily in debt." "What business of yours is that?" asked Pierce. "Well," said the stranger, "you can save your farms if you'll quit campaigning for public power." "And if I don't?" asked Pierce. "You'll lose your farm," was the answer.

Pierce, who died in 1954 at the age of ninety-two, was an old man when he told me this story. "What did you do?" I asked. The fire of the crusade was in his eyes. "What did I do?" he retorted. "I chased the guy off my place and kept talking for public power." And then he said, "I paid for it. In a few weeks they closed me out. Lost everything. Had to start again from scratch." After a pause he added wistfully, "I lost all my property for my convictions. But I didn't stop fighting."

The cause was in his blood. When he was over ninety, he wrote, "I shall *always* fight for public ownership and operation of public utilities."

History is filled with instances where the state has interfered in the affairs of a church, preferring one group over another, banishing an order, or prescribing standards for the clergy. Thus Bismarck expelled the Jesuits and undertook to purge the Catholic episcopate of men who might not be wholly sympathetic with his program.

The problem has had many manifestations on this continent, one example of which concerns the authority of the courts to settle disputes between warring groups within one church.

Last century, the Presbyterian Church was torn by the slavery issue. The anti-slavery group brought an action to obtain possession of the Walnut Street Church in Louisville. The court that could determine which group should have possession would choose the exponents of the true faith, by divesting one group of the temporal property that follows spiritual authority and vesting it in the other. The power to do that would throw the weight of the state to one or another faction, as shifting political or national interests might indicate. It would result in the courts doing here what Bismarck did in Germany.

On April 15, 1872, the Supreme Court ruled that it would enforce the rights of members in the Presbyterian Church, temporal and religious, only in accordance with the rulings of the highest church judicatory. Since the General Assembly of the Church had recognized the anti-slavery group as the lawful Walnut Street Church, the Court accepted that ruling as final and binding.

The same principle was used in 1952 to strike down a New York law which granted a cathedral to an American branch of the Russian Orthodox Church against the claim of the Moscow patriarchate. A cleric who undertakes subversive action is not protected by his robe or his pulpit. But there was no evidence that the Moscow patriarchate was using the New York cathedral for subversive purposes. Legislative determination of which group in the hierarchical church was entitled to the cathedral violated our rule of separation of church and state.

The *Bill of Rights* forbids Congress (and the States) not only from establishing a religion but also from prohibiting the "free exercise thereof." Suppose a religious cult made a rite out of the sacrifice of human beings. Could that practice be enjoined? Could a priest who killed a human being as part of a "religious" service be tried for murder? Once on a walking trip through the Mountains of Lebanon in the Middle East, I came to Afka, where there are ruins of an ancient temple of Venus. Centuries ago, worshipers of Aphrodite met there and as part of their rites indulged in promiscuous sexual intercourse, marked by frequent changes of partners. If a "religious" cult adopted that practice, would the members be immune from prosecution for fornication or adultery?

The Supreme Court gave a definitive answer to those questions in 1878, when it decided the famous Mormon cases. Once upon a time polygamy was part of the Mormon religion. Under the common law bigamy, i.e., marriage to more than one spouse, was a crime. Mormons with plural wives were prosecuted for bigamy under an Act of Congress applicable to the Territory of Utah. They defended that polygamy, being a "religious" duty, was protected from governmental interference by the First Amendment.

The Supreme Court rejected that defense. It reviewed the history of polygamy, showing that it had long been "odious" to Western civilization and therefore no proper part of a "religion." A "religious" rite which violates standards of Christian ethics and morality is not in the true sense, in the constitutional sense, included within "religion," the "free exercise" of which is guaranteed by the *Bill of Rights*.

Michigan was the first State to deal with destitute and delinquent children in a comprehensive manner. A committee headed by S. S. Cutler made a report in 1871. It found the insane, the idiots, the dissolute living with the other paupers. There were several hundred children with these paupers, mixed in with prostitutes, drunkards, and beggars.

Acting swiftly, on April 17, 1871, Michigan authorized a public school for these pauper children. It was established at Coldwater in 1874.

In 1874, William P. Letchworth of the New York State Board of Charities made an historic report. His report was based on a personal investigation. He found 615 children in poorhouses. Of these 348 were over two and under ten, 124 over ten and under sixteen. Seventy-nine had pauper grandparents, 546 had pauper parents, and 190 had been born in the poorhouse.

Letchworth found in the poorhouse "seeds of idleness, shiftlessness, immorality, and vice" that were "sown in the rich soil of childhood." The girl reared there was frequently the mother and grandmother "of a race of paupers or criminals." The boy became a "semi-vagrant" who frequently ended in prison.

He urged that children be removed "from association with paupers and poorhouse life and its stigma." He recommended a system of placing these children in homes, carefully selected; if not in private homes, then in orphan asylums.

As a result of Letchworth's report, New York passed its Children's Law of 1875, making it unlawful to put or keep children between the ages of three and sixteen in a poorhouse, with the exception of idiots, epileptics, paralytics, or others unfit for family care.

Michigan and New York opened a new chapter in child welfare history.

On April 18, 1933, Minnesota enacted a law placing a short-term moratorium on mortgage foreclosures, which in substance allowed mortgagors to remain temporarily in possession of the property after default, on payment of the reasonable rental value or income of the property as determined by the state court. The *Constitution* provides that no State shall pass any law impairing the obligation of contracts. The constitutionality of the mortgage moratorium law was challenged on that ground (April 6).

In 1934, the Supreme Court, in a five to four decision, sustained the law. It said that while a state could not repudiate debts or destroy contracts, it could interpose limited and temporary restraints on enforcement of contracts if that course was deemed necessary by physical disasters, such as fires and floods, or economic disasters, such as depressions.

From the beginning, the States passed stay laws for the relief of debtors. These laws suspended suits on claims for a period, extended the time for foreclosure of mortgages, enlarged the categories of property which creditors could not reach, etc. Periods of panic or depression usually produced a flood of these stay laws. Most of them were held invalid by the state courts. But usually it took years to get a court decision. In the interim, the stay laws gave temporary protection, and conserved the property of debtors from forced sales. Beginning in 1878, the Supreme Court struck down those stay laws, holding that a law of a State passed after a contract is executed, which so affects the remedy as to impair substantially the value of the contract, is forbidden.

The decision in 1934 concerning the Minnesota mortgage moratorium thus represented a swing away from the earlier decisions, in recognition of the fact that "vital public interests" may make it necessary in times of crises for a State to stay the hands of creditors while debtors get their breath. Hughes was the new spokesman.

Connecticut did not ratify the *Bill of Rights* until April 19, 1939. Georgia did the same only on March 18, 1939, and Massachusetts on March 2, 1939.

The failure of these States to ratify short of 150 years is no measure of their interest in civil liberties. Massachusetts failed to act because when the Amendments were submitted in 1790 the legislators became involved in an attempt to propose the inclusion of even more civil rights. The two legislative Houses in Connecticut were divided on the Amendments, both in 1789 and in 1790. In Georgia, the records are incomplete. The final word was in a report of a joint committee of the two Houses: ". . . the proposed amendments to the defective parts of the *Constitution* of the United States, and which are particularly the object of, and referred to in the said communication; cannot be effectually pointed out, but by experience, therefore . . ."

Ratification by these three States became unnecessary when Virginia's approval in 1791 made the *Bill of Rights* a part of the *Constitution.* That doubtless was the reason why the matter was forgotten. But 1939 was the 150th anniversary of the *Bill of Rights.* Forces were loose in the world which symbolized the mounting threat to the liberty of all men. As Governor Leverett Saltonstall of Massachusetts said in his message proposing ratification, "Totalitarian countries, where bills of right have been abandoned, are seeking to spread their rule ever wider. And there is the further danger of failure by some divisions of the government to respect the spirit of the *Bill of Rights* in their dealings with minorities and with individual citizens."

1939 was, indeed, an appropriate time for rededication to the principles of our *Bill of Rights.*

304

The Australian ballot has four features: It is printed by the government at public expense; it includes the names of all the candidates who have been lawfully nominated; it can be obtained only within the polling place from election officials; it is marked by the voter in the secrecy of the voting booth.

It was adopted by Victoria in 1856, New South Wales, South Australia, and Tasmania in 1858, New Zealand in 1870, England in 1872, and Western Australia in 1877.

In the early days, politics was a low-grade business. There was much bribery and intimidation at the polls, and there was much manipulation of the ballots by the bosses.

The failure to provide an official ballot gave rise to spurious ballots and ballot box stuffing. When the printing of the ballots was left to party managers, many frauds cropped up. Failure to print at public expense also increased the burden of campaigns. The absence of a requirement for secret ballots resulted in many voting places being riotous and disorderly. There was need of a secret ballot to protect laborers, since employers often stood watch to see which of their men voted the "wrong" way. Many a man had his mortgage foreclosed on him because his vote was known. When the balloting was not secret, bribery was encouraged. For the party supervisor, who had paid for the vote, could see to it that the voter performed his promise.

Today all States have the Australian ballot. It was first adopted for municipal elections in Louisville, Kentucky, early in 1888. Later that year Massachusetts adopted it on a state-wide basis. The last of the States—South Carolina—adopted it April 20, 1950.

On April 21, 1899, Illinois enacted the pioneer statute establishing a Juvenile Court. Thereafter the delinquent child was treated not as a criminal, but as a neglected or dependent person. That was the beginning of a revolutionary approach to the problems of the transgressor. Courts became less and less concerned with questions of criminal responsibility, guilt, and punishment of minors, and more and more with the causes of abnormal behavior, with guidance and protection, with correction or rehabilitation.

The other States followed Illinois' example. By the mid-twentieth century we had some outstanding judicial clinics on juvenile delinquency. Many people made notable contributions to the subject. But Sheldon and Eleanor Glueck of Harvard probably head the list.

The administration of a juvenile delinquency system calls more for knowledge of medicine, psychiatry, sociology, slums, unemployment, and marital problems than of law. The problems of human behavior, and the myriad motives behind it, touch all aspects of human nature. Some transgressors need only friendly admonishment; others need a tight rein and close supervision. Boy Scouts, boys' clubs, baseball and other sports and recreations are powerful preventives.

William G. Long, a wise judge who has presided over Seattle's Juvenile Court for many years, treats his courtroom as a clinic, his staff as orderlies and nurses, the jail as a temporary detention ward in a hospital.

Once I asked him how many mend their ways. He told how difficult it is to get reliable statistics, how nearly impossible it is to follow these delinquents into their maturity. At the end of our talk he summed up his long experience in these words, "Most boys and girls grow up."

Giving boys and girls a chance to "grow up," freed from the stigma of the criminal law, is perhaps the greatest advance the law has made this century.

In 1837, a butcher boy in England suffered a broken leg when a wagon he was driving collapsed. The accident occurred because the wagon was overloaded and in a bad state of repair. The butcher boy sued his employer for damages on account of the injury. He was denied recovery because another employee had been at fault. This was the fellow servant rule, under which an injured workman was denied damages from his employer, if a fellow servant in any way contributed to the injury.

The rule lost no time in crossing the Atlantic. Judges maintained that any other rule would encourage carelessness among employees, and subject employers to ruinous responsibilities. The courts also created the rule of assumption of risk. That rule placed on the employee all the known or obvious risks of the job. These included not only the accidents that were nobody's fault, but dangerous possibilities which, though created by the employer's negligence, were known to the workman. Moreover, the courts barred recovery even when the employer was negligent, if the employee's negligence contributed to the injury.

As Theodore Roosevelt said, these were oppressive rules, placing upon workmen a "frightful hardship," which employers, through insurance or otherwise, could the better bear.

These rules were gradually changed, mostly by the legislatures. Some of the changes date back to the middle of the last century. One of the most significant victories was on April 22, 1908, when, under Theodore Roosevelt's urging, the *Federal Employers' Liability Act,* governing the liability of interstate railroads, was passed. The fellow servant rule, assumption of risk, and contributory negligence were abolished as defenses. The carrier was liable for injury or death to its employees resulting in whole or in part from acts of negligence of any of its officers, agents, or employees. If the injured employee was also negligent, the amount of his recovery was reduced proportionately.

Thus, part of the dreadful load which industrial accidents and the law had placed on workmen was lifted.

In 1821, the Supreme Court upheld the power of the House of Representatives to hold in contempt a non-member for attempting to bribe the chairman of a committee. The right to imprison him, *so long as but no longer than the Congress was in session,* was also sustained.

On April 23, 1917, the Court held this power did not go to the extent of enabling the House to hold in contempt a United States Attorney, who wrote a letter, charging that a subcommittee of the Judiciary Committee was endeavoring to interfere with investigations being made by a grand jury. The writing of the letter was held to be no obstruction to the performance of the legislative functions of the House.

In 1935, the Court held the Senate had the power to punish for contempt a witness charged with having permitted the removal and destruction of papers which he had been subpoenaed to produce before a Senate committee. Here, the destruction of the papers was "of a nature to obstruct the legislative process." The fact that the witness later had repented and delivered all papers that remained was held to be without legal significance. The power of Congress "to punish a private citizen for a past and completed act" had been asserted from the beginning, even before the Revolution, by the colonial assemblies, which followed the precedent of the House of Commons.

The Court also held that either House of Congress could punish a citizen for contempt, even though the same act was an offense under a federal statute for which the citizen might also be prosecuted. Under the latter, he would, of course, get all the protection of a criminal trial, including the right to a jury. In a contempt proceeding before Congress, those safeguards would not be present; he would be tried in a summary way.

Were your parents born in the United States of America?
Are you a Gentile or Jew?
Do you believe in the principles of pure Americanism?
Do you owe ANY KIND of allegiance to any foreign nation,
government, institution, sect, people, ruler, or person?

This was the questionnaire sponsored by the Ku Klux Klan in the early 20's. It was aimed primarily at the Roman Catholics, secondarily at the Jews. In the 1920's, Alfred E. Smith, a Catholic, was being groomed for the Presidency. The Ku Klux Klan made violent protests. When the Democrats nominated Smith in 1928, the Klan helped defeat him.

One exponent of intolerance in those days was Senator Tom Heflin of Alabama. After the defeat of Smith, he continued the campaign against the Catholics and brought to the floor of the Senate a resolution asking the Senators to vote "whether they are for the American Government or for the Roman Catholic Church. . . . Romanism and Americanism! They are in deadly conflict in this country."

On April 24, 1929, Borah of Idaho answered Heflin in one of the great speeches in our annals:

"It is not enough that we merely refrain from passing laws which work intolerance, but in our social life, in our political life, we are to heed the spirit which is incorporated in the Constitution. There, too, intolerance should be banished. . . .

"There is nothing that dies so hard and rallies so often as intolerance. The vices and passions which it summons to its support are the most ruthless and the most persistent harbored in the human breast. They sometimes sleep but they never seem to die. Anything, any extraordinary situation, any unnecessary controversy, may light those fires again and plant in our Republic that which has destroyed every republic which undertook to nurse it."

In 1908, Taft was opposed for the Presidency on the grounds that he was a Unitarian. Roosevelt met the criticism head on:

"Is he a good man, and is he fit for the office? These are the only questions which there is a right to ask."

Censorship of the English stage is as old as the English drama. In the seventeenth century, the censor was the Master of the Revels. He would rewrite lines to take out ideas which were politically offensive or which offended the Church. Under Charles I, the censor struck out the following lines spoken by the heroine who was being pursued by a lecherous clergyman:

> *Helpe, angells, helpe*
> *To thrust this divell from your oracles,*
> *This forbids whoredom, lust, adulterie,*
> *And yet persuades to vilifie the bed*
> *Of holy wedlocke.*

The words "yfaith," "troth," and "by the Lord" were also stricken. Also all reference to political episodes that might annoy or embarrass the King.

In the days of the Star Chamber, that court punished those who made sport of the Church. One prosecution was against John Yorke, his wife, and others for permitting a traveling company to perform in Yorke's house a play which portrayed a dispute between a priest and a minister. The weapon of the minister was the *Bible*, that of the priest was the Cross. The priest won the argument and was carried off by an angel. The devil carried off the minister. The play was much applauded. Yorke was not a Catholic and he apparently did not know beforehand the nature of the play. But since he did not interrupt or reprove the players, he was fined £1,000. His wife and guests, who included Catholics, were also heavily fined.

Today, censorship of the stage in America is more subtle. A producer who has a large investment in a production will not want to take a chance on being closed down by the police. The theater owner does not want to lose his license. The experience in New York City with *The Captive* was warning enough. *The Captive* is a play about a Lesbian and her attachment to another woman who never appears on the stage. This attachment is stronger than the wife's love of her husband. It is indeed so great it ruins her marriage. Critics applauded the play. So did clergymen and psychiatrists. After it had run nearly five months, the District Attorney arrested the producers and the actors, including Basil Rathbone and Helen Menken, on the charge that the play tended to corrupt the morals. Later he withdrew the charge on condition that the play not be produced until some court decided it was not in violation of the law. The battle was transferred to the courts, where it ended inconclusively.

The power of these informal sanctions is great. It was the reason Mayor James M. Curley of Boston was able, forty years ago, to keep from the stage the Belasco play *Marie-Odile*. For he put a ban on suggestive jokes and songs and on "coochy" and "other suggestive dances."

"For ever the fat of the whole foundation hangeth on the priests' beards."

So wrote Simon Fish in 1529 in his famous tract, *A Supplication for the Beggars.* This tract, which Sir Thomas More answered in *Supplication of Souls,* is a violent attack on the monasteries.

Fish called the clergy "sturdy, idle, holy thieves." They had collected vast wealth for over 400 years through tithes and through fees for various church ceremonies. These "locusts," he said, also owned one third of all the land, although in number they were only a quarter of 1 per cent of the population.

Fish charged the clergy with immorality, as St. Bonaventura and Durand had done before him. He pointed out how they had woven church and state together for the perpetuation of their own power. They were strong politically, beating down their opposition through heresy trials and excommunication. What was the remedy? Whip "these holy, idle thieves," and make them get "their living with their labor in the sweat of their faces."

In 1536, Thomas Cromwell confiscated the smaller monasteries. Then to avoid the appearance of further confiscation, he negotiated with the larger monasteries for their surrender. He succeeded by hook or by crook, as he was resolved "to taste the fat priests." In 1539, an Act was passed confirming what had been done and vesting the surrendered properties in the King, who used the spoils to rebuild his political fences.

Today "the fat of the whole foundation hangeth" on the beards of priests, of princes, and of landlords in many parts of Asia and Africa. In some regions monasteries own 90 per cent of the land. In some nations a few families or a few people own practically the entire wealth. One man will own hundreds of villages; millions of people will work as virtual serfs for a few.

This is the kind of feudalism that Simon Fish proclaimed against in 1529. While Europe has had her revolution against it, Asia and Africa have not. That is why the most turbulent days are still to come. And when they do come, the diatribes of Simon Fish will seem calm and dispassionate compared with the forces which will be loosened.

An Act of Congress has long provided that no common carrier by rail should subject any person to any "undue or unreasonable prejudice or disadvantage." This was uniformly construed to mean that Negroes purchasing first-class tickets must be furnished with accommodations equal in comforts and conveniences to those afforded first-class white passengers.

On April 28, 1941, the Supreme Court enforced this statute on the complaint of a Negro Congressman, Arthur W. Mitchell, who was denied Pullman space in a car reserved for whites, and forcibly removed to a second-class coach reserved for Negroes.

The same result was later reached in a dining car case. Ten tables of four seats each were reserved exclusively and unconditionally for white passengers, and one table of four seats for Negroes. Between this table and the others, a curtain was drawn. The Court held this regulation to be in violation of the Act. If more than four Negroes wanted to eat at the same time, some would have to wait, even though there were vacancies elsewhere in the diner. A like deprivation would be imposed on whites if more than forty of them wanted to eat at the same time and there were vacancies at the Negro table. It was no answer to the particular passenger, who was denied service at an unoccupied place in the dining car that, on the average, persons like him were served. Under the statute each passenger is entitled to the right of equality of treatment.

In this country, Alaska is the pioneer in old age pensions. Arizona passed such a law in 1914, but it was declared unconstitutional. Berger, a Socialist, introduced an old age pension bill in Congress in 1911 providing for a maximum payment of $4.00 a week. It did not pass. The Alaska law, approved April 29, 1915, gave any "pioneer of Alaska, regardless of sex" who was sixty-five years old or more and in need, an option either to go to a government home or draw an amount not exceeding $12.50 a month.

By 1933, there were 25 States with old age pension plans, 19 of which were mandatory. The program got great impetus by the *Social Security Act* of 1935. By this Act, the federal government instituted a program of aid to those States which met prescribed standards. Employees and employers contributed to the plan. That law has been revised and broadened, but not basically changed. It applies today to people over sixty-five years old. Picking a month at random, during June 1953, 2,597,075 people in the forty-eight States and Territories received aid under the program, the average payment being $48.74.

One of the promoters of this program was Jane Addams of Hull House, who saw two forces—the prolongation of life and the tendency of industry to employ younger people—working to produce poverty in the aged and an attitude of indifference of the public toward them.

Another promoter was Abraham Epstein, dynamo of the American Association for Social Security. In the early '30's Dr. F. E. Townsend started a crusade for a federally guaranteed income of $200 a month for everyone over sixty who made less than $2,400 a year (provided he spent the money within thirty days in the United States). Others formed similar crusades. The driving power behind the federal old age pension plan that materialized was Franklin D. Roosevelt, who, in 1934, stated, "There is no tragedy in growing old, but there is tragedy in growing old without means of support."

During the American Revolution, North Carolina passed a law confiscating lands held by those sympathetic with the British cause and providing that if one who purchased the forfeited lands from the State were sued, the courts should dismiss the action.

In 1787, a North Carolina court held that the legislature could not finally determine that the buyer of the confiscated land had good title.

"Every citizen," it said, "had undoubtedly a right to a decision of his property by a trial by jury. For that if the Legislature could take away this right, and require him to stand condemned in his property without a trial, it might with as much authority require his life to be taken away without a trial by jury, and that he should stand condemned to die, without the formality of any trial at all; that if the members of the General Assembly could do this, they might with equal authority, not only render themselves the Legislators of the State for life, without any further election of the people, from thence transmit the dignity and authority of legislation down to their heirs male forever."

The right to a trial in a court of justice is deep in our tradition whether life, liberty, or property is at stake.

MAY

On May 1, 1946, a case was argued before the Supreme Court involving a novel question concerning the taking of private property for public use. A man had a small chicken farm near an airport in North Carolina. The Army used a runway ending not far from the farm, sending planes 67 feet above the house, 63 feet above the barn, and 18 feet above the highest tree. The noise was so great that many chickens were killed by flying into the walls from fright, and production fell off. The result was that the property could no longer be used as a chicken farm. The Court held that the government had taken an easement over the chicken farm for which it had to pay "just compensation," in accordance with the command of the Fifth Amendment.

The Supreme Court had held in 1833 that the Fifth Amendment barred only Congress, not the States, from confiscation. But after the Fourteenth Amendment was adopted (July 28), it ruled that the same guarantee had at last been furnished against state action also. Thus the emphasis in the *Constitution* upon property rights is great. A person may not be deprived of *property*, any more than *life* or *liberty*, without due process of law. Property rights are also involved in the Fourth Amendment (February 24). One's possessions are protected against unreasonable searches and seizures.

Property rights are important civil rights to the individual. His home, his library, his furniture and personal effects are part of his personality. His farm and office, his car and boat, his reputation and his right to work are his livelihood. "You take my life When you do take the means whereby I live," said Shylock. The *Magna Carta* is filled with safeguards against seizures of property. One provision reads, "No constable or other Our bailiff shall take corn or other chattels of any man without immediate payment for the same . . ."

The award to the North Carolina chicken farmer was therefore a response to influences deep in our law.

In 1880, the Supreme Court set aside a conviction of a Negro who was tried for murder in a State which, by statute, excluded Negroes from all juries. The Court held that the exclusion of Negroes from juries was a denial of the equal protection of the laws within the meaning of the Fourteenth Amendment. "The very idea of a jury," said the Court, "is a body of men composed of the peers or equals of the person whose rights it is selected or summoned to determine . . . his neighbors, fellows, associates, persons having the same legal status in society as that which he holds."

On May 2, 1881, the Court laid down the rule, since followed in a long line of cases, that convictions of Negroes will be set aside where members of that race have been purposefully and systematically excluded from either the grand jury (the one that returns the indictment) or the petit jury (the one that hears the case). In either case, Negroes are denied equal protection of the laws. This does not mean that a Negro defendant is entitled to have members of his race on the jury that indicts him or tries him. It does not mean that the jury must represent, proportionately, the various racial groups in the community. It only means that if the pool or panel from which juries are drawn is fairly to reflect the racial composition of the community, race or color cannot be the standard which determines eligibility for jury service.

One of the most recent devices for discrimination against Negroes in the selection of juries was through the use of white tickets for white people and yellow tickets for Negroes. The names of those eligible for jury duty would be placed on the tickets and the tickets placed in the jury box. The judge would then draw the required number from the box and hand them to the sheriff, who would prepare the list of those to be called for jury duty.

Of the sixty names drawn in one case to try a Negro for rape, the name of no Negro appeared, though 14 per cent of those eligible for jury duty were Negroes and though over 5 per cent of the tickets were yellow. Chief Justice Vinson held that the use of the white and yellow tickets gave such an opportunity for discrimination that their use to produce a panel of sixty on which there were no Negroes could not be taken as fortuitous, but established a *prima facie* case of discrimination. The conviction accordingly was set aside.

On May 3, 1954, the Supreme Court applied the same rule for the advantage of a Mexican convicted of murder in a Texas county. People of Mexican descent constituted 14 per cent of the population but they had been systematically excluded from juries.

"It taxes our credulity," said the Court, "to say that mere chance resulted in there being no members of this class among the over six thousand jurors called in the past 25 years."

The Fourteenth Amendment, adopted in 1868 (July 28), was designed to protect the Negroes in their newly won rights. That such was its purpose was too plain for argument when the first cases reached the courts. But in 1886, long before Negroes had received many of its blessings, the Amendment was suddenly construed by the Supreme Court to extend to corporations. The Court was so clear on the point that it announced its ruling without hearing argument.

The ruling was astounding. President Arthur T. Hadley of Yale wrote, "The Fourteenth Amendment was framed to protect the Negroes from oppression by the whites, not to protect corporations from oppression by the legislature." Whether or not the ruling was warranted has been debated to this day. Certain it is that it put the industrial corporation in the strongest constitutional position. That position was used to fight off wave after wave of social legislation.

The Fourteenth Amendment says that "persons born or naturalized" here are "citizens." A corporation cannot be such a "person." The Amendment bars a State from abridging the privileges or immunities of "citizens," which again excludes corporations. The Amendment commands the States not to deprive "any person of life, liberty, or property, without due process of law" nor to deny "any person" the equal protection of the laws. A corporation cannot be deprived of "life" or of "liberty" in the constitutional sense. Yet even though a corporation is not a "person" for most purposes of the Fourteenth Amendment, it suddenly emerges as a "person" when it comes to the protection afforded property interests.

Thus, a legal fiction exalted the corporate device and reshaped American life.

Life is filled with fictions—what Cardozo called "the consciously false." Adam Smith built a system of political science around an economic man. Karl Marx, Lenin, and Stalin took God and morality out of the cosmic scheme and constructed dialectical materialism. Our law has its reasonable man, its negligent man, its "for $1.00 and other valuable consideration."

We once recognized the liability of an inanimate thing. The instrument which caused a death was called a deodand. It was forfeited, valued, given to the church, and expended for the good of the soul of the deceased—whether the deodand was a knife or a horse. The liability of an inanimate thing survives in admiralty today. It is the ship that is liable. As the Court said long ago in an admiralty case, "The thing is here primarily considered as the offender; or rather the offense is primarily attached to the thing."

In 1774, a man sued in England for an assault committed on the Island of Minorca "to wit at London aforesaid, in the parish of St. Mary le Bow, in the ward of Cheap." Lord Mansfield held that placing the Island of Minorca in London was, of course, a fiction, but one which could not be rebutted. The court used the fiction to permit recovery in England for a wrong done beyond the seas.

The law often uses "the consciously false" to serve the ends of justice. Employers are held liable *as if* they were wrongdoers for injuries committed by those who work for them. Thus, injuries occurring in the course of employment are made part of the costs of doing business.

The struggle for liberty was not only against the executive; it was against the legislature as well. During the rule of Charles I, the *Petition of Right* was granted, establishing the principle that it was the legislature not the executive who had the power to determine the grounds on which men could be imprisoned (May 26). That issue was precipitated by the action of the King in jailing men who refused to loan him the money he wanted.

Robert Manwaring, a minister, defended the King in two sermons, saying that the King was not bound to observe the laws, that those who refused to make the loans did so "upon pain of eternal damnation," "offended against the law of God," and were "guilty of impiety, disloyalty, and rebellion," that the authority of Parliament was not necessary for the raising of money.

Parliament, flushed by its victory over the King, entertained a charge against Manwaring in 1629. The House of Lords impeached him. He was sentenced to jail and fined; suspended for three years from the ministry, disabled ever to hold office, and forced publicly to acknowledge his offense. Moreover, the books containing the sermons were burned (April 30).

Thus, the Framers of our *Bill of Rights* had reason to be fearful of encroachments by the legislature as well as by the executive. Manwaring's case was precluded here by the command of the First Amendment that Congress shall make no law abridging freedom of speech, the press, or religion.

The list of Englishmen and Americans who were punished for free speech is too long to be remembered. One long forgotten is Richard Chambers, who said publicly in London, "The merchants are in no part of the world so screwed and wrung as in England; in Turkey they have more encouragement."

He was convicted on May 6, 1629, for these "undutiful, seditious, and false words." He was fined £2,000 and imprisoned. He was denied relief by way of habeas corpus. He spent six years in prison for the offense, and years later died under the weight of an oppressive debt, which he could never pay.

Coal mines have taken a terrible toll in human lives. Cave-ins and the explosions of gas or coal dust created most of the accidents. Anthracosis, silicosis, and occupational pneumonia are the common diseases acquired by miners. Both the accidents and the occupational diseases are mostly preventable.

In 1869, Pennsylvania enacted a limited mine inspection law. In 1874, Ohio passed a more comprehensive one. Other States followed suit. For one reason or another, state inspections were ineffective. The mine owners controlled the inspectors; the state standards were lax.

It took a generation of agitation to establish in 1910 the federal Bureau of Mines. It did excellent work, providing standards of prevention and disseminating information. But the mining disasters continued to mount. When the Bureau of Mines asked to inspect a mine, it was often refused permission; and it had no recourse.

On May 7, 1941, a federal law was enacted making inspection of coal mines mandatory. This was a great step forward. But the mines were not required to comply with the federal requirements. In 1947, the explosion at the Centralia mine in Illinois killed 111 miners. In 1951, an explosion, plainly preventable, killed 119 at West Frankfort, Illinois. Time and time again the federal inspectors would give warnings that went unheeded. In one year in the early '50's, nearly a half of the mines inspected had serious hazards. Yet when the Bureau of Mines wrote the owners, 89 per cent of the letters went unanswered. It seemed that the dominant interests in the coal-mining industry were callous and indifferent.

In 1952, Congress was thoroughly aroused. The 1941 law was amended, giving the federal agency power to close unsafe mines, establishing safety standards, and applying criminal sanctions.

At long last the human rights in coal were given dignity and security.

Massachuetts led the way in social legislation protective of women and children. On May 8, 1874, it passed a pioneer law establishing a ten-hour day for minors under eighteen years of age and for women. The constitutionality of the law was sustained in 1876 by the Massachusetts courts.

In 1905, the Supreme Court struck down a New York law limiting the employment of *men* in bakeries to ten hours a day or sixty hours a week, on the ground that it deprived the employer of property (liberty of contract) without due process of law in violation of the Fourteenth Amendment. But in 1908, it sustained an Oregon law establishing a ten-hour day for *women* in laundries against the same claim of unconstitutionality. The Court said that "her physical structure and a proper discharge of her maternal functions—having in view not merely her own health, but the well-being of the race—justify legislation to protect her from the greed as well as the passion of man."

It was in this case that Louis D. Brandeis (later Justice) filed an historic brief. Of the 113 pages, only two contained legal argument in the conventional sense. The rest included history, the experience of other nations, a collection of scientific data and expert opinion on the bad effects of long hours of work on women, and an analysis of the conditions in laundries which justified protection of women workers.

Throughout history, innocent men have been punished for crimes they did not commit. Mistaken identities and perjured testimony have produced many miscarriages of justice. Occasionally, persons have even been convicted of murder where later on the "murdered" man turned up very much alive. Some innocent men have been executed; others have served long years for crimes they did not commit (November 14, 15).

Those who eventually were cleared and released from prison had no remedy against the government for the time they spent in prison in punishment for crimes they did not commit. For the legal maxim—the state (the King) can do no wrong—barred recovery. The *Constitution* provides that government may not take a person's *property* without compensation. But there is no comparable provision governing the taking of one's *liberty*.

Last century, many European countries enacted laws granting indemnity to innocent people convicted of crime and later cleared. But in this country the only relief afforded such persons was through special Acts of the legislature (November 15).

On May 9, 1913, Wisconsin made effective the first indemnity act in this country. California followed the same year, North Dakota in 1917, the federal government in 1938, and New York in 1946.

The first federal bill was introduced into Congress in 1912 by Senator (later Justice) Sutherland of Utah. The passage of the federal law was due largely to the efforts of two law professors—Edwin M. Borchard of Yale and John H. Wigmore of Northwestern.

The anti-Chinese movement in this country dates back to the middle of the last century, when the influx of Chinese into California resulted in laws discriminating against them. By 1870, a whole series of anti-Chinese measures were adopted. A tax on foreign miners and a head tax were imposed; a requirement was exacted that all ships bringing immigrants give bond that the newcomers would not become public charges; the legislature was given the power to protect the public from aliens who were "dangerous or detrimental"; corporations were prohibited from employing Chinese; Chinese were barred from public works. There was violence up and down the west coast, with an occasional Chinese being killed. In Los Angeles, a mob descended on Chinatown, laid it waste, and killed twenty-two Chinese. Hysteria about the "yellow peril" seized the west coast. Laborers, merchants, and others who felt the competition of the Chinese joined in the campaign.

San Francisco passed an innocent-looking ordinance, which required laundry operators to obtain licenses. As applied, no Chinese could get a license even though he met all the requirements demanded of other applicants.

One Yick Wo, an alien Chinese, was arrested and convicted for operating without a license. In an historic decision announced May 10, 1886, the Supreme Court set aside the conviction. The Fourteenth Amendment provides that no State shall deny "to any person within its jurisdiction the equal protection of the laws." The Court held (1) that "any person" included a resident alien as well as a citizen; and (2) that a man could not be barred from the laundry business merely because of his race and nationality (June 7).

Racism as a constitutional principle was emphatically rejected.

"I hereby establish an agency within the Government to be known as the Rural Electrification Administration," which shall have the duty "to initiate, formulate, administer, and supervise a program of approved projects with respect to the generation, transmission, and distribution of electric energy in rural areas." So wrote Franklin Roosevelt, May 11, 1935.

The private utilities issued a now famous statement, "There are very few farmers requiring electricity for major farm operations that are not now served." The R.E.A. proved that declaration wrong. In 1935, only 10 per cent of America's farms had electric service from central stations; in 1954, over 90 per cent.

Morris Cooke was the chief architect of this rural program. George Norris, John Rankin, Sam Rayburn, and Franklin Roosevelt were its main political sponsors.

The opposition of the private utility companies, with some exceptions, was severe and unending. The competition to get the huge market which R.E.A. revealed, the political tactics employed against R.E.A., the campaign to discredit it as "socialism" have been told in *The Farmer Takes a Hand* by Marquis Childs.

R.E.A., now permanent, makes loans to finance electric systems in rural areas—over 99 per cent of which have been repaid when due. It works mostly through co-operatives and public power districts. Public power districts (which own all of Nebraska's electric facilities) are authorized in about twenty States. R.E.A. has worked through them to some extent. But over 90 per cent of its loans have been made to co-operatives. The co-operatives were also bitterly fought by the private utilities. They have emerged, however, a strong, vigilant group in American life—reviving democracy in the rural areas, relieving farmers of drudgery and backaches, raising their standard of living, and at long last bringing them some leisure.

By 1954, R.E.A. was drawing its battle lines on a new front. It was fighting to maintain the preferences granted public power districts and co-operatives to the power generated at the federal dams (April 14). Those preferences mean low costs, without which R.E.A. would be seriously crippled.

In 1948, the American Library Association adopted the following Bill of Rights:

1. As a responsibility of library service, books and other reading matter selected should be chosen for values of interest, information and enlightenment of all the people of the community. In no case should any book be excluded because of the race or nationality, or the political or religious views of the writer.

2. There should be the fullest practicable provision of material presenting all points of view concerning the problems and issues of our times, international, national, and local; and books or other reading matter of sound factual authority should not be proscribed or removed from library shelves because of partisan or doctrinal disapproval.

3. Censorship of books, urged or practiced by volunteer arbiters of morals or political opinion or by organizations that would establish a coercive concept of Americanism, must be challenged by libraries in maintenance of their responsibility to provide public information and enlightenment through the printed word.

4. Libraries should enlist the cooperation of allied groups in the fields of science, of education, and of book publishing in resisting all abridgment of the free access to ideas and full freedom of expression that are the tradition and heritage of Americans.

5. As an institution of education for democratic living, the library should welcome the use of its meeting rooms for socially useful and cultural activities and discussion of current public questions. Such meeting places should be available on equal terms to all groups in the community regardless of the beliefs and affiliations of their members (November 29).

(In 1951, this Bill of Rights was extended "to all materials and media of communication used or collected by libraries.")

May 13, 1912, marked the end of a momentous debate in the Congress. On that date the House concurred in the Senate draft of a proposed constitutional Amendment, providing for the direct election of Senators. Ratification by the States came so rapidly that the necessary three-fourths vote was obtained by May 1913.

William E. Borah of Idaho led the fight. In 1903, Borah had been defeated for the United States Senate in the Idaho legislature. Four years later, the Idaho legislature elected him after he had won a majority of the popular vote. Referring to that popular vote, Borah said, "I have great affection for the bridge which carried me over."

Borah's report of 1911 to the Senate is a masterful document. It contains an historical analysis of the problem, a sober statement of the evils of logrolling and other sinister practices in state legislatures, and a plea for faith in the democratic processes.

It was Borah's dogged drive and astute determination that drove the bill through the Senate. He had eminent opponents— Root of New York, Lodge of Massachusetts. Root argued for "stability" and against "change." He pleaded that, as Ulysses asked "his followers to bind him to the mast" so that the sirens would not seduce him, so America should remain fast to the *Constitution*. He condemned the proposed Amendment as one of the "weaknesses of democracies," against which the *Constitution* was designed to guard. He extolled a Senate, elected by legislatures, as the conservative influence, the "guardian of the sober second thought."

Borah had stalwart allies. One was Beveridge of Indiana, who argued that the people were intelligent and informed and should be trusted, that the popular desire for the Amendment was overwhelming, that it was a part of "the deliberate and intelligent advance of all humanity."

Borah's plea for "faith in the source of all power, the people," won out. The final vote in the Senate was 64 yeas, 24 nays; in the House 238 yeas, 39 nays.

Last century, there were many paupers among the mass of immigrants coming to America. Caring for them placed quite a burden on cities like New York, which were ports of entry. The practice developed of collecting head taxes—$1.50 to $2.50—from the incoming ships to care for the needy immigrants. In 1876, the Supreme Court held these head taxes unconstitutional, since they were state taxes on the privilege of landing in this country. Such a regulation of foreign commerce, the Court held, was for Congress alone.

The decision gave impetus to federal legislation. As a result the first federal immigration law was passed by Congress in 1882. It imposed on ships a 50 cent head tax for each immigrant. Collection of the tax was vested in the Secretary of the Treasury, who was authorized to contract with state agencies for administration of the law and for support and relief of the immigrants. The division of authority between the federal government and the port of entry States did not work very well. Agitation for an exclusive federal law continued. That law finally was enacted in 1891. For the first time control of immigration was placed entirely in federal hands.

Up to this time, New York had a landing depot for immigrants at Castle Garden, an old fort at the foot of Manhattan Island. After enactment of the 1891 law, Castle Garden was abandoned; and the federal government opened Ellis Island.

Prior to that—in 1886—the Statue of Liberty (symbolizing the Mother of Exiles) was placed on Bedloe's Island. Frédéric Auguste Bartholdi, famous French sculptor, was the artist. Emma Lazarus has a poem graven there:

> *Give me your tired, your poor,*
> *Your huddled masses yearning to breathe free,*
> *The wretched refuse of your teeming shore,*
> *Send these, the homeless, tempest-tossed to me:*
> *I lift my lamp beside the golden door.*

May 15, 1893, was a dark day for aliens resident in this country. The Supreme Court held that Chinese, guilty of no crime, living lawful lives here, and having roots deep in the country, could be deported, merely because of their race and their birthplace. That decision, which subsequently has been reaffirmed in the case of aliens of other races, was over the dissent of three Justices, one of whom was David J. Brewer.

Brewer, who came to the Court in 1889 from Kansas, was known by his colleagues as a man of strong blood. Lawyers would call him competent and conservative. He was indeed the champion of property rights to a greater extent than his more famous successors. But when it came to issues involving the rights of Asians (particularly Chinese) who lived in this country or who sought admission to it, he usually was against the immigration officials. In one famous dissent, he warned that if the hostility in our laws toward the Chinese continued, China, "the most populous nation on earth," will become "the great antagonist of this republic."

Why did this Kansan have that tolerant attitude toward the Asians? There are inklings of the answer. Brewer, son of a missionary, was born in the Middle East and, to use his own words, he caught from his parents the message of their devotion "to the despised races" of Asia. Brewer also believed from childhood that the *Bible* "affirms the unity of the race" and "proclaims the brotherhood of man."

We Americans have long been an insular people, exploiting and enjoying the lush continent that we inherited. Asia has been unknown to us. Europe we knew largely through literature. Brewer, thanks to his parents, apparently saw America through Asian eyes, and, seeing it, realized that an insular attitude was hostile to America's interests, that if America was to maintain moral leadership in the world, she must, in concrete ways, identify herself with the dreams and aspirations of all mankind.

On May 16, 1868, Andrew Johnson, President of the United States, was found not guilty of the high crimes and misdemeanors for which the House had impeached him. He was tried by the Senate, Chief Justice Salmon P. Chase presiding. The trial started March 5, 1868 and ended May 26, 1868. The critical vote was taken May 16, when 35 Senators voted for conviction and 19 voted for acquittal. Conviction failed by 1 vote, as 36 constituted the necessary two thirds.

The charges against Johnson related largely to his removal of Edwin M. Stanton as Secretary of War. But the reasons for impeachment struck much deeper. Johnson followed Lincoln's course of moderation after the Civil War ended. The South was devastated. Her war casualties were a quarter million. Four million slaves had been freed. Her towns and plants were in ruin. So was her economy.

Johnson, like Lincoln, wanted the seceding States readmitted to the councils of the nation. The northern radicals—the Republicans—objected. Under the leadership of Thaddeus Stevens of Pennsylvania, they laid the lash on the South, treated the southern States as conquered territory, refused to seat their Senators and Congressmen, and passed the *Reconstruction Act* of March 2, 1867, which placed ten "rebel States" under military government.

Johnson vetoed this law. He also clashed again and again with the Republicans and others who wanted to punish the South. Stanton was opposed to Johnson. His removal was the occasion, not the basic cause, for the impeachment. Feelings in the North ran high. Seven Republican Senators had the courage to vote "not guilty." In so doing, they sacrificed their political careers. None was ever elected to any office again. But they saved the conscience of America from a cruel ordeal. For the compassion and understanding of Lincoln and Johnson were necessary to heal the wounds of that war.

In 1896, the Supreme Court in the famous *Plessy* case (December 11) held constitutional a state statute, which required segregation of the white and colored races while they were riding in passenger coaches. John M. Harlan of Kentucky was the lone dissenter. The *Plessy* case adopted the "separate but equal" doctrine (first formulated by a Massachusetts court in 1849), which permitted segregation of the races in public vehicles and other public places, provided the facilities furnished Negroes were substantially equal to those furnished the whites.

For decades public schools were segregated in many States, both north and south. By 1954, there were still 17 States that required them to be segregated, and 4 that in varying degrees permitted it.

In 1952, segregation cases from Delaware, Kansas, South Carolina, Virginia, and the District of Columbia reached the Supreme Court. These five cases, which were twice argued, involved the constitutionality of the segregation of Negro students from white students in public schools that were equal, so far as physical facilities and teaching staffs were concerned. Is segregation constitutional under the Fourteenth Amendment when the schools are separate but equal?

The Supreme Court in *unanimous* decisions rendered on May 17, 1954, held that racial segregation in public schools is unconstitutional.

The Court ruled that segregation in the schools has a detrimental effect on colored children irrespective of the quality of the buildings or instruction, that all separate education facilities are "inherently unequal," that segregation in public schools solely on the basis of race is unconstitutional.

So spoke the Supreme Court at a point of history when intolerance and racial hatreds were tearing some nations apart.

The Tennessee River and Muscle Shoals have long been in the public eye. Monroe, in 1824, urged their improvement for navigation. Roosevelt, on May 18, 1933, approved the bill creating the Tennessee Valley Authority. Between those dates the federal government initiated numerous projects on the river. Under Wilson, a dam and powerhouse were erected for the fixation of atmospheric nitrogen for war purposes and for use as a fertilizer. Sentiment grew for a more ambitious project. Different bills were introduced in the Congress during the 1920's. One that passed met a pocket veto by Coolidge; another was vetoed by Hoover. The one approved by Roosevelt had as its chief sponsor, Senator George W. Norris (February 6).

Roosevelt and Norris cenceived of the T.V.A. as an instrument for the management of a complete river watershed, involving seven States. T.V.A. has evolved in that manner. It has provided 630 miles of inland water transportation. By 1956, it will have a hydroelectric power capacity of 9,600,000 kilowatts. Transportation and power have brought a large degree of industrialization to the Valley, with substantial increases both in jobs for workers and in manufacturing income. T.V.A. is also important to flood control. It has operated its dams so as to reduce peak floods on the Ohio, saving millions of dollars. In dry seasons, it has released water into streams that in their natural state would have dwindled to trickles. Water control means protection of soil against erosion, and that requires afforestation and scientific agriculture.

The T.V.A. serves those ends also. It co-operates with the States in programs for the promotion of fishing, for the propagation and protection of ducks, geese, and quail, for the development of large recreation areas. This idea of the development of an entire watershed in the interests of all the people has traveled around the world. It has been adopted in India, and is projected for the Tigris and Euphrates. In the 1920's and '30's opponents called T.V.A. a "communistic experiment." Others denounce it as "creeping socialism." But the world knows it is a sensible way of putting a river system to work for all the people.

Before the Civil War, Congress had made land grants to turn-pike, canal, and railroad companies. In the 1850's, it granted 28 million acres of public lands to the States for the purpose of subsidizing railroad construction. But those gifts were minor compared with those to come. Beginning in 1862, Congress made lavish land grants direct to the roads to aid their westward construction. It also made loans. States and communities added to the subsidy. Never was an industry so heavily subsidized. In public lands alone they received (net) nearly 120 million acres. It was their energy that not only built the roads, but populated the land. The roads had their agents in Europe scouring that continent for settlers.

The roads also created a host of abuses. Railroad stocks were highly watered, and farmers paid extortionate rates based on the fraudulent inflation. The railroad magnates were feudal overlords. The wealth and the power of the roads were so great they overawed the States. The magnates bought legislators, gave secret rebates to powerful shippers, boosted rates or slashed them as their interests dictated. They were indeed a government unto themselves. They had at their command the only method of transportation, and they mostly monopolized warehouses as well. As a result, farmers, merchants, and whole communities could do business on their terms, or not at all.

The reaction was severe. The panic of 1873 brought a temporary halt to the ruthless use of the public domain for private gain. For the States set up regulatory laws to correct the abuses and the Supreme Court sustained them (March 1). But conservative Justices soon took the place of liberal ones and the reforms largely failed (March 2). That made inevitable the advent of federal regulation in 1887. While the Interstate Commerce Commission struggled to make its controls effective, the battle in the States continued under the aegis of men like Hiram Johnson of California and Bob La Follette of Wisconsin (September 12).

The advent of governmental control did not mark the eclipse of "free enterprise." The railroads were a "subsidized" business, drunk with power which they used without conscience.

On this day in 1785, the Continental Congress passed a law providing for the surveying and selling of public lands in the territory lying between the Alleghenies and the Mississippi. It provided that lot 16 of every township should be reserved "for the maintenance of public schools within the said township." By the 1802 enabling Act authorizing the admission of Ohio into the Union, the United States granted the sixteenth section in every township for the maintenance of schools within the township. With few exceptions (Texas, West Virginia, and Maine), that practice continued as each new State was admitted. With the admission of California in 1850, the grant was increased to two sections. And in a few of the more arid western states, four sections were granted for public schools. In all, Congress has granted the States approximately 145 million acres (226,562 square miles) of public lands for public schools—an area about four times the size of New England. It has pledged this sizable portion of the public domain to the faith expressed in the famous *Ordinance* of 1787, which created the Northwest Territorial government: "Religion, morality, and knowledge being necessary to good government and the happiness of mankind, schools and the means of education shall forever be encouraged." (July 13.)

It was in May 1862 that a basic change in American land policy took place. Prior to that time the public lands had been sold to settlers or donated to them for military service rendered along the frontier. The agitation for free land started early. One advocate said that land was "the gift of God to man," and "the gift of the government to its citizens."

Price or no price was an issue that grew between West and East. The voting strength of the East long kept the issue from coming to a head. The Free-Soil party sponsored free land in 1848. The Free-Soil Democrats proclaimed in 1852 that public lands were "a sacred trust" to be granted "in limited quantities, free of cost, to landless settlers." That was the position of the Republican party in 1860. It was a cause long sponsored by Horace Greeley.

The delay in getting a free homestead law through Congress was due to the fact that the issue of free land became caught up in the slavery issue. Slavery could not exist without the large plantation system. The free homesteads would establish a system of small farms. Settlement of the western lands by free whites would limit and curtail the extension of slavery. It would in time cast the full political balance of the country against the slave States.

The *Homestead Act* of 1862 gave settlers the right to acquire farms of 160 acres, free of all charges except a nominal filing fee, and required them to live on the homestead for five years before getting title to the land. West of the 100th meridian adjustments had to be made, because 160 acres was not enough. But east of that point the *Homestead Act* was a great success, a million and a third homesteads having been taken up and completed.

Abraham Lincoln also signed the *Morrill Act* in 1862. That Act granted public lands to each State (30,000 acres for each Senator and Congressman) for the endowment of "at least one college" whose "leading object" shall be the teaching of "such branches of learning as are related to agriculture and mechanic arts" in order to promote "the liberal and practical education of the industrial classes."

Under this Act some 13 million acres of the public domain were granted to the States for land grant colleges. In 1954, there were 69 such colleges, located in the forty-eight States and in Alaska, Hawaii, and Puerto Rico.

In the year 1950–1951, the endowment income from the land grants under the *Morrill Act* and under supplementary land grants was about two and a quarter million dollars. The endowment (not including unsold lands) was about 75 million dollars, and the value of the unsold land was about 24 million dollars.

Professor Jonathan B. Turner of Illinois College, Jacksonville, Illinois—father of the *Morrill Act*—speaking of the need for educating farmers and mechanics, said, "We wish them to read books only that they may the better read and understand the great volume of nature ever open before them." Congressman Justin S. Morrill of Vermont, the sponsor, stated that the existing colleges taught mostly the classics, "leaving farmers and mechanics and all those who must win their bread by labor to the hap-hazard of being self-taught or not scientifically taught at all. . . ."

On May 23, 1903, Wisconsin proposed a direct primary law which was approved by the voters in 1904. There had been earlier attempts made in several States to regulate primaries. But Wisconsin's law was the first one that was state-wide, comprehensive, and mandatory. So insistent was the demand, so swift the movement, that by 1917 all but 4 States had some form of direct primary laws; and in 32 of these the law was mandatory.

The reform gained impetus under disclosures of the abuses in the convention system. In Illinois, a Cook County convention in 1896 had 723 delegates of whom 84 had criminal records, 17 having been tried for homicide, 46 having served prison terms. Stories of the manipulation of the conventions by the bosses were lurid and alarming. The "muckraking" journalists added their disclosures. Investigations showed evil alliances manipulating party machines.

Charles Evans Hughes in New York, Woodrow Wilson in New Jersey, Hiram Johnson in California, Robert La Follette in Wisconsin led the fight (September 12). La Follette's fight against the machine began in 1894. He called the convention a "corrupt influence which was undermining and destroying every semblance of representative government in Wisconsin." He vowed to break it, and he did. He carried the fight to the people, shouting that the party convention served no purpose than "to give respectable form to political robbery."

In 1954, the direct primary in some form or other had been accepted by all the States, except Connecticut.

There were libraries in the Colonies from the beginning, and they were public, in the sense that they were not the exclusive property of any individual. Some were in colleges; some were town collections; others were owned by churches. In 1731, Benjamin Franklin founded a subscription library at Philadelphia. Others soon followed. By 1800, scores of New England towns had these book clubs. By 1850, there were 259 New England towns with more than one library. And there were, in addition, many circulating libraries run for profit on a rental basis.

These libraries were inadequate for the growing educational needs of the communities. Tax-supported libraries were established, following the example of Peterborough, New Hampshire, in 1833. By the mid-nineteenth century, the public library movement under George Ticknor of Boston was in full swing. The Massachusetts Library Act of May 24, 1851, which permitted towns to establish public libraries, marked its commencement.

Over the years, private gifts and public grants have produced more libraries and larger libraries than will be found in any other nation. There are today about 7,500 public libraries in the nation, with a total endowment of nearly 90 million dollars. And public funds constitute about 90 per cent of their income. Nearly two thirds of our public libraries are in communities with less than 5,000 population.

Library management has made the service of these libraries highly efficient. Today, they are an indispensable adjunct of community life and adult education. They have helped create an atmosphere of tolerance for new ideas; they have become sanctuaries where men can pursue problems to the periphery of knowledge; they are one of the important influences in our life which make any "book-burning" project offensive and shocking.

Douglas C. Macintosh was a Canadian by birth, educated at the University of Chicago, and Chaplain and Dwight Professor of Theology at Yale. In World War I, he saw service in the front lines as a Chaplain in the Canadian Army and as manager of an American Y.M.C.A. hut. In the 1920's, he sought naturalization in this country. His primary allegiance to God would not permit him to make a blanket promise to bear arms, without knowing the cause beforehand. Hence, he was denied citizenship. The Supreme Court upheld that decision, Hughes, Holmes, Brandeis, and Stone dissenting. Hughes rejected the idea that Congress had established a religious test for citizenship. Yet Macintosh, he wrote, was only asserting what was the "essence of religion," which is "belief in a relation to God involving superior duties to those arising from any human relation." Hughes also noted that in modern war the bearing of arms is not the only way to defend the *Constitution*. The aircraft worker and the scientist are full partners with the soldier in total war. This was on May 25, 1930.

In 1946, Hughes, retired from the bench, saw his view accepted. In the midst of another war, another Canadian, though willing to take the oath of allegiance, was not willing to do combatant military duty because he was a Seventh-Day Adventist. The Supreme Court, reversing Macintosh's case, adopted the dissenting view of Hughes. ". . . even in time of war one may truly support and defend our institutions though he stops short of using weapons of war."

Charles I, in order to finance some military ventures, required the wealthy to loan him the money. Since there was no prospect of repayment, the "loans" were, indeed, heavy taxes, parceled out by the King's agents. Those who refused to make the "loans" were jailed. Five of them applied for writs of habeas corpus, demanding to know what crime they had committed. The court granted the writ, and put the case down for hearing. The lawyer for the prisoners argued that no reason having been given for their confinement, it was unlawful; that if these men could be restrained at the whim and caprice of the King, then people could be "restrained of their liberties perpetually," without any remedy. Counsel for the King argued that if the King gave no reason for confining a man, it simply meant that it would endanger the state for him to make his reasons public.

The court agreed with counsel for the King and refused to release the five prisoners, saying that it would not act where it did not know what cause the King had for committing them; that the court trusted the King "in great matters."

Parliament considered the matter for months, and finally, on May 26, 1628, adopted the famous *Petition of Right*, which the King shortly agreed to. The *Petition* prayed that no man should be compelled to make a loan or pay a tax to the King, "without common consent by act of Parliament," nor be imprisoned or detained for his refusal.

This battle for the supremacy of the legislature, won in 1628, was partly lost in 1637, and had to be won again.

It was the 1637 episode that made John Hampden famous. The King insisted that he could assess his subjects for ship money to finance his navies. Hampden became the symbol of the opposition, though only twenty shillings were involved.

Hampden lost; and Burke said on another day, "Would twenty shillings have ruined Mr. Hampden's future? No, but the payment of half twenty shillings, on the principle it was demanded, would have made him a slave."

On May 27, 1679, England enacted her famous *Habeas Corpus Act* which made the Great Writ available to those arrested for "any criminal or supposed criminal matter." The judges had hemmed habeas corpus in by technical and narrow constructions, so that the liberty of the citizen was subject to the caprice of government. The 1679 Act liberalized the procedure, making the writ a ready means for testing the power of government to detain a citizen. Since that time, habeas corpus has become perhaps the greatest of all civil rights.

The sad plight of one Francis Jenkes hastened the passage of the 1679 Act. He was a trader who, in 1676, made a speech concerning the decline of trade in London and urging that Parliament be convened to consider the problem. He was summoned before the King and his Council to answer for his effrontery.

A LORD: How came you then to meddle with matters of state?

JENKES: I thought any of his Majesty's subjects, in an humble manner, might petition his Majesty for a remedy of any grievance whatsoever.

THE KING: I will take care that none such as you shall have to do with the government.

JENKES: I think my expression was no great absurdity. Yet, if I have failed in due expression, I beg his Majesty's pardon.

LORD CHANCELLOR: Sir, pray tell us, who advised you in this matter?

THE KING: Who advised you?

JENKES: To name any particular person (if there were such) would be a mean and unworthy thing, therefore I desire to be excused all farther answer to such questions, since the law doth provide that no man be put to answer to his own prejudice.

After several months in jail Jenkes was released on bail. It was his difficulty in obtaining habeas corpus that emphasized the need for reform.

The right to the writ of habeas corpus, guaranteed by the *Constitution*, is the procedure whereby a jailer is required to deliver a prisoner before a court so that the legality of his detention may be determined. Without some such procedure, men might be held in protective custody for years on end. Its importance is so great that the *Constitution* provides that it may not be suspended, except when in cases of rebellion or invasion the public safety may require it. The *Constitution*, however, does not say whether the President or the Congress may suspend it; and the question has never been resolved.

Lincoln suspended the writ in 1861, an action ratified by Congress two years later. But in between those dates, one John Merryman was arrested by the Army in Baltimore. Many people in Baltimore were pro-southern and interfered with the movement of northern troops to Washington, D.C. The mobbing of the troops and the destruction of bridges caused Lincoln to suspend the writ.

Merryman applied to Chief Justice Taney for a writ of habeas corpus. Taney issued it, ordering the Commanding General at Fort McHenry to produce the prisoner. Taney's view was that only Congress could suspend the writ. Lincoln refused to deliver the prisoner. Taney had no army to compel it. The authority of the Court was flouted; and its prestige suffered greatly.

Lincoln's homely philosophy on the case was this: "By general law, life and limb must be protected, yet often a limb must be amputated to save a life; but a life is never wisely given to save a limb." It was his way of saying that the preservation of the Union came first, even if one constitutional guaranty had to be disregarded.

On September 17, 1787, the delegates to the Constitutional Convention signed the *Constitution* and shortly submitted it to Congress. On September 28, 1787, Congress submitted it to the States for ratification. Delaware was the first of the thirteen States to ratify it. This was on December 7, 1787. Rhode Island, the last, approved it on May 29, 1790. By its terms, the *Constitution* was to be established when nine States ratified it. The ninth State was New Hampshire, which ratified it on June 21, 1788. Delaware, New Jersey, and Georgia were unanimous. But in the other States the vote was divided. For example, in Pennsylvania the vote was 46 to 23; in Massachusetts, 187 to 168; in New Hampshire, 57 to 47; in Virginia, 89 to 79; in New York, 30 to 27.

These close votes were due in large measure to two fears—first, the absence of a Bill of Rights restraining the powers of the national government; second, the fear of the power of this new central government. George Mason put the latter fear dramatically in the Virginia debates when he said:

"The very idea of converting what was formerly a confederation to a consolidated government is totally subversive of every principle which has hitherto governed us. This power is calculated to annihilate totally the state governments."

The fear of the loss of States' rights would have been greatly multiplied had Marshall's doctrine of implied powers been foreseen (March 7). For the doctrine of implied powers and the Commerce Clause—which also cast a shadow over the debates—have, indeed, made an extensive empire strong and powerful under our national government.

The first treason trials in this country took place in May 1795 in connection with the Whisky Rebellion. Several were convicted, but each was pardoned. In our history there have been less than two dozen treason trials prosecuted by the federal government; and no executions have resulted. The trial of Thomas Dorr by Rhode Island and John Brown by Virginia (December 2) are the only treason trials prosecuted by the States.

The federal *Constitution* says: "Treason against the United States, shall consist only in levying War against them, or in adhering to their Enemies, giving them Aid and Comfort. No Person shall be convicted of Treason unless on the Testimony of two Witnesses to the same overt Act, or on Confession in open Court."

This narrow definition reflects the fears which the fathers had of political prosecutions (July 17). The law of England allowed a man to be tried for treason if he "doth compass or imagine the death" of the King. This was called "constructive treason," for the accused did not have to lift his hand against the King to be guilty; all he need do was wish the King was dead.

The first treason case ever to be decided by the Supreme Court reached there in 1944 in the midst of World War II. It involved an American citizen charged with having given aid and comfort to Germany in time of war. His conviction was reversed by a divided Court.

Apart from levying war, the crime has two elements: (1) adherence to the enemy; and (2) rendering him aid and comfort. The accused must have more than an intent to betray; he must translate the intent into action. Each act must have two witnesses. And the act of adherence must confer some actual, tangible benefit on the enemy. So ruled the Court in 1944.

The construction given was so restrictive that some thought that no prosecutor would thereafter chance an indictment under the head of treason.

Each of the original States, except Delaware, had copyright laws. Hence, it is natural to find a copyright clause in the *Constitution*. It provides that Congress may secure to authors, for limited times, the exclusive right to their writings.

From the beginning, Congress was presented with numerous petitions by authors for the protection of their literary works. George Washington urged the First Congress to pass a law that would promote literature. Congress acted early, our first copyright law being dated May 31, 1790.

The copyright law has been amended many times, once to give the widow of Jeff Davis the benefit of the copyright of a book which he wrote, but failed to copyright by reason of a mistake in filing.

The first copyright law gave an author protection for fourteen years with an option to renew for another fourteen. Today a copyright extends for twenty-eight years with right of renewal.

The first right applied to maps, charts, or books. The present law extends not only to books, maps, papers and periodicals, lectures and dramatic compositions, but also to photographs, prints and pictorial illustrations, musical compositions, motion pictures, drawings and plastic works of a scientific or technical nature, works of art, and reproductions of a work of art.

Our early laws gave no protection to foreign authors. An American citizen could pirate a Frenchman's novel or a Britisher's poems, with no redress to the author. By a law passed in 1891, that policy was changed. Today, a resident alien may copyright his works under our law. So may a non-resident alien, when his nation grants equality of treatment to Americans by treaty or law, or when it is party to an international reciprocal agreement.

JUNE

An Oklahoma law, enacted in 1935, provided for the sterilization of "habitual criminals." One Skinner, who had been convicted once of stealing chickens and twice of robbery with
firearms, was ordered to submit to the operation of vasectomy
(March 20). He protested and carried the case to the Supreme
Court. On June 1, 1942, the Court held that the application of
the law to Skinner would deprive him of the equal protection of
the laws in violation of the Fourteenth Amendment.

"A clerk who appropriates over $20 from his employer's till . . .
and a stranger who steals the same amount are . . . both guilty
of felonies. If the latter repeats his act and is convicted three
times, he may be sterilized. But the clerk is not subject to the
pains and penalties of the Act no matter how large his embezzlement nor how frequent his convictions . . . When the law lays
an unequal hand on those who have committed intrinsically the
same quality of offense and sterilizes one and not the other, it
has made as invidious a discrimination as if it had selected a particular race or nationality for oppressive treatment."

On June 2, 1902, Oregon amended her constitution so as to provide for the initiative and referendum. Thus the people were given the power to propose and enact laws independently of the legislature, and to reject laws which the legislature had enacted. The initiative and referendum were means by which the people hoped to gain control over a boss-ridden legislature that would act only grudgingly and after long agitation.

Oregon was the first State to adopt the initiative and referendum in a comprehensive, detailed form. Today twenty States have it in one form or another on a state-wide basis; two States have the referendum alone.

In Oregon down to 1954, the initiative was used in proposing 198 measures, 75 being adopted and 123 rejected. The referendum was used 44 times, the laws being approved 26 times and rejected 18 times.

Oregon has used the initiative to get the direct primary, the recall of public officials, women's suffrage, a state income tax, reapportionment of the legislature, prohibition of the use of convict labor in private industry, the creation of public utility districts, and a World War II bonus for veterans.

Oregon has used the referendum against reactionary legislatures. Five times a sales tax was enacted; five times the referendum repealed it. Four times a cigarette tax was imposed; four times the people rejected it.

In Oregon, the threat of the initiative and referendum has made many legislatures behave. They have served the function promised by W. S. U'Ren, the man most responsible for Oregon's reform—the function of the "stick behind the door."

It was once suggested that the initiative and referendum worked so well in California that administration of the State be left to the Governor and a small board of comptrollers, and that all laws—general and special—be enacted by popular vote. But this system of direct legislation, important as it is, has its limitations. New York, where the initiative and referendum is not known, often has more enlightened laws than Oregon.

One of the most spirited controversies involving the rights of
conscience arose in connection with state laws requiring school
children to salute the Flag. In Pennsylvania, the requirement was
enforced against a child who claimed that the doing of the act
violated his religious scruples. He was a Jehovah's Witness who
was taught that the *Bible* commanded him, at the risk of God's
displeasure, not to go through the form of pledge. The Supreme
Court nevertheless held that the salute could be required of him.
Three years later in a case from West Virginia the Court overruled that decision, holding that the regulation could not, consistent with the freedom of conscience guaranteed by the First
Amendment, be enforced against one whose religious scruples
against saluting the Flag were genuine and real.

The first decision was rendered June 3, 1940. Harlan F. Stone
was the sole dissenter. But his dissent—that no government can
compel a person "to bear false witness to his religion"—was soon
to win over a majority of the Court.

It is hard to know what the influences are that shape up one's
philosophy of life. Some are in the genes of the bloodstream.
Some go back to happenings too distant to remember. Some come
raw from experience. Perhaps Stone's tolerance for the religious
scruples of an unpopular minority went back to World War I,
when he served on a board of inquiry to review cases of conscientious objectors who had refused to perform military service. I
knew from what he told me that it was for him a moving experience. Perhaps he learned from the quiet Quakers, or from those
who are more impassioned, the full meaning of religious freedom.
Perhaps he saw in the deep, burning eyes of some of the 2,000
drafted men whom he interviewed the message that there are
some who will die rather than bear false witness to their religious beliefs.

A majority of nine judges of the Supreme Court have thought that wire tapping violated the command of the Fourth Amendment against unreasonable searches and seizures, and infringed the guaranty of the Fifth Amendment that no one person shall be compelled to be a witness against himself. But these judges never sat on the Court at the same time, and the exponents of that view were in the minority whenever the issue arose.

The historic decision was rendered June 4, 1928, over the dissents of Holmes, Brandeis, Butler, and Stone. Wire tapping to Holmes was "dirty business." Brandeis denounced it in scathing terms, and, in a brilliant dissent, laid the constitutional basis for its condemnation. The Fourth and Fifth Amendments, he said, conferred as against government "the right to be let alone—the most comprehensive of rights and the right most valued by civilized men." Wire tapping, he maintained, was the most oppressive intrusion into the right of privacy that man had yet invented. He went on to say that the fact that wires were being tapped to catch criminals was no justification for letting down the barriers. "The greatest dangers to liberty lurk in insidious encroachment by men of zeal, well-meaning but without understanding."

In 1934, Congress passed a law which forbade telephone messages to be intercepted unless the interception was authorized by the sender, and which barred any person from divulging the message or its substance to any other person. The Supreme Court held that this law prevented use of evidence obtained by wire tapping in criminal trials in the federal courts, but not in state trials.

Federal agents, however, continue to tap wires. The F.B.I. uses wire tapping in cases of espionage, sabotage, internal security, and instances where human lives are in jeopardy, the theory being that divulging the results of wire tapping by one federal agent to another is not a "divulging" within the meaning of the Act of Congress. Though the evidence is inadmissible, it may give leads to other evidence which is used. Thus the prosecution often gets an enormous advantage by doing indirectly what it may not do directly. The burden of showing that wire tapping is used against the accused is on the accused. And it is a burden difficult in practice to maintain.

Relaxation of the 1934 federal law has been repeatedly sought. Wire tapping, it is said, is essential or important in detection of crime. The use of torture is also effective in getting confessions from suspects. But a civilized society does not sanction it. Wire tapping may catch criminals who might otherwise escape. But a degree of inefficiency is a price we necessarily pay for a civilized, decent society. The free state offers what a police state denies—the privacy of the home, the dignity and peace of mind of the individual. That precious right to be let alone is violated once the police enter our conversations.

Most states have legislation prohibiting wire tapping. But they generally admit evidence so obtained in criminal trials.

New York became the first state to provide a procedure for supervised wire tapping. A constitutional amendment in 1938, together with legislation subsequently enacted, permits a judge to issue an order allowing the prosecution or the police to tap telegraph or telephone wires on a showing that there is reasonable ground to believe that evidence of crime may be thus obtained and on identifying the lines to be tapped, the persons involved, and the purpose of the tap. These orders may be issued in the judge's chambers, secretly and without notice.

During 1952, there were in New York City alone at least 58,000 orders issued which allowed wire tapping—over 150 a day every day in the year. The New York system has in practice been oppressive; it has been used as the means whereby police have obtained guarded confidences of people and used the information for corrupt purposes.

Wire tapping, wherever used, has a black record. The invasion of privacy is ominous. It is dragnet in character, recording everything that is said, by the innocent as well as by the guilty. It ransacks their private lives, overhears their confessions, and probes their innermost secrets. It is specially severe in labor espionage, in loyalty investigations, in probes to find out what people think.

Someday controls may be worked out. But today, wire tapping is a blight on the civil liberties of the citizen.

JUNE 7   *Discrimination against the Japanese*

In the 1800's, anti-Japanese sentiment began to appear on the west coast. "The Japs Must Go" became a political slogan. Trade unionists later organized an Asiatic Exclusion League. In San Francisco, Asian students were segregated in public schools. At first the Japanese were laborers. Soon they became farmers, merchants, and fishermen. Then their competition was felt and the crusade against them mounted in intensity. Land laws were passed making aliens from Asia ineligible to own land, or to lease it for more than short terms. Californians promoted a federal law making all Asians ineligible for citizenship. The restrictions which the western States placed on land ownership by Japanese aliens were sustained by the Supreme Court in 1923, control of land ownership, in the opinion of the Justices, being fundamental to the sovereignty of the States. But early in 1948, the discrimination against Japanese aliens was not allowed to be extended to the children born here, for those children are citizens regardless of race. And on June 7, 1948, the Court held that a State could not disqualify an alien Japanese from getting a license as a commercial fisherman merely because he was Japanese. The Equal Protection Clause of the Fourteenth Amendment once more protected the right of aliens to earn a living in a lawful occupation. Once more racism as a political creed was nullified (May 10, 17).

Under the *Constitution,* Congress has power to regulate commerce among the States. From the earliest days that power was broadly construed. Today it is a vital source of authority for the federal government.

It was soon argued that effective regulation of *interstate* commerce also required some control of *intrastate* activities. The controversy took many forms, one of the earliest being an attempt by the federal government to regulate intrastate freight rates.

There was competition between Shreveport, Louisiana, and Dallas and Houston, Texas, for business in East Texas. The comparative freight rates from East Texas to the three cities often determined which city Texans used as a market. Texas sought to stimulate growth in Dallas and Houston by setting rates from those cities to East Texas much lower than those from Shreveport to East Texas. For instance, sixty cents would carry an amount of freight 160 miles eastward from Dallas, but only 55 miles westward from Shreveport.

The Interstate Commerce Commission ordered the railroads to end this discrimination against Shreveport by raising their intrastate rates. Texas argued that these shipments, being wholly within Texas, were not subject to federal control. On June 8, 1914, the Court held that the power of Congress includes the right to control intrastate trade where otherwise interstate commerce would be discriminated against.

That opinion was written by Hughes. It was Hughes who again wrote for the Court in 1937, upholding the *National Labor Relations Act* against the claim of States' rights. Factories that produce goods for interstate commerce are engaged in a local activity. But even so, their activities may so "affect" interstate commerce (for example, by paralyzing strikes) as to give Congress control over them.

This theory of Hughes opened broad vistas for federal power. It laid the basis for many controls over business which Congress imposed in the 1930's and 1940's.

One of the bitterest contests over the Commerce Clause related to the effort of Congress to regulate hours of work and conditions of labor in factories producing goods for interstate commerce. In 1916, it prohibited interstate shipments from mines or factories that employed children under 14 years of age, or that permitted children between 14 and 16 to work more than 8 hours a day or more than 6 days a week. In 1918, the Act was declared unconstitutional by a five to four decision of the Supreme Court. The Court held that the production of goods was exclusively a matter for local regulation.

Congress then tried to tax the products of child labor out of existence. But in 1922, the Court struck the tax down. There followed a nearly successful attempt to amend the *Constitution* so as to give Congress the power. Meanwhile, the Court was holding in a long line of decisions that Congress could close the channels of interstate commerce to certain harmful or odious traffic—lottery tickets, liquor, "white slaves," stolen motor vehicles, filled milk, convict-made goods.

If these could be barred, why not goods made by child labor?

If these prohibitions did not invade States' rights, why did a prohibition against child labor goods?

In 1938, Congress prescribed minimum wages and maximum hours of work for employees "engaged in commerce, or the production of goods for commerce," and barred from commerce goods of a manufacturer employing child labor. In 1941, a unanimous Court, speaking through Stone, overruled the 1918 decision and held that the regulation of labor standards in industries producing goods for commerce was an appropriate means of protecting interstate commerce from unfair competition due to substandard labor conditions, and was therefore within the commerce power of Congress.

The 1918 decision fitted the policy notion of judges who never shared the expansive interpretation of the Commerce Clause that both Marshall and Hughes had championed.

Should one man be able to act as prosecutor, judge, and jury, and sentence a person to jail, or fine him? Judges have often done just that—convicting men for contempt of court in summary trials without a jury (July 24). Some bitter contests have raged over those episodes (March 17).

One of the earliest was in 1831. One Lawless, who lost a case before Judge James H. Peck, a federal judge in Missouri, printed in a newspaper a "concise statement of some of the principal errors." Peck summarily sentenced Lawless to one day in prison, and suspended him from the practice of law for eighteen months for contempt. Congress tried Peck for impeachment, and finally acquitted him by a vote of 22 to 21. Thereupon, Congress restricted the power to punish for contempt to cases of misbehavior in the presence of the court, or so near thereto as to obstruct the administration of justice. All other cases of contempt had to be tried like any other criminal case—before an impartial judge and jury.

In 1918, the Supreme Court had before it a case involving the editor of a Toledo newspaper who had been held in contempt by a federal judge for intimating in an editorial that the judge was too biased to sit in a particular case. On June 10, the Court, over the dissent of Holmes and Brandeis, held that newspapers could be summarily convicted for making statements derogatory of the court prior to or during a trial, when, in the judge's opinion, the article or editorial had a "reasonable tendency" to "obstruct the administration of justice."

The dissent in the Toledo case became the law in a series of decisions beginning in 1941. Newspaper comment on trials, though ill-tempered or prejudiced, is part of our freedom of speech and of press. A judge denounced or attacked by a paper may not drag the editor in by the heels and summarily punish him. If newspapers violate a law in what they print, they are entitled to trial, with all the safeguards of our criminal procedure.

In 1841, a British publisher was found guilty of blasphemy for printing Shelley's *Queen Mab,* a philosophical poem which makes an attack on religion, particularly on the story of Adam and Eve and on the divinity of Christ.

The judge charged the jury: "Were the lines indicted calculated to shock the feelings of any Christian reader? Were their points of offence explained, or was their vice neutralized by any remarks in the margin, by any note of explanation or apology? If not, they were libels on God, and indictable."

The jury found the defendant guilty, but he was never sentenced.

Since the adoption of the *Constitution,* there have been only a few blasphemy convictions in this country. On June 11, 1811, Ruggles was found guilty in New York. Updegraph was convicted in Pennsylvania in 1822, Kneeland in Massachusetts in 1834, Chandler in Delaware in 1837, Mockus in Maine in 1921.

Ruggles and Chandler had attacked the character of Jesus in vile language. Updegraph (who won on appeal by reason of a defective indictment) said that the Scriptures were a mere fable, containing a number of good things, but also a great many lies. Kneeland said, "Universalists believe in a god which I do not; but believe that their god, with all his moral attributes (aside from nature itself) is nothing more than a mere chimera of their own imagination." Mockus impugned the Immaculate Conception in coarse and vulgar language.

Blasphemy, insofar as it employs vile language, overlaps obscenity. Insofar as it involves bona fide theological discourse or argumentation, it is tangled with questions of freedom of religion.

Our most famous Bill of Rights goes back to June 12, 1776, the date Virginia adopted a *Declaration of Rights*, drafted by George Mason. It guaranteed freedom of press and religion, right to jury trial, and most of the procedural safeguards for criminal trials now contained in the Fifth and Sixth Amendments. It subordinated the military to the civil power. It provided for free elections, and placed the taxing power in the hands of elected officials. It proclaimed against unreasonable searches and seizures. Beyond these specific measures, it stated a profound, though revolutionary, concept of government:

1. That all men are by nature equally free and independent, and have certain inherent rights, of which, when they enter into a state of society, they cannot by any compact deprive or divest their posterity; namely, the enjoyment of life and liberty, with the means of acquiring and possessing property, and pursuing and obtaining happiness and safety.

2. That all power is vested in, and consequently derived from, the people; that magistrates are their trustees and servants, and at all times amenable to them.

3. That government is, or ought to be instituted for the common benefit, protection, and security of the people, nation, or community; . . . that when any government shall be found inadequate or contrary to these purposes, a majority of the community hath an indubitable, unalienable and indefeasible right to reform, alter or abolish it, in such manner as shall be judged most conductive to the public weal.

On June 13, 1779, Thomas Jefferson wrote his famous article of faith on free speech:

"The opinions of men are not the object of civil government, nor under its jurisdiction; that to suffer the civil magistrate to intrude his powers into the field of opinion and to restrain the profession or propagation of principles on supposition of their ill tendency is a dangerous fallacy, which at once destroys all religious liberty, because he being of course judge of that tendency will make his opinions the rule of judgment, and approve or condemn the sentiments of others only as they shall square with or differ from his own; that it is time enough for the rightful purposes of civil government for its officers to interfere when principles break out into overt acts against peace and good order; and finally, that truth is great and will prevail if left to herself; that she is the proper and sufficient antagonist to error, and has nothing to fear from the conflict unless by human interposition disarmed of her natural weapons, free argument and debate; errors ceasing to be dangerous when it is permitted freely to contradict them."

Most of this is in the preamble of an Act sponsored by Jefferson and Madison and finally passed by Virginia in 1786. It is the essence of the provision in the First Amendment that "Congress shall make no law . . . abridging the freedom of speech, or of the press . . ."

Courts have not always been faithful to that command. They have read "no law" as meaning "some law" and at times have allowed the legislature to curb speech when the courts thought the legislature had grounds for believing that the public interest required it (October 28, 29, 30). Jefferson placed no restraints on discussion of political, social, or economic affairs, whether the ideas expressed were popular or unpopular. His idea was that even rash and violent talk should be allowed; that debate and argument, no matter how revolutionary the sound, were sacrosanct. Only when speech moved into the realm of action against peace and security could it constitutionally be punished.

Freedom of speech protects various interests. First, there is the interest of the speaker. The right of conscience—the right to think and believe as one chooses—does not amount to much if there is no right to give expression to one's ideas. Life in a police state is a suffocating experience.

There is, secondly, the public interest in allowing people to "blow off steam." It is good therapy for the individual, and for society as well. Grievances that are aired do not become as virulent as grievances that are suppressed or driven underground. The British experience at Hyde Park—where sage or crackpot can speak as he will—is evidence enough.

But the most important aspect of freedom of speech is freedom to learn (September 2). All education is a continuing dialogue—questions and answers that pursue every problem to the horizon. That is the essence of academic freedom, of all scientific inquiry. Pursuit of that ideal caused Socrates his death. He was the "gadfly" whose mission was to rouse, reprove, and argue with people. He plagued their consciences and challenged their prejudices. He taught that "virtue does not spring from riches but riches and all other human blessings, both private and public, from virtue." Hence, he was charged with "corrupting the youth."

Once limits are put on discussion people do not develop their capacities. They cease to learn and become saturated with the prevailing orthodox creed. They are apt to become minions of one political sect. New ideas become fearful or dangerous. That is why totalitarian governments dare not allow free universities, free speech, free churches. That is also why any totalitarian government cannot long endure. For the mind of man can never be long kept in chains.

Richard the Lion-Hearted was dead and his brother John ruled England as the thirteenth century began. John was talented and aggressive. He increased the taxes on the barons and the Church, confiscated estates, limited landowners' rights to leave their property to their children, deprived the barons of their right to hold court for their tenants, and appropriated the food and provisions of the monasteries. The barons and the clergy were not the only ones who suffered. The mercantile class paid heavy taxes and in return were oppressed by an evil government. And John's appropriation of the food of the monasteries destroyed the chief provision for poor relief of that day.

John had a quarrel with the Church that aroused the people even more. Pope Innocent III appointed Stephen Langton as Archbishop of Canterbury. John showed his displeasure by exiling all the monks. The Pope countered by interdicting all of England, excommunicating John, and persuading France and Scotland to make war on him. At the last minute, John capitulated to the Pope. But that did not stop the seething unrest in England. Even lower-class Englishmen were aroused against him. Public sentiment and the urgency of the situation united, for the moment, all of John's opponents. The barons and clergy under the guidance of Stephen Langton drew up their demands. On the banks of the Thames at Runnymede, John capitulated. On June 15, 1215, he accepted the *Magna Carta*—a document that was an affirmation that free men had fundamental rights.

The *Magna Carta* has 61 Articles, most of which merely enumerate the feudal rights of the barons, and are no longer of interest. But Articles 39 and 40 went further:

39. No freeman shall be taken, or imprisoned, or outlawed, or exiled, or in any way harmed, nor will we go upon or send upon him, save by the lawful judgment of his peers or by the law of the land.
40. To none will we sell, to none deny or delay, right or justice.

These were the antecedents—more remote than commonly thought—of due process of law and the guarantee of trial by jury.

A committee of twenty-five barons was established to enforce the charter. This opened the way for the barons to work as a class rather than as individuals in their political struggle against the King. Thus the way was paved for the entry of new classes into the political arena. First the nobles, then the bourgeois used the *Magna Carta* to defend their interests against the royal power. This precedent was of some importance in the forces that eventually produced the British Parliament.

But the *Magna Carta* had values more intangible and yet greater. It signified that the King was not above the law, but subservient to it. The idea grew with each infringement of rights. A King who thereafter transgressed was palpably wrong. A citizen who pleaded for the rights of man found the *Magna Carta* the rallying point for public opinion. The *Magna Carta* grew in symbolism with the passing centuries, and came to have more powerful moral authority than the barons who drew it ever dreamed.

When Thomas Cromwell and Henry VIII brought the Reformation to England, vast reforms were undertaken. The monasteries that owned great wealth and wielded political power were dissolved (April 27). Then came regulations of religious matters. The clergy were forbidden to promote belief in miracles or in pilgrimages for saints. They were admonished to teach the Protestant faith and to warn their hearers not to count their beads or offer money to images. It was forbidden to light candles before images or pictures.

Laws were passed defining heresy. Heresy included denial that in communion "the natural body and blood" of Christ is "present really under the form of bread and wine." One convicted "shall for his first Offence recant, for his second adjure and bear a Faggot, and for his third shall be adjudged an Heretick, and be burned and lose all his Goods and Chattels."

Moreover, the clergy were enjoined to provide a *Bible* for each church and to encourage the people to read it, for it is "the word of God" that every Christian must believe "if he look to be saved."

This was in 1538. But in 1543, a great change took place. A law was passed which said:

"The *Bible* shall not be read in English in any Church. No Women or Artificers, Prentices, Journeymen, Servingmen of the Degree of Yeomen or under, Husbandmen, nor Labourers, shall read the New Testament in English. Nothing shall be taught or maintained contrary to the King's Instructions."

Why did Henry VIII first introduce the *Bible* and then restrict its use, confining it to the nobility and gentlemen, and letting them read it privately but not publicly?

First, people in general, the common folks, are not to be trusted.

Second, the *Bible* promotes a diversity of ideas. People who read it may end up with strongly dissident views. That is always a dangerous condition for those who want to establish one orthodox view and indoctrinate the common people with it.

On June 18, 1940, a federal court in Virginia rendered an historic decision. A Negro schoolteacher of Norfolk sued the school board, charging that the salaries fixed for him and other Negro teachers in the public schools were lower than those paid white teachers and that the difference was not based on qualifications, experience, or the duties and services rendered, but solely on race and color.

The court did not determine whether the charges were or were not true. It did rule, however, that if they were proven, a violation of the Fourteenth Amendment would be established. No one has a right to teach for the State. Employment of teachers rests on the discretion of the school authorities. But an applicant has the constitutional right to a salary fixed on the merits, not reduced or diminished by reason of his race or color.

"If a man be taken in execution and lie in prison for debt, neither the plaintiff at whose suit he is arrested, nor the sheriff who took him, is bound to find him meat, drink, or clothes; but he must live on his own, or on the charity of others; and if no man will relieve him, let him die in the name of God, says the law; and so say I." Thus spoke Mr. Justice Hyde on June 19, 1663.

Beginning in 1283, England allowed merchants to have their debtors arrested for non-payment. Imprisonment for debt was gradually extended by legislation and judicial rulings until in most civil cases a defendant could be arrested *before* judgment and kept in prison until he paid.

No opportunity was afforded him to work. He was closely guarded, for if he escaped the sheriff had to pay the debt. Even if the plaintiff felt sorry for the debtor, he would be reluctant to consent to his release, for release from prison was an irrevocable payment of the debt.

The Fleet was the most famous of debtors' prisons. The Warden of the Fleet was an office that was contracted out; the prison was a vile place. The plight of debtors cast a shadow over the land. Dickens told some of the horrors in *Little Dorrit* and *The Pickwick Papers*. Shakespeare expressed the popular revulsion in *The Comedy of Errors*.

ADRIANA: Where is thy master, Dromio? is he well?
DROMIO: No, he's in Tartar limbo, worse than Hell.
    A Devil in an everlasting garment hath him;
    One whose hard heart is button'd up with steel;
    A Fiend, a Fairy pitiless and rough;
    A wolf, nay, worse, a fellow all in buff;
    A back-friend, a shoulder-clapper, one that countermands
    The passages of alleys, creeks and narrow lands;
    A hound that runs counter and yet draws dry-foot well;
    One that before the Judgment carries poor souls to Hell.

Silas M. Stilwell is a name for Americans to honor. He led the fight in New York in one of the great battles for humanity—abolition of imprisonment for debt. The law he sponsored was enacted in 1831. It allowed imprisonment for debt only in case of fraud. Other States followed in a wave of reform that swept the country. Today a few States forbid imprisonment for debt without exception. Usually fraud is an exception; cases of willful injury are common exceptions. Absconding debtors and those in arrears for alimony are also exceptions. Defendants are usually entitled to bail; and even when they are placed in jail, the "jail" may be a prescribed area such as Manhattan Island, New York City.

Only one State today recognizes bondage for all forms of debt. That State is Vermont. But even there, a debtor (except in cases of fraud) "shall not be continued in prison after his delivering up and assigning over, *bona fide,* all his estate, real and personal."

England finally abolished imprisonment for debt (with the exception of cases of fraud) in 1869.

The northern and middle States were the worst offenders in this country. In 1830 those States had three to five times as many persons in jail for debt as for crime. Only 10 per cent owed more than $100; about 15 per cent owed less than $5.00.

There was very little imprisonment for debt in the South. The great philanthropist, James Edward Oglethorpe, had indeed undertaken to colonize Georgia with those who fled the fearful debtors' jails of England. That is doubtless one reason the South showed more compassion than the North.

The Fifteenth Amendment, adopted in 1870, provides that the right of citizens to vote shall not be denied by the federal government nor by the States "on account of race, color, or previous condition of servitude." Since that time numerous devices have been tried to prevent Negroes from voting (April 3). The Grandfather Clause was one. It is illustrated by a 1910 amendment to the constitution of Oklahoma. This amendment provided a literacy test for voting; but it went on to say that the literacy test would not be required of anyone who was on January 1, 1866 (that is to say, prior to the Fifteenth Amendment), entitled to vote or who at that time resided in some foreign nation, or of any lineal descendent of such person.

On June 21, 1915, the Supreme Court held this provision unconstitutional as an unmistakable, though somewhat disguised, refusal to give effect to the Fifteenth Amendment, since in Oklahoma, Negroes were not entitled to vote in 1866. It was, in other words, a way of keeping illiterate Negroes from voting, though allowing the privilege to illiterate whites.

The Oklahoma formula, if successful, would have had a serious impact. In Oklahoma 3.5 per cent of the whites, as against 17.7 per cent of the Negroes, were illiterate. Moreover, the 1866 voting test would have wide ramifications. In that year Negroes could vote in only eight of the States, where only about 2 per cent of all the Negroes in the United States lived.

James Sommersett was a slave whom his owner took with him to England on a business trip. The owner's purpose was to take Sommersett to Jamaica and sell him. While Sommersett was in England under the custody of the ship's captain, he applied for a writ of habeas corpus.

On June 22, 1772, Lord Mansfield ordered the Negro discharged, saying that no law of England sanctioned slavery, that there were no moral or political reasons which could justify it, that it was "so odious that nothing can be suffered to support it."

The decision had one important effect overseas: it illustrated to the people on this side of the Atlantic, who were yet to have their revolution, the importance of habeas corpus in a system of liberty under law.

Two years earlier a Massachusetts court had reached the same conclusion, a result reaffirmed in 1783 by the Massachusetts Supreme Court in a decision which held that the American ideas of equality, freedom, and liberty were wholly repugnant to slavery.

Guilt by association is a dangerous doctrine. It condemns one man for the unlawful conduct of another. It draws ugly insinuations from an association that may be wholly innocent. In June 1945, the Supreme Court stated the American philosophy concerning this concept:

". . . Individuals, like nations, may cooperate in a common cause over a period of months or years though their ultimate aims do not coincide. Alliances for limited objectives are well known. Certainly those who joined forces with Russia to defeat the Nazis may not be said to have made an alliance to spread the cause of Communism. An individual who makes contributions to feed hungry men does not become 'affiliated' with the Communist cause because those men are Communists. A different result is not necessarily indicated if aid is given to or received from a proscribed organization in order to win a legitimate objective in a domestic controversy. Whether intermittent or repeated, the act or acts tending to prove 'affiliation' must be of that quality which indicates an adherence to or a furtherance of the purposes or objectives of the proscribed organization as distinguished from mere cooperation with it in lawful activities. The act or acts must evidence a working alliance to bring the program to fruition. . . ."

The occasion for this statement was an order directing Harry Bridges to be deported because he was "affiliated" with the communist party. But *the record in the proceeding* showed only cooperation with communist groups for the attainment of wholly lawful objectives.

Guilt by association was also denounced in a 1952 decision of the Court involving an oath exacted of teachers in Oklahoma. They were barred from employment, if during the prior five years they had been members of an organization listed by the Attorney General as "subversive." The law disqualified from employment those whose membership was wholly innocent of any unlawful purpose. It was therefore struck down as an unconstitutional interference with a teacher's liberty.

California, like many other States, long had a law making it a crime for anyone to bring into the State an indigent person, i.e., a person destitute of property, without resources to obtain the necessities of life, and without friends or relatives able and willing to support him. On June 24, 1940, the California courts sustained a conviction of one Edwards for bringing his wife's brother, Frank Duncan, from Texas to California, Duncan being unemployed, without funds, and ending up being supported by a federal relief agency.

That conviction was set aside by a unanimous Supreme Court. Some of the Justices held that the movement of people across state lines was interstate commerce, which Congress alone had authority to regulate. Other Justices thought the right of migration was one of the rights of national citizenship. Disease might enable a State to stop a migrant at her borders, but not poverty. Poverty was a powerful impetus in all our migrations, and migrations are an historic American method for seeking new opportunities elsewhere. Statistics showed that more than one fifth of all native-born Americans had migrated from the States of their birth to other States.

The Supreme Court in the *Edwards* case repudiated the dictum of the Court, announced in 1837, that it was as competent for a State "to provide precautionary measures against the moral pestilence of paupers" as it was "to guard against the physical pestilence."

The poor were long considered aliens in the parish where they lived, and deportable by the authorities. The dark story of their being passed round and round in England and, wherever practicable, sent across the border to Scotland or across the waters to Ireland or Jersey, was told by Sidney and Beatrice Webb in *English Poor Law History*. Worse still was the practice of "farming out the poor" to contractors, who, to increase their profits, often turned their workhouses into houses of terror that soon shocked the conscience of England.

We followed some of those precedents to a shameful extent: paupers were removed from towns where they went to better their condition; people were punished for harboring paupers deemed undesirable by the city authorities; the poor were "let out" to contractors; citizens were disfranchised when they became so destitute that they had to seek public aid (January 22). For example, down to 1947 no pauper could vote in New Jersey.

An interesting episode happened in North Dakota in the 1930's. The Hulms came to North Dakota from South Dakota looking for work. Roy Hulm was paralyzed and unable to do hard labor. He had a wife and ten children. They settled in Burleigh County, where they lived over a year. Shortly after Hulm applied for work on a W.P.A. project, the sheriff got an order from the local court directing removal of the Hulms to South Dakota because they were indigent. The South Dakota authorities would not receive the Hulms, so they were deposited in Adams County, North Dakota, where they lived on charity.

Adams County thereupon sued Burleigh County, asking that the latter be required to take the Hulms back and also to reimburse Adams County for the support of the family. The North Dakota Supreme Court granted the relief, saying:

"Somewhere and somehow the wellsprings of humanity and brotherhood appear to be dried up. Sick and impoverished creatures against whom there is no indication of crime, laziness, or willfulness, have no place to lay their weary heads."

In 1886, there was great industrial strife around Chicago over the attempt to introduce an eight-hour day. On May 3, a bloody encounter took place between police and laborers in which several workers were killed. An anarchist group printed a circular headed "Revenge! Revenge! Workmen to Arms" and called a meeting at Haymarket Square the next night. The meeting was orderly; even Chicago's Mayor attended. But the police undertook to break it up. Some unknown person threw a bomb, killing several policemen. Four of the convicted men were hanged on November 11, 1887. The sentences of two were commuted to life; one received fifteen years. In 1892, John Peter Altgeld was elected Governor of Illinois, and one of his first acts was to entertain a petition for pardon of the three—Samuel Fielden, Michael Schwab, and Oscar Neebe.

Altgeld found that the jury which convicted the men had been "packed," i.e., made up of men selected (with the help of a special bailiff) because of their prejudice; that there was no evidence connecting the three men with the crime; that they had not received a fair trial. They *had* made incendiary talks; they *had* perhaps been "anarchists." But there was *no shred of proof* connecting them with the bomb. Altgeld felt they were victims of the frenzy of passion that had swept Chicago in those days. His pardon message was issued June 26, 1893. It served the cause of justice, but it ruined Altgeld politically. He knew the bitter years. He lost his health and his wealth under the pressure of his enemies. The man who had the courage to give a despised minority the protection of the *Bill of Rights* was hounded to his death.

In 1947, Carl Sandburg and I were at a dinner in Chicago honoring the 100th Anniversary of Altgeld's birth. Sandburg—America's beloved poet and biographer of Lincoln—read Vachel Lindsay's poem, *The Eagle That Is Forgotten,* which eulogizes Altgeld. In the middle of the reading his voice broke so that it seemed he would not be able to finish. Afterwards, I spoke to Sandburg about the incident.

Sandburg's explanation was this:

"When the four anarchists were hanged on November 11, 1887, I was a boy in Chicago, nine years old. When I heard the news, 'Well, they hanged 'em,' I felt good. I felt as if Chicago had been saved from evil men. Six years later I read Altgeld's pardon message and realized that the hanging of those men had been an act of great injustice—an act that could not be undone."

There were tears in Sandburg's eyes as he added:

"Tonight when I read *The Eagle That Is Forgotten,* I suddenly remembered that as a boy I had been a victim of the frenzy of passion that swept Chicago in the '80's. It was the awful realization that I had felt elated over an act of injustice. That's why I choked up on the radio and almost lost my voice."

376

In 1864, Congress recognized the legality of "contract labor," by providing that those who brought emigrants here might have a lien on their wages "for a term not exceeding twelve months to repay the expenses of their emigration" and, if the contract so provides, on the land the emigrants might thereafter acquire. That law was repealed in 1868. But the practice itself was not outlawed until 1885.

A Congressional committee condemned the practice in a report dated June 28, 1884. It did not want to restrict free immigration; but it felt that he who came, not "by his own initiative but by that of the capitalist," created special problems:

"This class of immigrants are men whose passage is paid by the importers. . . . They are generally from the lowest social stratum, and live upon the coarsest food and in hovels of a character before unknown to American workmen. Being bound by contract they are unable, even were they so disposed, to take advantage of the facilities afforded by the country to which they have been imported. They, as a rule, do not become citizens, and are certainly not a desirable acquisition to the body public. When their term of contract servitude expires, their place is supplied by fresh importations. The inevitable tendency of their presence amongst us is to degrade American labor and reduce it to the level of the imported pauper labor.

"The demand for the enactment of some restrictive measure of this character comes not alone from American workingmen, but also from employers. . . . The employers of labor, who . . . employ only American workingmen, are unable to compete in the markets with the corporations who employ the cheap imported labor.

"As an evidence of the truth of this proposition, the glass manufacturers of Pittsburgh, including all the large employers of labor in that industry, in January, 1880, denounced the action of the manufacturers west of Pittsburgh in importing European workmen in place of discharged American workmen."

A great host of indentured servants came to America during the eighteenth century. Many came from Germany; many more from England, Scotland, and Ireland. They were tailors, weavers, farm hands, clerks, shoemakers, teachers, doctors, lawyers. Some fled war-stricken regions; others sought escape from poverty, want, and persecution. In 1774, John Harrower became an articled schoolteacher to a Virginia family: "This day I being reduced to the last shilling was obliged to engage to go to Virginia for four years as a schoolteacher for Bedd, Board, washing and five pounds during the whole time."

Those who brought them here under contract were the "white slavers" of that century. The business was a brisk one, the profits great. Sometimes the indentured servants would be sold prior to shipment, the American owner paying the transportation and the brokerage. At other times the risk of the venture was on the contractor who would advertise, "Lately arrived from London, a parcel of very likely English servants, men and women to be sold reasonable and time allowed for payments."

Tens of thousands of emigrants came in this fashion. Most worked out their contracts with their masters, whom they called "soul drivers"; many slipped away into the frontier to make with an ax a home of their own.

These indentured servants, though derelicts, plebeians, and commoners, conditioned American thought in an important way. They easily suspected the motives behind Tory programs and Tory pronouncements. They had experienced the sufferings of underlings in an aristocratic society; they had piled up grievance after grievance; they were receptive to the democratic ideas which political agitators such as Samuel Adams (July 11) were promoting.

We have had a glorious list of "muckrakers" in America—Henry Demarest Lloyd, Lincoln Steffens, Ray Stannard Baker, Ida M. Tarbell, Samuel Hopkins Adams, Upton Sinclair, to mention only a few. They conducted many wars against social, financial, and political evils. Perhaps the most important of all was their war against poison, which resulted in the *Pure Food and Drug Act* and the *Meat Inspection Act,* both enacted June 30, 1906.

The most powerful document was *The Jungle* by Upton Sinclair, which in novel form laid bare the awful picture of contaminated food turned out by the meat-packing houses. Dr. Harvey W. Wiley, Dr. E. F. Ladd, Dr. James H. Shepard revealed an amazing use of adulterants and preservatives in other canned and prepared foods.

Dr. Wiley submitted twelve healthy young men (dubbed the "poison squad") to tests to show that preservatives used in food were harmful to health. In other studies, it was shown how from an average breakfast one got eight doses of harmful chemicals and dyes, at lunch, sixteen, at dinner, sixteen. In patent medicines, one often got poisons or habit-forming drugs.

Collier's, the *Ladies Home Journal, McClure's* took up the cudgel. The New York *Evening Post* lampooned the packers:

> *Mary had a little lamb,*
> *And when she saw it sicken,*
> *She shipped it off to Packing-town,*
> *And now it's labelled chicken.*

Theodore Roosevelt made the issue a political one. The disclosures of the muckrakers and of a commission appointed by Roosevelt were revolting. Public indignation reached the boiling point. The country resolved to have done with the practices of merchants who built fortunes by undermining the health of the nation. The passage of these laws was a victory of the muckrakers over some of the most powerful lobbies ever brought to Washington, D.C.

JULY

Racism cuts deeper into human relations the world over than any other force. Racial prejudices are present in every nation. They often make political outlaws out of racial minorities, and even close avenues of employment to certain groups.

We in this country have sometimes carried discrimination into our factories and shops, the Negroes, Jews, and Mexicans feeling the main brunt of it. The practice has been nationwide, though not all trades have been affected. Employers are not the only offenders. Unions too have shown a racial bias.

There have been numerous victories in the battle for equality of opportunity in employment. Private groups such as The National Conference of Christians and Jews, founded by Charles E. Hughes and Newton D. Baker, have made progress. Roosevelt's Fair Employment Practice Committee did notable work during World War II. In 1944, the Supreme Court ruled that under the *Railway Labor Act* a union must act for all the employees whom it represents, colored as well as white, and may be enjoined from taking discriminatory action against members based on race. Some unions have changed their policies, no longer making membership turn on race or color.

By 1954, a dozen States, Alaska, and over two dozen municipalities had some form of fair employment practice legislation. The most comprehensive is New York's, effective July 1, 1945. It established a state commission to police discrimination, and prohibited employers and unions alike from discriminating against any employee because of his "race, creed, color, or national origin."

Vaclav Hlavaty, a refugee from communist Czechoslovakia, is the brilliant mathematician who, in 1953, solved the equations of Albert Einstein's unified field theory. In commenting on man's efforts to understand the universe, Hlavaty said, "The farther we go the more the ultimate explanation recedes from us, and all we have left is faith."

This question of faith goes to the very heart of the problem of survival. Faith in men of opposing political creeds—faith in people who worship God from a temple too strange for us to call a church—faith in those who reject institutions and ways of thought which we hold dear—faith in the great and exciting diversity of man—faith in the inevitability of the failure of communism or any other form of dictatorship which leaves out of account God and His ethical principles—faith that there is a community of human need in the world that cuts across all barriers of race, creed, or color—faith that ideas of liberty will always command the market place when there is freedom of speech and of press.

Faith of people in each other has suffered greatly since World War II. At home, the campaigns of hate and suspicion have taken a devastating toll. The illicit methods of the witch hunt tore communities apart, and set faction against faction, until at times any but the orthodox was suspect. What we did at home had powerful repercussions abroad. We became in Europe and Asia more and more the symbol of intolerance. Our emphasis on guns and dollars, rather than on fraternity and democracy, alienated us more and more from the peoples of the world. The deterioration has been alarming. An Asian friend, who hates communism with all his being, had tears in his eyes as he said farewell in 1954 after a year's visit here. "All of us in Asia will be solidly aligned against America in a few years."

Our faith in Asia would generate Asia's faith in us. Without faith, there is nothing but the bomb. And the bomb leads only to the crucible.

Our freedom is the product of countless episodes, the gradual accretion of precedents, the slow growth of habits and attitudes. No one event has marked its victory; no one event, its decline. It has been retained or lost, depending on the intensity of the efforts continuously to renew it—in our villages as well as in our capitals. Its vigor or decline has often been marked by a pattern of deeds so small as hardly to be seen in the mosaic.

In days ahead, the dependency of freedom at home on events abroad will increase. Though the menace of Soviet imperialism were suddenly removed, there would still be alarming problems, problems we have yet hardly comprehended. They are reflected in the calculus of increasing population, limitation of food, depletion of raw materials, and the pressing need for industrialization in Asia. The liberty of one man will hereafter be closely linked with the hunger of another. The world community is more and more the testing ground for every man's freedom.

If liberty is to prevail, the prayer of Rabindranath Tagore must be our ideal:

> *Where the mind is without fear and*
> *the head is held high;*
> > *Where knowledge is free;*
> > *Where the world has not been broken*
> *up into fragments by narrow domestic walls;*
> > *Where words come out from the*
> *depth of truth;*
> > *Where tireless striving stretches its*
> *arms towards perfection;*
> > *Where the clear stream of reason has*
> *not lost its way into the dreary desert*
> *sand of dead habit;*
> > *Where the mind is led forward by*
> *Thee into ever-widening thought and*
> *action——*
> > *Into that heaven of freedom, my*
> *Father, let my country awake.*

KINGS AND QUEENS OF ENGLAND

Reign Began

WILLIAM I	OCTOBER 14, 1066
WILLIAM II	SEPTEMBER 26, 1087
HENRY I	AUGUST 5, 1100
STEPHEN	DECEMBER 26, 1135
HENRY II	DECEMBER 19, 1154
RICHARD I	SEPTEMBER 23, 1189
JOHN	MAY 27, 1199
HENRY III	OCTOBER 28, 1216
EDWARD I	NOVEMBER 20, 1272
EDWARD II	JULY 8, 1307
EDWARD III	JANUARY 25, 1326
RICHARD II	JUNE 22, 1377
HENRY IV	SEPTEMBER 30, 1399
HENRY V	MARCH 21, 1413
HENRY VI	SEPTEMBER 1, 1422
EDWARD IV	MARCH 4, 1461
EDWARD V	APRIL 9, 1483
RICHARD III	JUNE 26, 1483
HENRY VII	AUGUST 22, 1485
HENRY VIII	APRIL 22, 1509

Reign Begun

EDWARD VI	JANUARY 28, 1547
MARY	JULY 6, 1553
ELIZABETH I	NOVEMBER 17, 1558
JAMES I	MARCH 24, 1603
CHARLES I	MARCH 27, 1625
CHARLES II	JANUARY 30, 1649
JAMES II	FEBRUARY 6, 1685
WILLIAM & MARY	FEBRUARY 13, 1689
ANNE	MARCH 8, 1702
GEORGE I	AUGUST 1, 1714
GEORGE II	JUNE 11, 1727
GEORGE III	OCTOBER 25, 1760
GEORGE IV	JANUARY 29, 1820
WILLIAM IV	JUNE 26, 1830
VICTORIA	JUNE 20, 1837
EDWARD VII	JANUARY 22, 1901
GEORGE V	MAY 6, 1910
EDWARD VIII	JANUARY 20, 1936
GEORGE VI	DECEMBER 10, 1936
ELIZABETH II	FEBRUARY 6, 1952

PRESIDENTS OF THE UNITED STATES

	Term Began
GEORGE WASHINGTON	APRIL 30, 1789
JOHN ADAMS	MARCH 4, 1797
THOMAS JEFFERSON	MARCH 4, 1801
JAMES MADISON	MARCH 4, 1809
JAMES MONROE	MARCH 4, 1817
JOHN QUINCY ADAMS	MARCH 4, 1825
ANDREW JACKSON	MARCH 4, 1829
MARTIN VAN BUREN	MARCH 4, 1837
WILLIAM HENRY HARRISON	MARCH 4, 1841
JOHN TYLER	APRIL 6, 1841
JAMES K. POLK	MARCH 4, 1845
ZACHARY TAYLOR	MARCH 5, 1849
MILLARD FILLMORE	JULY 10, 1850
FRANKLIN PIERCE	MARCH 4, 1853
JAMES BUCHANAN	MARCH 4, 1857
ABRAHAM LINCOLN	MARCH 4, 1861
ANDREW JOHNSON	APRIL 15, 1865
ULYSSES S. GRANT	MARCH 4, 1869
RUTHERFORD B. HAYES	MARCH 4, 1877
JAMES A. GARFIELD	MARCH 4, 1881

Presidents of the United States

Term Began

CHESTER A. ARTHUR	SEPTEMBER 20, 1881
GROVER CLEVELAND	MARCH 4, 1885
BENJAMIN HARRISON	MARCH 4, 1889
GROVER CLEVELAND	MARCH 4, 1893
WILLIAM MCKINLEY	MARCH 4, 1897
THEODORE ROOSEVELT	SEPTEMBER 14, 1901
WILLIAM H. TAFT	MARCH 4, 1909
WOODROW WILSON	MARCH 4, 1913
WARREN G. HARDING	MARCH 4, 1921
CALVIN COOLIDGE	AUGUST 3, 1923
HERBERT C. HOOVER	MARCH 4, 1929
FRANKLIN D. ROOSEVELT	MARCH 4, 1933
HARRY S. TRUMAN	APRIL 12, 1945
DWIGHT D. EISENHOWER	JANUARY 20, 1953

JUSTICES OF THE SUPREME COURT OF THE UNITED STATES

CHIEF JUSTICES IN ITALICS

	Term
John Jay	1789–1795
JOHN RUTLEDGE	1789–1791
WILLIAM CUSHING	1789–1810
JAMES WILSON	1789–1798
JOHN BLAIR	1789–1796
JAMES IREDELL	1790–1799
THOMAS JOHNSON	1791–1793
WILLIAM PATERSON	1793–1806
John Rutledge	1795–1795
SAMUEL CHASE	1796–1811
Oliver Ellsworth	1796–1800
BUSHROD WASHINGTON	1798–1829
ALFRED MOORE	1799–1804
John Marshall	1801–1835
WILLIAM JOHNSON	1804–1834
BROCKHOLST LIVINGSTON	1806–1823
THOMAS TODD	1807–1826
JOSEPH STORY	1811–1845
GABRIEL DUVAL	1811–1835
SMITH THOMPSON	1823–1843
ROBERT TRIMBLE	1826–1828
JOHN MCLEAN	1829–1861

	Term
HENRY BALDWIN	1830–1844
JAMES M. WAYNE	1835–1867
Roger B. Taney	**1836–1864**
PHILIP P. BARBOUR	1836–1841
JOHN CATRON	1837–1865
JOHN MCKINLEY	1837–1852
PETER V. DANIEL	1841–1860
SAMUEL NELSON	1845–1872
LEVI WOODBURY	1845–1851
ROBERT C. GRIER	1846–1870
BENJAMIN R. CURTIS	1851–1857
JOHN A. CAMPBELL	1853–1861
NATHAN CLIFFORD	1858–1881
NOAH H. SWAYNE	1862–1881
SAMUEL F. MILLER	1862–1890
DAVID DAVIS	1862–1877
STEPHEN J. FIELD	1863–1897
Salmon P. Chase	**1864–1873**
WILLIAM STRONG	1870–1880
JOSEPH P. BRADLEY	1870–1892
WARD HUNT	1872–1882
Morrison R. Waite	**1874–1888**
JOHN M. HARLAN	1877–1911
WILLIAM B. WOODS	1880–1887
STANLEY MATTHEWS	1881–1889
HORACE GRAY	1881–1902
SAMUEL BLATCHFORD	1882–1893
LUCIUS Q. C. LAMAR	1888–1893
Melville W. Fuller	**1888–1910**
DAVID J. BREWER	1889–1910
HENRY B. BROWN	1890–1906
GEORGE SHIRAS, JR.	1892–1903
HOWELL E. JACKSON	1893–1895
EDWARD D. WHITE	1894–1910
RUFUS W. PECKHAM	1895–1909

	Term
JOSEPH MCKENNA	1898–1925
OLIVER W. HOLMES	1902–1932
WILLIAM R. DAY	1903–1922
WILLIAM H. MOODY	1906–1910
HORACE H. LURTON	1909–1914
CHARLES E. HUGHES	1910–1916
Edward D. White	1910–1921
WILLIS VAN DEVANTER	1910–1937
JOSEPH R. LAMAR	1910–1916
MAHLON PITNEY	1912–1922
JAMES C. MCREYNOLDS	1914–1941
LOUIS D. BRANDEIS	1916–1939
JOHN H. CLARKE	1916–1922
William H. Taft	1921–1930
GEORGE SUTHERLAND	1922–1938
PIERCE BUTLER	1922–1939
EDWARD T. SANFORD	1923–1930
HARLAN F. STONE	1925–1941
Charles E. Hughes	1930–1941
OWEN J. ROBERTS	1930–1945
BENJAMIN N. CARDOZO	1932–1938
HUGO L. BLACK	1937–
STANLEY F. REED	1938–
FELIX FRANKFURTER	1939–
WILLIAM O. DOUGLAS	1939–
FRANK MURPHY	1940–1949
JAMES F. BYRNES	1941–1942
Harlan F. Stone	1941–1946
ROBERT H. JACKSON	1941–
WILEY B. RUTLEDGE	1943–1949
HAROLD H. BURTON	1945–
Fred M. Vinson	1946–1953
THOMAS C. CLARK	1949–
SHERMAN MINTON	1949–
Earl Warren	1954–

AAA (Agricultural Adjustment Administration), 77, 197
Abbott, Edith, 18
Abolitionists. *See* Slavery
Academic freedom. *See* Education, freedom of
Accusation, right to know, 148
Accuser, right to be confronted with, 144–46, 271, 274
Adams, John, 2–3, 101, 126; and Alien and Sedition Laws, 12; on denunciation of British writs of assistance, 247; on international role of American independence, 114; Supreme Court appointments of, 227; on Tom Paine, 21
Adams, Samuel, 9
Adams, Samuel Hopkins, 379
Adamson Act, 214
Addams, Jane, 18, 314
A.F. of L., Boston police union affiliated with, 74
Africa, American foreign policy in, 114–15; self-government drive in, 6
Agricultural program of F. D. Roosevelt, 47, 50, 77, 197, 328
Aguinaldo, Emilio, 8
Aitken, James, London incendiary, 4
Alien and Sedition Laws, 12–14
Aliens, copyright privileges for, 348; deportation of, 332; registration of, 211; right to work, 327, 356
Allen, William, 51
Alsop, Joseph and Stewart, 275
Altgeld, John Peter, 375–76
Amendments to *Constitution,* procedure for effecting, 174; *see also* under separate amendments
American Bar Association, on expulsion of Socialist legislators, 200; on publicity seeking by lawyers, 181
American Colonies, free grammar schools in, 138; freedom of press in, 52, 131, 190, 235, 244; freedom of speech in, 190; home rule in, 6, 9, 190, 277; judicial proceedings in, 55, 110–11, 190, 235; judicial supremacy in, 228; judiciary in, 51; juries in, 55, 110–11; religion in, 106, 135, 184; taxation by England of, 110, 128, 234; trial juries in, 55, 110–11; witchcraft in, 85
American Library Association, on censorship, 156, 329
American Mercury, censorship of, 39
American Revolution, class conflict in, 76; *Declaration of Independence,* 2–5; forces behind, 6, 110–

11; October *Resolution* of First Continental Congress, 109; Paine's *Common Sense,* 101; *Quebec Letter,* 121; role of Sam Adams in, 9; *Stamp Act,* 234
American Weekly Mercury, 52
Anderson, George W., 193
Andrews, Bert, *Washington Witch Hunt,* banned by State Department, 155
Anglican Church, in England, under James II, 186; in Virginia, 183
Anne, Queen of England, 234
Anthony, Susan Brownell, 57
Anti-Peonage Act, 194, 222; *see also* Servitude, involuntary; Slavery
Anti-Semitism in Maryland, 49; *see also* Discrimination; Religion, tolerance in
Anti-trust legislation. *See* Monopolies
Appeal, criminal, 56, 141–42
Arbitration of labor disputes. *See* Labor unions
Archbald, Robert W., impeachment of, 59
Arrest and imprisonment, *Bill of Rights* on, 88; in Colonies, 190; for debt, 368–69; in England, 91, 198, 323, 343–44; excessive bail, 137; F.B.I. raid of 1920, 193; Fourteenth Amendment on, 26; habeas corpus, 108, 249, 345; *Northwest Ordinance* on, 11; *see also* Searches and seizures
Arthur, Chester, federal civil service established under, 207
Articles of Confederation, 9; government under, 183, 216–17, 232, 237
Ashton, John, 17
Asia, American policy on, 82, 115, 383; *Declaration of Independence* as influence in, 4; self-government drive in, 6
Asians, discrimination against, 212, 327, 332, 356
Assembly, right of, 195; Bonus Army, 27; First Amendment on, 109; state authority over, 123
Atheists as witnesses, 66
Atomic energy, control of, 168; Eisenhower on, 167; and international law, 169
Attorneys, disbarment of, 71
Australian ballot, 305

Babcock, Joshua, 213
Bail, 137, 198; *Bill of Rights* on, 88; in Massachusetts Colony, 190; *Northwest Ordinance* on, 11
Bailey, Dorothy, trial of, 145

393

Navigable streams, ownership of power in, 246
Nazi war criminals, 96
Neebe, Oscar, 375
Negroes, citizenship for, 26, 212; educational facilities for, 170, 334; employment practices, 367, 382; housing restrictions, 132–33; jury duty, 319–20; political rights, 283, 288, 292, 370; travel facilities, 170, 313; see also Racism; Slavery
New England. See American Colonies; American Revolution
New England Courant, 52
New York Evening Post, 379
New York State, Tweed ring in, 102
New York Times, exposure of Tweed ring, 102
Newspapers, Tweed ring exposed by, 102; see also Press
Nineteenth Amendment, 57
Ninth Amendment. See Bill of Rights
Norris, George W., 197, 229, 328; and T.V.A., 335
Norris-La Guardia Act, 276
Northwest Ordinance, 11, 337
Nuclear fission. See Atomic energy
Nuremberg trials, 96
Nutter, Christopher, 143

Oates, Titus, 16, 91
Oaths, loyalty, 245; of religious conformity, 245, 264; of self-incrimination, 33, 236, 245
Obscenity laws, 37–38; see also Censorship
October Resolution of First Continental Congress, 109; events behind, 110–11
Odell, Jonathan, 76
Odyssey, suppression of, 154
Oglethorpe, James Edward, 369
Old age pensions, 314
Oneida Community, N.Y., 209
Ordeal, trial by, 91
Orientals. See Asians
Otis, James, 51, 184, 247
Overthrow of government by force, 123–24, 238
Ovid, Art of Love, suppressed, 154

Pacifism. See Conscientious objectors
Page, J. W., pro-slavery novel by, 28
Paine, Thomas, 101; trial of, in England, 179
Palmer, A. Mitchell, 193
Parker, Theodore, 209
Parks, William R., Soil Conservation Districts in Action, 50
Parliament, encroachment on liberties by, 323
Parliamentary immunity, 265–66

Parochial schools, 139; and public funds, 296, 298
Parrington, Vernon L., Main Currents in American Thought, 101
Patent laws, 44–45; and monopolies, 157
Paul, St., 185
Paupers. See Poor
Peck, James H., impeachment of, 59, 359
Peineforte et dure, 86
Pendleton Act, 207
Penn, William, 184; Frame of Government, 250; trial of, in England, 68–69, 136
Pennsylvania Constitution of 1776, 264
Peonage. See Anti-Peonage Act
Petition, right of: Bonus Army, 27; First Amendment on, 109
Petition of Right, England, 148, 323, 343
Philippine Islands, American policy in, 8
Phillips, Wendell, 189
Pickering, John, impeachment of, 59
Pierce, Walter M., 299
Pinchot, Gifford, and forest conservation, 162
Pinckney, Charles, 99, 232
Plessy segregation case, 170, 334
Police power, state and federal, 93
Police strike in Boston, 74
Political asylum, Wilson on, 219
Political controversies, judicial abstinence from, 100
Political freedom, Jefferson on, 257; Hughes on, 200; Lippmann on, 258; principle of, 125; Smith, Alfred E., on, 256
Poll tax, 165, 229
Polygamy and religious freedom, 301
Poor, treatment of, 213, 374; children institutionalized with, 302; pauper schools for, 295
Popish Plot, England, 91
Populism, restrains on, 217, 224
Populist party, and anti-trust laws, 189
Port of Boston, closing of, by Crown, 110
Post Office Department, censorship by, 153
Prejudicial conduct, in congressional investigations, 268–69, 271; in trials, 54, 56, 68–70, 181, 270, 375
Presbyterian Manifesto of 1953, 116
President, constitutional oath of, 264; limitation of terms, 250; veto power of, 220; see also Federal authority

Presidents listed, 287–88
Press, freedom of, 128: Alien and Sedition Laws, 12–14; in Colonies, 52, 131, 190, 235, 244; First Amendment on, 88; legal abridgment of, 124–25; under Lincoln, 163; Lovejoy, martyr to, 130; Milton on, 152; newspapers in contempt of court, 358; obscenity laws, 37–38; prior restraints on publication, 149; *Quebec Letter* on, 121; religious literature, 150; state authority over, 123, 233; Wilson on, 163; Zenger trial, 35; *see also* Censorship; Speech
Press, power of, 9, 101–2, 126
Press in England, restraints on: High Commission, 34; licensing of, 34, 151–52; Star Chamber, 32; taxes on printed matter, 234; trial of author Tom Paine, 179; trial of editor Richard Carlile, 201
Price controls, 93
Priests as witnesses, immunity of, 24
Primary elections, direct, 340; white, 288
Progressive party campaign of 1912, 36
Property rights, decision by trial, 315; federal seizure of struck plants, 293; Fifth Amendment on, 204, 318; Fourth Amendment on, 318; Fourteenth Amendment on, 26, 318; and martial law, 98; in Massachusetts Colony, 190; *Northwest Ordinance* on, 11; of opulent minority, 217, 224; *Quebec Letter* on, 121; racial discrimination in, 132–33, 356; and right to strike, 214; and state authority, 93; and "yellow dog" contracts, 118; *see also* Agricultural program of F. D. Roosevelt
Protective custody, 97; *see also* Arrest and imprisonment
Protestants, persecution of, in England, 68
Public lands, given to railroads, 336; *Homestead Act,* 338; for schools, 337, 339
Public libraries, 341
Public nuisance, defamatory periodical as, 149
Public power, 299, 328
Public school system, 138
Public trial, 20; *see also* Mob influence
Public Utility Act, 221
Public works programs, 278
Publications. *See* Books; Newspapers; Press

Publick Occurences, suppression of, 52
Pujo Report of 1913, 182
Pullman strike of 1894, 104
Punishment: banishment, 73; cruel and inhuman, 17; Eighth Amendment on, 17; legal requirements for, 270; in Massachusetts Colony, 190; *Northwest Ordinance* on, 11
Pure Food and Drug Act, 379

Quakers, persecution of, in England, 68
Quartering Act, colonial, 277
Quebec Letter of Continental Congress, 121

Racism, Stephen Douglas on, 29; Supreme Court on, 132, 170, 313, 319–20, 327, 334, 356, 370, 382; *see also* Discrimination; Slavery
Radin, Max, *The Day of Reckoning,* 96
Railroads, discrimination in accommodations, 313; subsidization of, 336; wage-and-hour law, 214
Railway Labor Act, 282, 382
Raleigh, Sir Walter, trial of, 144, 181
Randolph, Edmund, 58, 220
Rankin, John, 328
Rathbone, Basil, 311
Rayburn, Sam, 328
R.E.A. (Rural Electrification Administration), 328
Recall of judges, 53
Reconstruction Acts, 100, 333
Redfearne, Anne, trial of, 143
Referendum, 351
Reformation in England, 366
Religion, church and state: under *Articles of Confederation,* 183; clergymen as public officials, 23; in Colonies, 106, 184; governmental interference in church affairs, 300; national fast days, 7; public schools, 261, 296–98; religious qualifications for public office, 264; Sunday laws, 25
Religion, freedom of, 172, 210: atheists as witnesses, 66; under Calvin Genevan government, 122; in Colonies, 135; conscientious objectors, 342, 352; distribution of literature, 150; immunity of priests as witnesses, 24; *Northwest Ordinance* on, 11; polygamy, 301; state authority over, 123; Unitarian tenets on, 209
Religion, tolerance in: development of, 49; pleas for, 309
Religion in England: Bible reading, 366; *Declaration for Liberty of*

404

sions, 84, 86, 240; wire-tap evidence as, 353
Senate. *See* Congress; Congressional investigations; Federal authority
"Separate but equal" doctrine, 170, 334
Servetus, Michael, 122, 154
Servitude: contract labor, 377; indentured servants, 378
Servitude, involuntary: abolition of, 194, 222; *Northwest Ordinance* on, 11; of paupers, 213; of seamen, 180; *see also* Slavery
Seventh Amendment. *See Bill of Rights*
Shakespeare, *The Comedy of Errors,* 368; *Henry IV,* 22; *Measure for Measure,* 112
Shaw, Bernard, 154; *Saint Joan,* 15
Shays' Rebellion, 96, 216–17
Sheil, Bishop Bernard J., 269
Shelley, P. B., *Queen Mab,* 360
Shepard, Dr. James H., 379
Sherman, Roger, 2
Sherman Act, 189; and labor unions, 226
Shute, Samuel, 131
Sinclair, Upton, 154, 379
Sixteenth Amendment, 46
Sixth Amendment, rights under: place of trial, 21; knowing accusation, 148; speedy and public trial, 19; witnesses, 16, 144; *see also Bill of Rights*
Skinner case on sterilization, 350
Slater, Oscar, 56
Slavery, 371; conflicting views on, 28; and Constitutional Convention, 79; *Dred Scott* case, 259; *Emancipation Proclamation,* 192; *Fugitive Slave Act,* 81; Garrison campaign against, 242; and *Homestead Act,* 338; Jackson and literature against, 166; Lincoln approach to, 225; Lincoln-Douglas debates on, 29; in Massachusetts Colony, 190; *Northwest Ordinance* on, 11; Thirteenth Amendment on, 192, 222; *see also* Servitude, involuntary
Slum clearance, 18
Smith, Adam, 322
Smith, Alfred E., 309; on loyalty certificates for teachers, 64; on political freedom, 256
Social legislation, 254–55
Social Security Act, 230, 314
Socialists outlawed in New York, 200
Society of Sisters, 139
Soil conservation program, 50, 196, 335
Sommersett, James, 371

South Carolina, home rule restored after Reconstruction, 173
Sovereign immunity, 204
Spanish-American War, 8
Speech, freedom of, 199, 363: Alien and Sedition Laws, 12–14; in Colonies, 190; congressional immunity, 267; First Amendment on, 88; Jefferson on, 362; legal abridgment of, 124–25; state authority over, 123; *see also* Press
Speech in England, restraints on: High Commission, 34; parliamentary immunity, 265–66; Star Chamber, 32; trial of clergyman Robert Manwaring, 323
Spoils system, 206
Stamp Act, 128, 234
Stanton, Edwin M., 333
Star Chamber, England, 32, 310
Stare decisis, nonobservance by Supreme Court of, 48
Starkey, Marion L., *The Devil in Massachusetts,* 85
State authority, over debtors' relief, 303; First Amendment Rights, 123; Fourteenth Amendment limitations, 26; interpretation of Due Process Clause, 240; interstate commerce, 231; legislating for general welfare, 93; municipal bankruptcies, 291; nullification, 14; property rights, 356; river beds, 246; social legislation, 254–55; speech and press, 14; suffrage rights, 67, 165, 288; under Supremacy Clause, 211; taxing for public purpose, 129; under Tenth Amendment, 230
State Department, books banned by, 155
States, controversies between, 169
Stationers, Company of, printing monopoly of, 152
Stearne, John, 84
Steel mills, seizure of, 293
Steffens, Lincoln, 379
Steinbeck, John, 77
Sterilization, of habitual criminals, 350; of imbeciles, 273
Stevens, Isaac I., 97
Stevens, Thaddeus, 280, 295, 333
Stilwell, Silas M., 369
Stock market, reforms in, 221
Stone, Harlan Fiske, 104, 157, 353; on *Agricultural Adjustment Act,* 197; on bearing false witness to religion, 352; on railroad company unions, 282; on regulation of wages, 92
Stowe, Harriet Beecher, *Uncle Tom's Cabin,* 28, 154

Strikes, action against, 10, 75, 104, 113, 293; compulsory arbitration of, 214
Strong, William, 48
Stuart, Lady Arabella, 144
Subversive activity. See Communism; Communists; Loyalty procedures
Suffrage rights, Fifteenth Amendment on, 283; of paupers, 374; property qualifications for, 292; provisions for exercise of, 67; racial discrimination in, 288, 370; state authority over, 165; women's, 57
Sunday laws, 25
Supremacy Clause in *Constitution*, 211
Supreme Court, and advisory opinions, 99; dissenting opinions, 42–43; jurisdiction in controversies between States, 169; justices listed, 389–91; prejudicial decisions, 104; reorganization under F. D. Roosevelt, 47, 252; and *stare decisis*, 48
Supreme Court decisions: on advocating overthrow of government by force, 123–24; assembly rights, 195; bail, excessive, 137; Bank charter, 260; bankruptcies, 290–91; bills of attainder, 103; censorship, 149, 153; citizenship, 212, 342; communists barred from ballot, 284; congressional immunity, 267; congressional investigations, 215, 268; congressional power to deny jurisdiction, 280; contempt of Congress, 308; contempt of court, 104; convictions of indebted laborers, 222; corporations, 321; counsel, right to, 134; currency, 48, 241; dam site ownership, 246; debtors' relief, 303; deportation of aliens, 332; education and religion, 261, 298; educational facilities for Negroes, 170, 334; educational freedom, 139, 294; evidence obtained unlawfully, 178, 248, 353; executive seizure of struck plants, 293; flag salute, 352; freedom of press, 149–50, 233, 359; freedom of speech, 199; guilt by association, 372; interstate commerce, 231, 358; interstate migration, 373; intrastate commerce, 357; judicial supremacy, 227; jury panels, 112, 319–20; labor rights, 92, 113, 118, 214, 226, 255, 282, 325; loyalty cases, 145, 177, 205; martial law, 98, 176; mob influence in trial, 105; one-man grand jury, 270; patent system, 45, 157; political activity of gov-

ernment employees, 89; racial discrimination, 132, 319–20, 327, 356, 370, 382; racial segregation, 170, 313, 334; religion and government, 261, 298, 300; religious freedom, 301; self-incrimination, 202, 238; slavery and involuntary servitude, 29, 180, 194, 259; social legislation, 254–55; sterilization, 273, 350; suffrage restrictions by States, 165, 288; suffrage rights of employees, 67; taxation, 46, 47, 129; third degree, 240; treason, 347; vague and obscure laws, 251
Sutherland, George, 233, 326
Swartwout, Samuel, 206
Swayne, Charles, impeachment of, 59
Sweatshop, freedom of, 92; *see also* Labor
Swendsen, Haagen, trial of, 70

Taft, William Howard, 309; as Chief Justice, 70, 214; and literacy tests for immigrants, 219; on recall of judges, 53
Tagore, Rabindranath, 384
Taney, Roger B., 259, 345
Tarbell, Ida M., 379
Taxation, of American Colonies, 110, 128, 234; of English press, 234; federal authority in, 46, 78, 93; Hamilton on, 164; of newspapers, 233; for public purposes, 129; for religious activities, 183, 296, 298
Teachers. See Education
Tenement house laws, 18
Tennessee Valley Authority, 335
Tenth Amendment, 230; *see also Bill of Rights*
Texas, University of, and academic freedom, 61
Thanksgiving Day, constitutional aspects of, 7
Third Amendment. *See Bill of Rights*
Third degree, 240
Thirteenth Amendment, 192, 222; and runaway seamen, 180
Ticknor, George, 341
Tieton irrigation project, 171
Totalitarian government, rights of man under, 5
Townsend, Dr. F. E., 314
Trade unions. See Labor unions
Trammell, Park, 142
Treason, under *Constitution*, 15; trials for, 96, 347
Trials. See Judicial proceedings; Court decisions
Truman, Harry, 8, 220; loyalty pro-

We the People

Article. I.

Section. 1. All legislative Powers herein granted shall be vested in a Congress of the United States, which shall consist of a Senate and House of Representatives.

Section. 2. The House of Representatives shall be composed of Members chosen every second Year by the People of the several States...

Section. 3. The Senate of the United States shall be composed of two Senators from each State, chosen by the Legislature thereof, for six Years; and each Senator shall have one Vote.

Section. 4. The Times, Places and Manner of holding Elections for Senators and Representatives, shall be prescribed in each State by the Legislature thereof...

Section. 5. Each House shall be the Judge of the Elections, Returns and Qualifications of its own Members...

Section. 6. The Senators and Representatives shall receive a Compensation for their Services...

Section. 7. All Bills for raising Revenue shall originate in the House of Representatives; but the Senate may propose or concur with Amendments as on other Bills.

THE CONSTITUTION